The Vision of the Fool

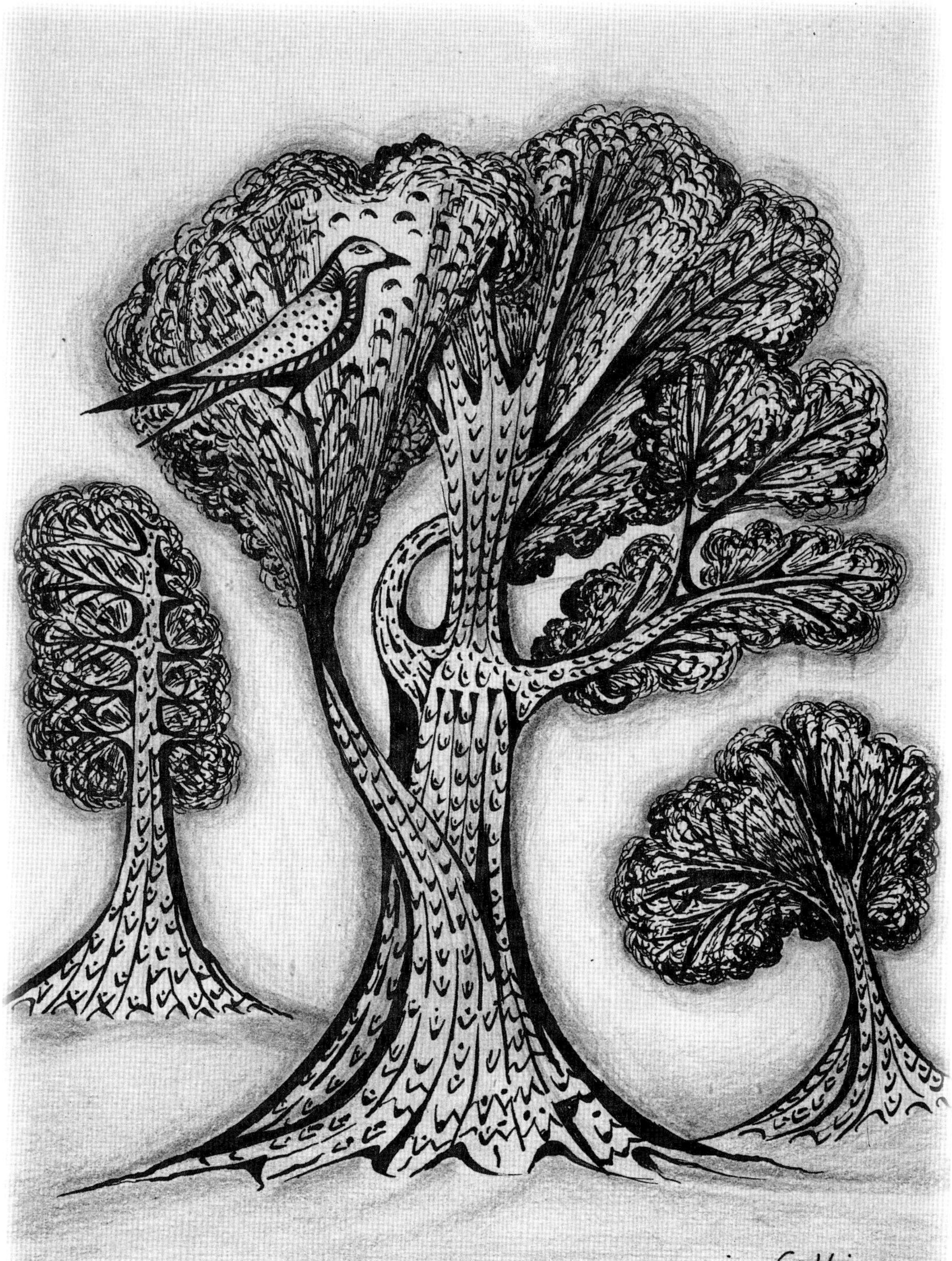
Cecil Collins, 1944

CECIL COLLINS

The Vision of the Fool and other writings

EDITED, WITH AN INTRODUCTION,
BY BRIAN KEEBLE

GOLGONOOZA PRESS

First published by Golgonooza Press
3 Cambridge Drive, Ipswich, IP2 9EP, UK

British Library Cataloguing-in-Publication Data.
A catalogue record for this book is available
from the British Library.

ISBN 0 903880 63 6 *cased*
ISBN 0 903880 64 4 *paper*

Typeset by Goodfellow & Egan, Cambridge
Printed by BAS Printers, Over Wallop

Contents

Chronology 7
Introduction 11
Foreword 27
Hymn of Life 29
The Artist in Society 44
The Eternal Presence 65
The Vision of the Fool 70
Art and Modern Man 82
The Artist in the New Age 93
Theatre of the Soul 104
Selected Bibliography 142
The Plates 144
Acknowledgements 192

Chronology

1908 Born in Plymouth 23 March.

1924 Begins four year study at Plymouth School of Art.

1927 Begins three year study at the Royal College of Art, London. Won the William Rothenstein Life Drawing Prize.

1931 Married Elisabeth Ramsden 3 April. Met Eric Gill and David Jones.

1933 Visited Paris where he saw works by Paul Klee.

1935 First one-man exhibition at Bloomsbury Gallery, London.

1936 Begins friendship with American artist Mark Tobey who encourages Collins's interest in Far Eastern philosophy. First poem published in *New English Weekly*. Two works included in the *International Surrealist Exhibition*.

1937 Exhibition of Paintings and Drawings in Barn Studio, Dartington.

1939 Teaches painting at Dartington Hall Summer School in August.

1940 Becomes tutor in painting and drawing at Arts Department, Dartington Hall.

1942 Begins essay 'Vision of the Fool'.

1944 Stays in London and Yorkshire and later moves to Cambridge. Exhibition of Paintings and Drawings at Lefevre Gallery, London.

1945 Stays in Yorkshire and London. Exhibition of New Watercolours and Drawings at Lefvre Gallery.

1946 Stays in Oxford. Publication of Alex Comfort's book *Cecil Collins: Paintings and Drawings, 1935–45* published.

1947 *The Vision of the Fool* published.

1948 Exhibition of New Paintings (shared with Robert Medley) at Lefvre Gallery. Lives in Cambridge, occupying studio belonging to Enid Welsford, author of *The Fool: His Social and Literary History* (1935).

1949 Tapestry 'The Garden of the Fools' woven by Edinburgh Tapestry Company.

1950 Short visits to France over next 3 years. Exhibition of New Paintings at Heffer Gallery, Cambridge.

1951 Exhibition at Leicester Galleries, London. Begins part-time teaching at the Central School of Art, sharing life class with Mervyn Peake. *The Sleeping Fool* presented by the Contemporary Art Society to Tate Gallery.

1953 Exhibits with Society of Mural Painters, London, and at Ashmolean Museum, Oxford.

1954 Travels in Italy and Germany. Tapestry 'The Fools of Summer' completed.

1956 Exhibition at Leicester Galleries. The Edinburgh Weavers produce two linen fabrics, 'The Herdsman' and 'The Fools'.

1958 *Christ Before the Judge* wins prize of £100 in first *John Moores Liverpool Exhibition*. Visits France.

1959 Fabric depicting eight Shakespearian characters produced for curtains of the New Conference Hall, British Embassy in Washington, USA. Major retrospective exhibition (227 works) at Whitechapel Art Gallery, London.

1961 Exhibition at Gallery Zygos, Athens, arranged through the poet George Seferis. Four works purchased by Greek National Gallery.

1963 Delivers talk 'Art and Modern Man' at annual conference of the Centre for Spiritual and Psychological Studies.

1965 Exhibition of Recent Paintings at Arthur Tooth Gallery, London.

1967 Exhibition of Gouaches and Watercolours at Crane Kalman Gallery, London.

1968 Oxford University Press commission pencil drawings for the *Oxford Illustrated Old Testament*.

1970 Moves permanently to London. Begins teaching at City Literary Institute.

1971 Exhibition of Recent Paintings at Arthur Tooth Gallery.

1972 Retrospective Exhibition (62 works) at Hamet Gallery, London.

1973 3 November, Consecration of altarpiece 'The Ikon of Divine Light' at Chichester Cathedral.

1975 Lectures at Tate Gallery.

1976 Exhibition of New Drawings at Anthony d'Offay Gallery, London.

1978 'The Eye of the Heart', by Stephen Cross; film on Collins's work commissioned by Arts Council.

1979 Awarded MBE. *Cecil Collins: Painter of Paradise* by Kathleen Raine published.

1981 Retrospective of Prints (55 works) Tate Gallery. Exhibition of New Works, Anthony d'Offay Gallery. BBC broadcast interview with Edward Lucie-Smith. New edition of *The Vision of the Fool* published. *In the Solitude of This Land*: (Poems 1940–81) published. *Theatre of the Soul*, a conversation with the artist published in *Temenos 1*, Richard Morphet's *The Prints of Cecil Collins* published.

1983 Retrospective Exhibition (40 works) at Plymouth Arts Centre.

1984 Exhibition of Paintings at Festival Gallery, Aldeburgh.

1985 1 November, Consecration of side windows at Church of St Michael and All Saints, Basingstoke.

1986 Lectures at Dartington in March. Exhibits in *The Temenos Exhibition* at Dartington as part of the Temenos Conference in October.

1987 Exhibits (19 works) in *A Paradise Lost: The Neo-Romantic Imagination in Britain, 1935–55*, Barbican Art Gallery, London.

1988 Eightieth birthday celebrations at the Central School of Art, Royal College of Art, and Chelsea Arts Club. Elected RA. 26 May, Consecration of West window, 'The Mystery of the Holy Spirit' at Church of St Michael and All Saints, Basingstoke. Exhibition of Recent Paintings, Anthony d'Offay Gallery. William Anderson's *Cecil Collins: The Quest for the Great Happiness* published.

1989 Major Retrospective Exhibition (147 works) at Tate Gallery. Judith Collins's *Cecil Collins: A Retrospective Exhibition* published. Dies in London 4 June.

Introduction

By the opening years of the 1930s, when Cecil Collins was a student at the Royal College of Art in London, European art, in the wake of Impressionism, had given rise to a whole range of artistic styles each of which made its particular contribution to a general tendency towards abstraction. For the young artist seeking to form a pictorial language sufficient to accommodate a visionary intuition these must have been exciting years, rich, if also bewildering, in the number of stylistic possibilities they opened up. Yet all these artistic movements had one thing in common, their lack of concern with the Divine as the ultimate subject of art. They were, more or less and in their different ways and not withstanding any idealistic, anarchic, or socio-political tendencies, variants of the thesis 'art for art's sake'; in the final analysis they all served the idea that there are criteria of truth and intelligence that belong exclusively to the aesthetic realm.

Cecil Collins seems always to have held the view that 'art is not about art'. 'Aesthetics by themselves have no meaning.' And, as we are now able to see from the writings collected here, a profound spiritual intuition led him to the belief that 'man is a metaphysical being' and therefore 'art is a metaphysical experience'. This above all should be the touchstone of our understanding of his work as it was for him the fundamental principle with which he steered a solitary course through the many modes of individualism that comprise the world of modern art. So, from the start and *in principle* we are in the thick of those issues which have occupied the deepest aspirations of human culture. We are engaged with a view of man and art that owes little to the humanist and increasingly secular culture of the last four centuries.

From the beginning Collins ackowledges that art must engage the whole of human nature. These writings attempt to establish the terms by which the aesthetic dimension of art must serve the thesis that is for Collins the divine dimension of art. For this reason no account of Collins's art that confines him to the modern movement can do justice to a visionary intuition that aligns the artist with the saint, the mystic and the priest. Whereas during the years of his working life it may have been expedient to demonstrate the artist's links with his contemporaries a deepening appreciation of his work is bound to see such links diminish in importance to reveal the extent to which he stood spiritually and artistically alone. Given the nature of his gifts and the substance of his art, his debts of his age can be seen as less important than the strength of his affirmation of the ageless and eternal. That modernism contributed to his development is true. That he grew beyond modernism as such is equally true.

If, as A. K. Coomaraswamy has rightly insisted, the evaluation of works of art must be based on a ratio of intention to result, then the importance of these texts in showing the artist's intentions are invaluable. A key part of our understanding of his intentions (what might be called the submerged strata in the production of works of art), must be that whole network and interplay of contingent factors that contribute to the final result. Unlike his traditional forebears who could rely upon a measure of consensus as to the nature of reality and of man, as well as to the function of the artist in his relationship to the wider social context, the modern artist is in this respect without lineage and true patronage. This accounts for Collins's repeated attempts in these texts to map out his artistic territory and define the terms of his actions within it.

Traditionally, as Collins recognises in several places, the artist's vocation and value are those of service to the spiritual and therefore 'truly functional' needs of the community; 'giving to humanity the deepest experience of reality'. But when this service is replaced by individualism and self-expression then art becomes a disembodied commmodity, something that requires artificial stimulation instead of arising organically out of a communal interplay of talent, responsibility and need. In this respect the modern artist is bound to be seen as, in Collins's phrase, 'an illegitimate child' whose 'self' so expressed is superfluous to the needs of his neighbours. He must then hawk his wares as chance decides in a society from which he is in exile. Such an isolation Collins certainly suffered and such was the burden of his complaint in 'The Artist in the New Age'.

With the exception of Eric Gill and David Jones no other modern British artist has so categorically affirmed the central role of art as the means of transfiguring human consciousness in accordance with an objective truth, sometimes called by Collins 'purity of consciousness', or 'the unknown that refreshens our lives': precisely because it is above and beyond all expedient and intellectual contrivance. In Collins's view this 'purity of consciousness' is the ultimate redemption of the human subject. The vocation of the artist is to create vision and the purpose of vision 'is to awaken man's real self, for in Art there is a hidden inviolate instinct for freedom, for eternity'.

Most of the material gathered here has never appeared in print. The artist seems to have made little or no effort to secure its publication. There would therefore be some justification in concluding that these texts form a series of self-clarifications as much as they are any sort of artistic credo.

In the earliest piece, published originally as the Foreword to his first one-man exhibition in 1935, we find in embryo many of the ideas that were to preoccupy him for the rest of his career: his rejection of the scientific world-view and socio-political agendas and allegiences, his conception of art as the language of a visual music articulating spiritual imagination, the idea that art is supremely functional in serving the inner god in each person, the rejection of abstraction as an insufficient visual means for conveying spiritual truth, that art is the inner vision of the real, the rejection of the 'isms of the modern movement, a belief in the objective and eternal value of first principles and above all, the idea that the art of true vision has a dialectic in accordance with eternal reality. Over the next five decades such ideas were expanded, clarified and refined but never foresaken.

The text 'The Artist in Society' is of special interest for here the artist draws out the implications of his own artistic vision by way of measuring himself against the surrealist achievement. We must read this text against the background of the First World War, whose dark shadow is cast over its whole length. This is presumably Collins's first attempt on an extended scale to put together his artistic testament. It is in part and variously, a cry of near despair, a declaration of comradeship, a prophecy, an indictment of the age—the ages!—a prescriptive analysis as well as a lyrical evocation of the artist's belief in the redemptive power of the artistic consciousness. It is certainly immature in places and many of its ideas were later to be handled with more clarity and spiritual maturity. But above all the whole text reflects the artist's need to formalise his own sense of direction by confronting and coming to terms with what was then the most significant modern artistic impulse, Surrealism.

If in this text he could speak of the 'surreal emotion of beauty' as being 'above good and evil', and as having a 'universal quality and attribute of creative power', we have to recognise this as very much his own interpretation of how Surrealism's concentration on the infra-rational nature of the inner psychic world could permit the activation of deeper currents of creative intuition. We can recognise in this, and in such phrases and ideas as that 'the poetic imagination' or 'poetic principle' is flowing in the direction of 'the creative God in man'—that is in the direction of the unknown inner universe just beginning to be explored, as he believed, by artists and poets—the emerging terminology of that visionary dialectic so evident in his later writings.

As a result of his early readings in mystical literature, especially his readings of Blake, as well as, no doubt, from inborn aptitude, Collins at all times sought a bulwark against what he called the 'psychic flux'. As he states in 'The Eternal Presence', '[Art], like all the acts of man, needs an absolute to relate its activity to . . . God is the only absolute.' This should caution us against a too overtly psychological interpretation whenever he speaks of the 'unconscious mind'. During the course of the interview included here the artist claimed he had never read Jung. But on the evidence of this essay there can hardly be any doubt that he was familiar with the then current ideas that the great discovery of the modern age is the subconscious and its seemingly natural corollary, the Jungian 'collective unconscious'. Collins's understanding of the 'unconscious', however, does not have the reductive contours of the Surrealists for whom the purpose of art was to fathom the subconscious for 'significant' (significant of what?) psychic forms and energies. The apparent triumph of scientific rationalism had certainly led to the need to rehabilitate the soul in the modern world. This task it inherited from the Romantics in the face of the Enlightenment. The lancing of the boil of the putrid psyche of the modern world was, in Collins's view, Surrealism's cathartic achievement. But his enthusiasm for its achievement did not prevent him from recognising that 'Surrealism is over. It's work is done'. And the recognition left him with the question of what the artist who comes after it is to do.

It was a presupposition (even if unconscious) of the philosophy of Surrealism that it should mend the breach between what had in the post-Cartesian world become irreconcilable opposites: man and nature, subject and object—a breach that Herbert Read's argument for an evolution of supernaturalism to superrealism did nothing to heal. For Surrealism confused phantasy and reality. 'It is the avowed aim of the surrealist movement to reduce and finally dispose of the flagrant contradictions that exist between dream and waking life, the "unreal" and the "real", the unconscious and the conscious' for, as André Breton claimed, 'The word *surrealism* . . . is employed by us with a precise meaning. We have agreed to refer by it to a certain psychic automatism'. But this is to forget that the 'phantasy' of the dream is the 'unreal' self-elaboration of the subjective psyche, whereas the 'real' is the self-elaboration of God (the divine play—*Līlā*—that Collins speaks of in the interview), and as such it is the supra-natural object of cognition.

David Cascoyne, *A Short Survey of Surrealism*, London: 1935, p.x and pp.47–8.

Cognition has no choice but to integrate itself with the real if we are to have an intelligible grasp of the motivation and purpose of our thoughts and actions. To 'invent' reality, as does Surrealism, by allowing it a psychic autonomy, is by implication to suppose that truth has no objective measure and that there is no distinction between falsehood and experience. ('[In] modern psychology . . . the cure and the disease, the patient and the doctor, are the same phenomenon', in Collins's own words.) Experiment and conclusion then become one and the same since there is no objective thesis for cognition to embrace. Thus consciousness has no point of orientation or, in Collins's terms (in, for instance, 'Art and Modern Man'), consciousness has no *context*. Breton's belief in the superior reality of 'the omnipotence of the dream and in the disinterested play of thought', makes the ruinous assumption that the source of cognition is *below* consciousness. But this is to have the principle of cognition determined by its own issue, in which case what Collins calls 'psychic furniture' becomes the measure of intelligibility. How can that be! Surrealism's attempt to throw off the yoke of rationalism by undermining it from below surrenders intelligence to illogicality and throws intelligibility upon the uncertainties of chance, freeing 'the real process of thought', as Breton called it, from all objective criteria. All this is done in the name of raising psycho-effluent to the status of art!

'Reason – the great prostitute', Andre Masson called it. One is inclined to think that Goya understood such things with greater precision: 'When reason dreams, monsters are born'.

It should be sufficient to quote Breton's words that Surrealism adheres 'to the theory of dialectical materialism . . . in all its points: supremacy of matter over thought . . . the materialistic conception of history', to make clear the fundamental incompatibility between Surrealism and the English painter's vision, whatever passing resemblances may have existed between them on a purely pictorial level at a time when Collins had yet to realise fully the visual analogues of his visionary art. In such phrases as 'trying to get into contact with the unconscious origins' and 'trying to unmask them, and to give them signs and symbols' (i.e. the inner experience of the psyche), Collins is surely groping for some objective bulwark against solipsism, instead of capitulating to the forces that would have him merely going with the 'psychic flow'. It was

Surrealism's inability to found itself upon a permanent principle of the real that led, even necessitated, Collins's rejection of it; a rejection which implicitly recognises that the soul's true life is finally vindicated by the divine: the intuitions of pure consciousness—The Fool, no less!

> I do not believe in surrealism precisely because I do believe in a surreality, universal and eternal, above and beyond the world of the intellect and the senses; but not beyond the reach of the humility and hunger of the human heart. And the human heart will find no meaning in life until it returns to eat of the source from which it came; and that source is the Eternal Person of all persons—God. For there is no meaning in life or art excepting that which springs from the immortal surreality of that Eternal Person.°

This quotation appears in the collection of writings and statements by the artist printed in Judith Collins's Tate Gallery catalogue.

Collins's rejection of Surrealism was no less decisive than was his rejection of abstraction and for reasons inherently consistent with his belief that 'art is a metaphysical experience'. It certainly was not that he simply chose to travel a path other than the self-destructive path of modern painting, 'oscillating between abstraction and figuration', as he described it in his interview with John Lane.

Although he did not actually paint any abstract works, David Jones welcomed abstraction as having released painting from the domination of naturalism and in the process reinstating the idea that the value of art is 'abstract' in so far as it is not to be judged according to criteria derived from the imitation of appearances. But for Cecil Collins the fact that 'art is not about art' means that the matter goes much deeper. Already in 1955, in the 'Foreword', he had written, 'I am opposed to contemporary, sterile, geometric art', and in 1944, in 'Hymn of Life' he elaborated the point: 'I do not believe in abstract painting. Subject or theme, thesis, which is the "place" of a work of art, is obviously of vital importance in generating a painting that is to give complete and whole experience. The thesis or theme or subject is the focus and energising which generates the pictorial elements.' To fully grasp all that is implied in this passage we must link it to two other statements taken from 'Theatre of the Soul'. 'There are no objects in my paintings'; and 'there is no such thing really as space values or abstract space'.

There are, then, no imitations of external visible objects, but there are images of internal forms whose symbolic, meditative 'content' are eternal ideas that are sources of being in their own right. Blake spoke of these self-same ideas in a passage of his *A Vision of the Last Judgement*—surely known to Collins—where he called them 'ever Existent Images' that return 'by the seed of Contemplative Thought; the Writings of the Prophets illustrate these conceptions of the Visionary Fancy by their various sublime and Divine Images as seen in the Worlds of Vision.' For Cecil Collins the beauty of these representations precipitates 'inner nuance, rapport and sensitivity to the vibrations and rays of livingness which are at the heart of things' in order to transform our consciousness. The artist has to be concerned with something *beyond* his art since knowledge of externals 'is meaningless unless it has a context'. The context of external knowledge (grasp of formalities) is internal significance which indicates that man cannot really know the 'how' of anything (its nature in itself), unless he can understand the 'why' of it (its nature as a part of that unity which is the essence of all knowable things). That is to say, consciousness is mediative in respect of a reality that is beyond cognition as such. That reality is the wholeness, the mysterious unity of life itself; which explains why for Collins a picture must 'live on many different levels at once, it is an interpenetration of planes of reality', and 'can only be realised as a total experience'.

'Space values', so called, arise out of the attempt to denote the *relationship* between the formal qualities of line, shape, colour and volume. Collins's objection to such a notion rest on the fact that such values have no basis in truth because they are without an objective context. The value of abstract works is simply hedonistic in that they have as their subject (or thesis) nothing other than the power inherent in the pleasure of attractiveness. What a 'space value' *is* may evoke feelings of pleasure, but what it *means* must be something beyond its formal expression as such. It is essential, as Collins says, for there to be a 'space *of* something'. Thus it is 'simply delusion to suppose there can be values apart from understanding a subject'—how else could Collins claim, as he does in the course of the interview, 'my vision has a dialectic'? Understanding presupposes the act of assimilating what is to be known as distinct from the subjective cognitive process by means of which this assimilation takes place. But the *value* of this process does not reside in the process itself, for that would be to exercise the process for its own sake (art for art's sake). There has to be an objective context (criteria) to lend cognitive validity to the process. And that, in the artist's words, is the 'whole inner world' which is the spiritual 'space of human imagination' in which the truth of the Eternal Person resides. All this is no doubt an intellectualisation of what was for the artist a state of the subtlest visionary instantiation. But we

The much maligned supposed naïvety of the question, 'what is it?', has behind it the power of an inescapable cognitive obligation.

have to grasp the profound implications which flow from his view that the imagination as being an organ of active spiritual transformation and not just an acquiescent mirror of the senses. As to the paintings themselves, this 'space' of the inner world is the purity of the Fool's consciousness; 'virginal' in being unseeded (undetermined) by the outer world of reflective experience.

Collins confessed many times that he was set to face the dawn. A significant proportion of these pages finds him speculating on the coming spiritual maturity of humankind; of a future universal civilisation. The subject is most overtly treated in 'The Artist in the New Age', where he entertains the idea of a world art more from the standpoint of one seeking to understand the breakdown of the religious cultures of the past than from the viewpoint of one prepared to delineate the coming order. What possible form such a global culture might take remains here largely undefined.

Yet clearly the artist envisaged emerging archetypal patterns of mythic structure for the future rather than an homogenisation of 'personal mythologies' (as he at one point calls them). But having broached the subject once he did not return to it. Moreover, his acute perception as to the nature of the cinematic and photographic image—in 'Hymn of Life'—must leave us in no doubt that he did not expect a culture of any symbolic depth from the age of television. We are living the failed experiment of secularism that is destructive of true culture. Nationalist fervour, scientific expansionism, political coercion or persuasion, democratic *laissez faire*, capitalist (or marxist) 'market forces', all seem to settle eventually for utilitarian expediency by way of what might be termed historical precipitation. All are proven infertile ground for the culture of spiritual vocation such as Collins envisaged.

Cecil Collins possessed a wide appreciation of the whole range of modern art, an appreciation that allowed him to draw from the work of many artists what he needed for his own purposes. But his appreciation was not confined to the twentieth century. His knowledge of many of the world's arts of all periods was considerable. This, coupled with his readings from the Bible, Eckhart, Blake, Traherne, Dionysius, Vaughan, Boehme, *The Cloud of Unknowning*, Coleridge, Shelley and the like not only influenced his thinking but might be said to have contributed as much to his pictorial language as did any visual influence.

This breadth of perspective must have lead him to view the whole question of the vocational place of the artist in society in a way in part shared by Gill and Jones. Here he would have found support for his preoccupation with the need to transcend that occupational hazard of the modern artist, solipsism, by drawing upon symbols and images whose significance and value derive from consecrated spiritual tradition rather than from artistic innovation and individual expressiveness. Throughout the pages of 'The Artist in the New Age' it is not difficult to discern the presence of earlier traditional societies whose underpinning by an hieratic culture was a model for his own vision of the coincidence of spiritual vocation and the arts common to all men where metaphysics, work and imagination can be held in a single grasp.

Although he did not share Jones's Catholic faith and therefore his subscription to its liturgical form, the fact that for Collins, as for Jones, the essential thesis of art is the sacred, made it inevitable that their recognition of the issues to be confronted by the twentieth-century artist would have much in common. Collins would have acknowledged the validity of Jones's observation in 'Religion and the Muses'—an essay written in the same year as 'The Artist in Society'—that, 'today we live in a world where the symbolic life (the life of true cultures, of "institutional" religion, and of *all artists*, in the last resort—however much we may disavow the association) is progressively eliminated.'

As a Catholic Jones found his 'solution' to this dilemma in working with the sacramental symbols of the Eucharist, the Incarnation and the Crucifixion. Collins, on the other hand, thought of such symbols as having been exhausted of their symbolic resonances to the extent of their having become, at least from the artist's point of view, pictorial cliches; a view that reflects the fact that twentieth-century artistic practice is somewhat removed from the spiritual and therefore operative context of canonic symbolism. In these matters there are no absolutes. The formal and aesthetic possibilities available to the artist in one age in the name of the spirit are not current for another. For Collins there could be no mediation of the living spirit in the mere repetition of such symbols.

Only for a short period in the 50s, in such works as *The Crucifixion* (1952), *Resurrection* (1952), *The Agony in the Garden* (1956), and *Christ Before the Judge* (1956), did he embrace the 'official' images of the Christian Faith.

Sacramental symbols, by their very nature, have one face turned towards the Divine and another face towards the human—a face that regards the Immutable Reality and a face that reflects the world of mutable realities, in order that there be a dialogue between them. Working as a painter in the margin of a consecrated tradition and having concern for the artistic validity of his representation of inner realities explains Collins's resort to such terms as 'lyric', 'fragrance', 'perfume', and 'inner nuance' in referring to the way in which a work of art may precipitate the process he held to be the central function of art: the spiritual transformation of consciousness. The dangers of serving a false mysticism not withstanding, no doubt the divine providence allows a measure of artistic conjecture that would be inappropriate within the context of consecrated worship in order to win consent to the sacred from the imponderables of artistic inspiration. How else are we to approach such a characteristic passage as this from 'Hymn of Life':

> The Art of Painting I believe is essentially a contemplative art; dealing... with the quality of ideas and their form. For the *quality* of a form is its reality. Essence reveals itself in the concrete reality of things. Aesthetics are the mode or art of giving the correct flavour of reality. An image of a transcendental reality, no matter how correctly the iconography is drawn, is not real, nor does it represent reality, unless the correct and actual quality of that reality is given in the image.

The artist, in the twentieth century, has to work with different conditions than those of his predecessors. However he may feel a kinship with the masters—anonymous or named—who have created the hieratic marvels of the past, from icons to cathedrals, the modern artist knows that such masters are not now his neighbours.

In Collins's paintings the Fool as emblem of the pure mystery of consciousness, of 'visionary intention'; the Angel as 'intermediary, the winged thoughts of the divine intelligence'; the Anima, soul as woman, the 'eternal bride' as receptical to the divine mystery, these and their compatriots are 'instruments of evocation' that are, so to say, lent a warranty from the known formalisation of mystic experience. And by this much they are saved from the charge of being merely the apparatus of a 'private mythology'—reductionist subjectivism that is. If what these symbols invoke has any power to save it is because they possess a common measure with revealed gnosis and here, in the beauty of the artist's realisation, are a living presence. To this extent they have, in the artist's words, the 'hint of redemption'.

Among his contemporaries Collins always considered Francis Bacon something of a polar opposite on an axis running from Heaven to Hell. Undoubtedly Bacon's images are powerful and, as with Collins, are the instruments of an inward search. But in going *in* we need to know whether thereafter the direction is 'up' or 'down'—possession or dispossession of our humanity! Bacon's images endeavour to suggest something of the dark side of human nature. But from Collins's point of view, in which art is an adjunct to the prayer and worship of God that 'opens up our nature [to] receive that which is higher than our nature, that which is wiser than our nature', Bacon's images express the subhuman. To concede that they express the truth of human nature would be to invite the belief that there are spiritual values that can be nourished by something other than the divine. This would amount to thinking that there could be some sort of reparation (why else should such images be made?), through appealing to the concatenation of passions and appetites that comprise and motivate the empirical levels of our humanity. If Bacon's images are about the disintegration of the human subject (for that is what it comes to), then Cecil Collins's images are about its redemption for the very reason that they exist to precipitate in the soul a movement of realisation in the direction of its natural vocation towards sanctity.

There is an implicit question, more or less hidden, in every work of art and which addresses us whenever we are touched by the beauty of the work in question. It is this. What am I asked to *be* in the presence of such beauty? The presence of artistic beauty is always a challenge to our humanity. So it is with the greatest works of Cecil Collins. Faced with his vision, one that runs counter to most contemporary expectations, we would be justified in asking for a guide. The authenticity of the following texts to perform that service can hardly be questioned.

'There are no objects in my paintings.' With what eyes then are we to look at the art of Cecil Collins? Surely eyes of flesh will never penetrate such images that testify to a seeing *into* vision rather than seeing *with* vision. Only the 'eye of the heart' will suffice the transformation of consciousness that such resonant symbols demand. How else are we to be moved by the infallible presence of the Anima of *The Invocation*? How else are we to know ourselves pierced by the resolute vision of the Angel in *The Angel of the Flowing Light*? To be present to their living reality requires an interior silence commensurate with the purity of their birth.

EDITORIAL NOTE

In order to err on the side of caution I have chosen a title for this book which suggests it contains only a selection of the artist's writings. But, with the exception of one essay-length piece, his poetry, and many hundreds of loose sheets of writings and jottings now in the Tate Gallery archives, this 'selection' includes all the larger writings that are known and therefore it might be considered, effectively, a 'collected' writings of Cecil Collins. A talk called 'The Rediscovery of the Sacred' exists in the Tate archives in the form of its original pencil manuscript and as a typed transcript, different in some detail. It is undated but internal evidence suggests it could not have been prepared prior to 1976. It is omitted here since it reads like an alternative draft of 'Art and Modern Man' and in addition covers much the same ground, in much the same manner, as 'The Artist in Society'. The provenance of the papers included here is as follows.

Foreword This reproduces the text of the 'Foreword' to the catalogue of the artist's first one-man Exhibition of Paintings and Drawings held at the Bloomsbury Gallery, London, 16–29 October 1935.

Hymn of Life Previously unpublished. The manuscript is contained in a ruled notebook now in the Tate archives. It is in the artist's handwriting throughout and has evidently been added to over several years. The earliest date given after an entry is May 1944, Cambridge. The last December 1955. The titlepage announces 'Hymn of Life by Cecil Collins'. The first four words are vigorously cancelled and the word 'Meditations' has been added at a later date, possibly 1947. This too has been vigorously cancelled. Various addresses (to which the plea 'please return to' is attached), recording the artist's movements from Devon to Yorkshire to Cambridge, are given.

In view of the style as well as the contents of this notebook it seems appropriate to retain both titles. In transcribing the manuscript I have applied the lightest editorial touch. Obvious and insignificant misspellings have been silently corrected. A few words and phrases deleted by the author have been silently omitted. The some time prose- some time verse-like layout of the lines has been adhered to in the present layout. One or two words—in square brackets—have been added where it seemed necessary, as have one or two words where I have 'interpreted' the handwriting. Like Blake, the artist frequently employs his own style of orthography. Because of this it is all but impossible to determine exactly where a capital at the beginning of a word is intended. I have added them only where, due to the handwriting, they seem obviously meant.

The Artist in Society Previously unpublished. Originally entitled 'Art and Modern Man; a study and interpretation of the problems of modern painting'. I have re-titled this to avoid confusion with the later 'Art and Modern Man' published in 1964. A reference at the end of the typed carbon copy in the Tate archives I have worked from states October 1st, 1941, Dartington Hall, Totnes, Devon. It was delivered as a talk, with slide illustrations, to 'a young arts club', according to a passage here omitted and was intended to promote discussion among members. I have left in at the beginning the commentary to some of the slide illustrations even though it is not altogether necessary to know what they were, whereas reference to them allows the author to establish his categorisation of the Apollonian and Dionysian types of the artist. My editorial notes—in square brackets—to the first four of these illustrations are based on the author's separate brief notes attached to the transcript. The discussion of other illustrations—not as many as the length of the talk might suggest—have been omitted as it is not possible to identify the paintings in question. I have also deleted small sections as being of too little interest, as well as several other longer passages that have the manner of digressions. There is some re-phrasing throughout in the interests of concision and clarity. Rather oddly, there are a few corrections of single words in the author's hand, but no attempt has been made to correct other obvious faults.

The Eternal Presence Previously unpublished. Like 'Hymn to Life' this text is written into a ruled notebook now in the Tate archives. From the handwritten titlepage it seems likely that the author first intended the work to be called 'The Eternal Presence; The Reality of Poetry', 1943. But, possibly at a later date, and after having completed the manuscript, the words 'Notes for' have been added before the title and a further subtitle, 'Studies of Art, Painting, The Birth of the Poetic Principle', with its Blakean overtones, has been added at the bottom of the page. The handwriting is consistent throughout except for the last three short paragraphs, which are heavier and may be of a later date. The same editorial practice has been applied as with 'Hymn to Life'.

The Vision of the Fool The present text, originally written in 1944, reproduces, with a few corrections, that of the second edition published by Anthony Kedros in 1981, itself a reprint with minor changes of the first edition by Grey Walls Press of 1947.

Art and Modern Man Published in *Tomorrow: the Journal of Parapsychology, Cosmology and Traditional Studies*, Autumn 1964, Vol. 12, no. 4, pp. 319–26, and reproduced here. Originally given as a lecture to the Centre for Spiritual and Psychological Studies at their conference 'Communion and Communication: the Role of the Symbol', 26–28 July 1963 at Cranfield.

The Artist in the New Age Previously unpublished. The text is from a typed carbon copy in the Tate archives. The heading states that it was delivered as a talk at the Attingham Park Adult College as part of a conference 'Pointers to the New Age', held on 11 to 15 June 1965. A handwritten pencil manuscript also exists, being somewhat different from the typed copy and is also largely unreadable. The typed copy has been prepared either from a recording or, more likely, from a shorthand account of the delivered talk. As with 'The Artist in Society' there are a number of additions in the author's hand which leave uncorrected other obvious errors. A few cuts have been made to the present text to avoid repetition and in parts, where there is some ambiguity of meaning (possibly due to the shorthand account), I have re-phrased the text on the basis of my experience of the author's conversation.

Theatre of the Soul Early in 1979 Kathleen Raine, Philip Sherrard, Keith Critchlow and myself formed the editorial board of the Journal *Temenos*. In preparation for the first issue it was proposed that I should interview the artist; a proposal he accepted with some alacrity. At the, then, age of 71 it became clear that he wanted the interview to be a major summary statement of his thought and experience. Accordingly, on two Saturday afternoons in September of that year, in his Chelsea studio, the range of topics to be covered was discussed and mapped out in some detail. A first conversation (for me a remarkable event still etched deeply into my memory), took place on 21 September. It was recorded, transcribed and on the basis of this transcription we decided there was a need to cover further ground in a series of supplementary questions. A second recorded conversation took place on 13 October, with the intention of editing the material into the first transcription. From this now 81 pages of typescript, owing to limitations of space, a much shortened version was prepared, with the approval of the artist. This was published as 'Theatre of the Soul' in *Temenos I*.

Much valuable material was left out of this version and in preparing the present text I have returned to the original transcripts to prepare a fuller version along the lines envisaged during the two planning meetings. I have made cuts where the exchanges became either too scrappy, too superficially opinionated, or the line of thought wanders into irrelevancies. Where relevant I have retained the artist's ammendations to the typescript and have edited, re-phrased, re-grouped according to our original plan. But also to make the results readable, clear and faithful on the basis of my many, many hours of conversation with the artist over seventeen years of friendship. The results, I believe, embody the artist's most mature reflections on the diverse and complex matters that were germane to his art.

In preparing the present volume I have, so far as possible, bearing in mind the above mentioned contingencies, kept editorial interference and accretion to a minimum, prefering to let the artist speak for himself. All side notes are by the editor with the exception of those on pages 50 and 71. Additional editorial matter within the text is enclosed in square brackets. For a more detailed Chronology and exhaustive Bibliography up to 1988 the reader is directed to Judith Collins's excellently thorough *Cecil Collins: A Retrospective Exhibition*, Tate Gallery, London, 1989.

Foreword

I THINK the time has come when the people of the world, artists and poets in particular, should turn a sceptical eye upon the stereotyped actualities of the scientist and the politician.

My works are visual music of the kingdoms of the imagination. There is in all human beings a secret, personal life—untouched, protected—won from communal life; and of which all public life is the enemy. It is this sensitive life which my art is created to feed and sustain, this real life deep in each person. Thus my art is truly functional.

I am opposed to contemporary sterile geometric art with its tyrannical cultural snobbery. I believe the time has come for severe re-valuation: re-valuation that will expose this barren stereometry as the new academic art with its popular function that of industrial design and its aesthetic, no more than a creed for minor artists.

I write this not with malice, but to express my vision. Enough of feverishness: art is not a rocket—it is a star that can be looked at through a telescope and be measured, talked about, and yet still live in inviolate eternity.

The art of the future shall be to feed the interior life of individuals and will not be dominated by any theory: political, philosophical or religious.

Beware of crowd-consciousness.

Keep away from all crowd movements.

All crowd movements are hypnosis.

The crowd is ant-psychology.

Throw over in yourself the herding, gregarious human idealism.

Be something: an individual: a personal entity. There are no such things as movements in art—there are only individuals.

There must be in the world a spiritual revolution NOW. A spiritual revolution is the movement of the human consciousness from the ideas of fear and desire, victory and defeat, courage and cowardice, possessions—on to the idea of intelligence which is humility.

All force is evil.

Intelligence is divine.

All mass revolutions are not action—but reaction.

Revolution begins in you.

These are not original ideas, but eternal values.

Hymn of Life

Meditations 1939–55

THE clock in the night. The passing of centuries, passing. Dust gathering in the rooms, on the ledges and corners of the windows. Outside. Night; ages, ages.

He sat bowed, full of an intense pain, an invisible pain without form. The book on the table had no healing in it. And there was no healing in all the books upon the shelves in the room, books of wisdom, books by all men. No healing.

Sunlight entered the room with a sudden ray. Cold, wintry, then opening in warmth over the window, softly moving upon the floor. Outside the window, deep in the wood, a bird sang. Ringing under the dark leaves the affirming rejoicing song rose into the wide sky, soaring.
The golden hand.
Remember.
Rejoice.

I am a messenger.
Sometimes it seems to me that I have spent all my life walking along lonely country roads, hearing in the cities a long way off, the murmuring and activity of men.

In the sunlight on the wall in the morning, in the sunlight upon the bark of the tree in the afternoon, there is something speaking, of something to be recovered, a forgotten beauty, a kingdom.

The long eternal afternoons robed in blue, with the white compassionate temples of the clouds floating in wise happiness and detached love.

Over our striving, our rooms, our houses; the beautiful ritual of the rain falling against the window, the voice of the wind, makes us remember a journey older than thought, deeper than death, a triumph, the secret ascension of love. The tasting of these things in our days and nights is the partaking of the sacrament of existence.

In the distance came the poignant rejoicing of the sea birds, and from far below the town arose the sound of the waves, deep, and eternal.

As a child I remember walking at night in a town by the sea, hearing the wind move through some dark pines, and far out in the darkness came the distant roar of the waves, and it seemed to me to be like a great unfolding of the history of world soul, a great poem, veiled and eternal.

The secret is, conversion to life.
Man has not yet become converted to life.

There are two definite things in this life that we can do—we can by our attitude, in life, and work, either stimulate people to live, or depress them to die.

Thinking, and thinking out explanations of life, are a waste of life.

The doubts and hopes of the intellect are irrelevant, for life is, and always will be a mystery.

The answer is, Life is love (Creative Imagination) and absence of love is death.

Science can never comprehend the meaning of existence, because science only understands facts, and facts are not reality, that is a scientific superstition. It is the significance of facts that is reality, not facts. And the significance of facts can only be understood by love, the greater the love, the greater the understanding.

Superstition in Religion is the literal acceptance of mythology and allegory, and not realising that it is the significance of a myth that is its reality.

Superstition in science is thinking that facts are reality.

Superstition in Art is believing that Art is the literal copying and imitating of nature.

The real creative nature is one which reconciles opposites by absorbing them into a third thing, an absolute. This is not a concept, but an attitude of livingness. Just as the body needs to reconcile opposites in order to function, so the soul needs to reconcile the opposites of Authority (i.e. form) and Freedom (i.e. energy). No really living creative human being can therefore take sides, because this is not life, but only a process in which one side destroys another. A living human being can only take the side of life and in doing so sees clearly that there is in everything political, philosophy, religion, art, some ideas which favour life, give life, stimulate life, praise life, and in all of them there are ideas which are against life, and depress life.

Thus by nature I am an authoritarian, and by nature I am an anarchist. These two opposites are in me. I have long recognised that the essential nature of life is a paradox. Man to live must be free, but man can only obtain freedom in authority, and he can only obtain authority through freedom. Only he who is free can have authority, just as only he who has authority can be free. The reconciling of freedom and authority is a major creative act in any field of human activity, and one without the other produces an inhuman world. These two things can be reconciled by the God in us.

Absence of life is the mercy of life for it creates the desire for life.

God is creativeness, poetry, love, happiness, life. Unhappiness, uncreativeness is non-existence, absence of life.

God, creativeness, love, happiness, is the meaning of life, because it is life.

The meaning of life is to come to fruition, to bear the fruit of life, which is happiness. But this fruition can only be obtained through growth, and growth is suffering—Hell. Hell is a state of growth, and growth is a process of purification. The seed of a flower in order to purify itself, makes the painful act of growth, through which it suffers, it then attains through this suffering a purer form of matter—the stem. And after still [further] creative movement and growth it attains its purest form, the flower itself. It has attained this purity and fruition by seeking the light, light purifies.

So the pilgrimage of life for all beings is through Hell, that is suffering, growth to Heaven, which is purification, fruition, Happiness, and the accomplishment of this is existence.

Happiness has to be accomplished, that is you cannot force it to you; you have to work hard to grow by your own creative efforts to purify your nature so that it attracts happiness. For like attracts like. God, happiness, exist all the time in rays and vibrations that pour forth abundantly, eternally, what we have to do, and all we can do, is to magnetise our natures by purity of heart, so that we attract these rays and vibrations to us, for love attracts love, it is the Godlike in us that desires God.

Life is love, communion.

I love and worship the mystical livingness of all life, the immortal sacrament purified and sanctified from the world.

The purpose of life is to live, and to live is realisation, and realisation is living, living is growth, growth is realisation. A tree is the realisation by the seed of its own nature.

The more living we are, the more we realise. We are alive according to the degree we are in contact with our fundamental nature, our essential self, our essence. This self, this essence, is that within us which knows everything, which has experienced everything, is everything. Therefore in searching for knowledge, for beauty outside, we are wasting our life, for we have within us that which knows all, is all, the Person, the God in us.

Religions are means and ways of contacting that essential self, that Person in us, but when a human being really contacts that God within us, then he becomes a real living person through which the God of life shines, and a really alive person is one who is free from religions, philosophies, politics, because these are organised concepts that imprison the eternally mobile essence in fixed form, whereas the freed man knows and experiences that essence in its organic empirical flowing, in its naked essentialness, uncrippled by fixture. So we must slowly free ourselves from these things.

We must regain the idea of the Person, the more real a thing is, the more Person it is.
The personality of the elements, the sea, the world, the earth, stars, trees, people.
The mythos of Person in everything.

If we don't love and worship life, life will not love and worship us.

Man's capacity for sacrifice has too long been exploited, we must develop his capacity for joy in life.

Art exists to destroy the world and to create a kingdom which is eternal.

My way to God is through the devotion of poetic imagination.

There is something more important than being wise, and that is to love freely and unendingly, letting everything grow and flow in its own nature, not trying to impose our nature, but by being alive oneself in such a way as to bring others alive too.

Conception in poetry is vanity, and the corruption of poetic sensation.

Painting is the language of sensation, words the language of thought. Words approach the language of sensation when they become poetry, this is the highest form of words. It is the highest form of anything, for the deepest reality is a sensation.

Symbol in painting is poetic sensation.

I am concerned with poetic painting.

The purpose of poetic painting is [to] arouse poetic emotion in those who behold it, by means of symbols.

Emotion is the actual recognition of some element or quality in existence, and poetic emotion is the recognition of one of the deepest and most universal elements in the world—the element of poetry.

To create is to make eternal.

Images arise from the fountainhead of human life—the heart, the solar centre from ancient memories in the blood, and from the polarity and fire of the spirit.

A man's deepest self speaks to him in dreams and parables. The awakening and liberation of that deepest self can only come in a more wide and general sense, with the return of the belief in the contemplative life as a vital element in human society.

The other day I saw and heard a bird singing on the branch of a tree, and suddenly realised that the tree was the shape of the birds song, they were one.

The drawing inspired by this event is reproduced as the frontispiece.

Now, I can gaze at the beautiful nakedness of stones, put my forehead against the rough bark of the trees, and feel the soft girl thigh feeling of leaves, and hear after the waves have fallen upon the shore, the hollow eternal sound echoing inward and away further and further mingling at a great distance inside of me, until it is already among the voices of other kingdoms.

I believe in a new and virgin romanticism, *a cosmic romanticism*, based on contact with the rhythm of eternal life. To give one's self up to the mercy and grace of our deepest self, the spring of life in us, deep and eternal, the profound flowing God in us, of whom Heraclitus speaks.

Not work, not sorrow, not knowledge, not wisdom, success or failure, not victory, not truth, but creative joy is the God of life, and until we desire that God, He will not appear.

The nourishment of Eternal silence.

Before we can enjoy the language of Heaven which is an eternal ecstasy and peace, we have to learn that language in bitterness and sorrow. This is life as we know it in this world, the learning in pain and sorrow of the language of peace and eternal joy.

The creative power of a symbol is not the symbol but the quality of the symbol, it's the same with everything, it's quality is its livingness, its reality.

Simple basic cosmic romantic pure deep flowing clear light communing expanding piercing exalting magic eternal peace wonder nuance romance of the moods of nature, the elements their mystical drama, the chorus of worlds watching, everything speaking through its own nature of one thing, endless pilgrim feeling of visiting as a stranger all the worlds. Different people, different natures, each person is a universe, the music of raindrops, the mystery of attraction.

Totnes, Devon, 1943

Prayer. Worship is one of the elements in happiness. And in a certain mystical happiness life fulfills its purpose. Happiness like everything else is dependant on a source. We cannot create happiness as such, but we can create the condition for happiness, that is fully a creative act. Happiness is given, it is grace, all true happiness is supernatural.

The idea of a source means that the source is greater than that which comes from the source, it is something higher than that which needs to feed from the source, something more potent than our potency. True personal happiness comes from superpersonal happiness. When we pray and worship God, we open up our nature and receive that which is higher than our nature, that which is wiser than our nature, that which is happier than our nature; we open up our nature to receive a portion of the happiness of all Happiness. We eat and drink of an absolute universal joy. It is the God in us that desires to eat and drink the God of life. We only live when we turn toward our source. But we must first create the conditions within ourselves in which we can receive this life. And part of the act of prayer, is the clearing, the washing away of the waste matter of negative thoughts and feelings, so that the living rays can enter us.

Prayer ought to be an eternal fact in our lives, independant of mood, or inclination, or inspiration. Creating in us a continuity of orientation towards our source, the Holy Sun of life.

May 1944, Cambridge

It is inexpressible. Today in the sun, I feel such an aristocrat of the spirit. The light in the curtains, the summer light, distant and all around, and the sounds, soft, piercing; the thick foliage, the voices. A gentle wind stirs the curtains with the implication of far off happiness, the threads and clues of a mysterious sacrament; and I know how deep within, the wide sea breaks in foam and waves; and I know that the bread of life is ready.

Behind the golden smile of the day, is the cool shadow, the white bones, and the cruel signs. A king alone can recognise how each lives in each, because wearing the crown of life, he reigns knowing the open burden and the secret fulfillment. All crumbles away, or falls slowly; as in the silence of an empty room, the fragrance of memory lives in the calm light; while outside, at the ending of day, young and urgent cries go forward with life, and far in the distance there is youthful praise, banners and flames starting out, with the old clouds behind them.

These are the wise thoughts of love. Young and magical grass yielding to the sun, everywhere starts up in shafts of plenitude. In spite of the cruel wounds, it is necessary for the curtains to be drawn back, the table laid, and the cups to be placed upon the white cloth, and for the old and compassionate hands to welcome the rising of the sun.

June 1944, Cambridge

In the moving of the years there is often a quietude, when something is trying to be remembered. If only we could believe, would not our sorrow turn upwards and remember?

Out of the window, in the garden, a wintry branch stretches itself into the white sky; and behind the trees, the choir of hills gather together in silence.

To know and to speak with the higher ones.

Early April 1944

Morning: the trees slowly and delicately move their leaves and branches reflected in the pure face of the glass of the window open to the early air and light of appearing day. The same thoughts: solitude, to what kindred, to what race do we belong? What king is our king? Yet it is the life of solitude which reveals to us our race and our king. My beloved one who is my wife, and I, know the solitude. In solitude the secrets speak their music.

July – August 1944, Cambridge

Despair, despair; machines roll through the cities with iron cries. An utter emptiness. A cold wind blowing in the streets and the rime of frost on the lips.

1944

A work of art is a perfection which feeds a thousand imperfect explanations.

There are two ways of life open to the artist. The way of the bohemian which is the open detachment from the world. And the way of the mystic which is the subtle detachment from the world.

July 1944

A flash of white in the lovely blue air. Then a murmur from the distance as all the leaves tremble before the freshness of the coming wind that moves and stirs along the empty avenues, whispering in secret language to the dust that shines in humility beneath the sun, whose royal and tender rays search the trees.

The clouds like clean white linen have wiped the tears from the windows of the houses. The rain has passed like the shadow and meditation of a sorrow, leaving a light and brilliant air of infinite peace. As I walk, all is, and ever shall be. Yet the realisation is brief, and soon the thirst will begin again. The rose wither [whether] left solitary, or crushed by passion, will leave the inheritance of the thorn for the gaze of the year.

Evening August 1944, Cambridge

The cinema and the camera have killed only that which is unessential in the art of painting. And have therefore done it a great service. For it has helped to restore the art of painting to its rightful function. A function altogether profounder than that of the cinema; (for it is no accident that the cinema is the most popular form of visual experience in the degenerate mechanisation of modern society, it is its rightful form of visual communication).

The Art of Painting I believe is essentially a contemplative art; dealing not with the narration of ideas and their forms, but with the quality of ideas and their forms. For the *quality* of a form is its reality. Essence reveals itself in the concrete quality of a thing. Aesthetics are the mode or art of giving the correct flavour of reality. An image of a transcendental reality, no matter how correctly the iconography is drawn, is not real, nor does it represent reality, unless the correct and actual quality of that reality is given in the image. This means that ultimately the reality can only be realized through sensibility, i.e. sympathy, like to like. Like to like is a state of consciousness above understanding. Because understanding still lives by need of knowledge. Whereas like to like has no more need of the method of knowledge, any more than love has need of reason to justify its activity. So that incidentally the cinema cannot communicate reality, because essence cannot be photographed. While it can record the physical geography of an object and its movements, the essence is of necessity absent, hence the curious emptiness of photographs. They are eventually unsatisfactory because fundamentally they are unreal. In the cinema, and the photograph, the image although it may often excite our surface consciousness, it does not take root in our consciousness, it does not remain actual in us. This is often shown if one goes to see the same film for five or six times, a revulsion sets in, no matter how good the film is. Unlike good painting, sculpture and theatre, to which one can return again and again, and the work actually grows and improves by continuous re-acquaintance.

The reason why painting has not an important place in the consciousness of most people in our own time, is that they have lost the art of contemplation, and of contemplating and experiencing the quality of images. They are mostly concerned with being drugged by the movement of the narration of forms. Hence the popularity of the cinema. It is because our society today holds a corrupt view of life, and of the Arts, that they have lost the very attitude of mind necessary to the enjoying of an understanding of them.

I do not believe in abstract painting. Subject or theme, thesis, which is the 'place' of a work of art, is obviously of vital importance in generating a painting that is to give complete and whole experience. The thesis or theme or subject is the focus and energising which generates the pictorial elements. Because a good artist can make a good pictorial design out of the most insignificant theme or subject, this does not invalidate theme, or thesis, but on the contrary shows that such an artist if he goes on all the time in this way, is superficial, because he is satisfied with making what is ultimately only pictorial exercises compared with the wonderful possibilities of pictorial structure when based on, and generated by the theme and deed of the subject.

1944

I am only interested in productive emotion.

How strange it is to be alive.

Theories are derived from life,
not life from theories.

This is the culture of the Spirit; Art must be sacrificed to the elements of Nature, and Nature must be sacrificed to the elements of Art. From these two divine sacrifices the mystery of life flashes its eternal poetry.

August 1944

Innocence, Innocence, Innocence.

Perhaps, what I seek is the immortal blue flower spoken of by Novalis. But it is not only a flower I seek, but a cup. I seek it everywhere, in rooms, in writings, in cities. Sometimes its immortal presence seems behind the clouds that move over the city, and sometimes it seems behind the trees and the leaves of the trees, when they rejoice in summer; or when they fall to the ground with the oncoming of winter; the cup of life; to drink of the unknown, the setting out place of the soul, an eternal birth.

Peace is a condition of spiritual war through which mankind can grow and evolve into life. Therefore military war is a blasphemy against life, because it destroys peace.

December 1944

Night, silence, darkness, openness, fulfillment, peace.

December 1944

The world has hurt the truth,
and now the truth hurts the world.

O Light, O Light, the world is nearly dark enough to welcome you.

December 14th 1944

Last night as I went out to post a letter, I heard high up in the darkness of the sky, a liquid cry, poignant and yearning, it was answered by another cry deep in the darkness, a cry of peace. These voices continued on into the night, becoming far, then faint, then silent. My letter was pale in my hand under the lamplight. I posted it, and walked by the dark trees and street lamps, up the street quiet with the night.

Saturday, December 16th 1944, Cambridge

It is the impossible that makes life possible.

January 1st (New Year's Day) 1945

Some more reflections on this. The possible is kept alive by the impossible. For the possible grows and keeps alive by striving and desiring in some degree, for the impossible. Life is a process of making the impossible, possible. Impossibility is a potent symbol of creation, as the unknown is a potent image of wisdom and vision. The whole of possible life feeds from the impossible, and owes its existence to it, either knowingly, or unknowingly. True life for the possible, is to extend itself to expand its consciousness; it does this by expanding itself towards the impossible, inspired and moved by the impossible. To believe only in the possible is ultimately to deny life.

January 2nd 1945, Cambridge

It is the most gentle wind that stirs the deepest feelings.

January 10th 1945, Totnes, Devonshire

The stars stretch over the night sky. They are the lamps of the blessed dead.

January 11th 1945, Totnes, Devonshire

Anger is a kind of intelligence to the stupid.

January 14th 1945, Totnes, Devonshire

To those the higher ones we must constantly turn, communing with them. Their beauty and compassion is invisible to impurity. But there is something in all of us that desires their company and their love.

O holy ones I long for you, I long for my race, I long for my kingdom; we are all exiles. I know of your existence, I remember you, and my life with you. But here I wander, and I know nothing. But you exist, and most holy are you O beautiful servants.

January 14th 1945, Totnes, Devonshire

What an age to live in! It bites into you with a formless denying of the life in us. A frustration of all that which is growing, of all that which desires to give, to come to fruition. Our time denies, denies all who have inward fruit. Denies the artist, the contemplative, the human being. A winter of the spirit is over all society. The coldness of the vanity of the intellect on one side, and cheap vulgarity of attitude towards life on the other side. It is this official denial of life that confronts us in everything. But deep underneath flows the secret stream.

January 22nd 1945, Cambridge

Snow on the roofs outside, on the trees, on the fields; and the heart's thoughts hidden.

Water slowly trickles down the window panes. The frost yielding to the passion of the sun, flows in gradual ecstasy down the glass of the window, free at last. So too the heart warmed by the sun of love, melts in tears, and flows free, free.

January 22nd 1945, Cambridge

It is only the conventional life that enables us to think unconventional thoughts.

The real barbarians are those who want to reform the world by destroying it. Or to destroy the world by reforming it.

The world is made inhuman by reform. And is reformed by being human.

The less we suffer, the more we suffer.

It is the ambitious who are truly boring.

August 1946, Luddenden, Yorkshire

The so-called realism of modern life has succeeded in making everything unreal. Whereas the so-called superstitions of the ancient religions made life real, so real that the little remaining culture in our society today is based on them and on the faint shadows of their original wonder.

We are beings before we are men and women, and it is from being that all Art and Poetry spring, and not from man or woman. The Being within us contains the covenant that we made with God before the world began.

Cambridge, 1951

Wish is recollection.

The utter naivety and ignorance of modern psychology in its lack of understanding of the Reality of the *Wish* in the human heart, is shown in the way they [psychologists] dismiss it as wish-fulfillment, as something wrong, and of no good. In this they show that they do not understand the real nature of wish, and what wish-fulfillment really is, and of the mysterious nature of the wish, for example, which appears from the world's point of view, impossible to fulfill, and remains just a wish.

And of the creative energy of the wish. *It is important to wish.* Wish springs from the very foundation of the creative will, it is the will itself. Wish does not spring from what we have not got, but from a recollection of what we once had, wishing is an act of recollection.

Is this not the meaning [of] Pascal's saying, 'You would not have sought me if you had not already found me'.

Art is wish-fulfillment and recollection. We desire and wish for that beauty we once had. We cannot wish for what we have never known; we cannot paint forms we have never seen. We are, all of us, haunted by the wish to recollect what we once were, what we have known and experienced, in a word, we seek to recreate this real life in our Art and Life. This runs through life in all its aspects from the man in the brothel house, to the saint in prayer, they are all concerned to recollect their real life, and all their life is a wish fulfilled in acts. It is in everything, even the most common ordinary everyday wish is an aspect of this magical process by which human life transforms its being and its world. We are in our ordinary life surrounded by a great mystery of world flux living and transforming itself by the energy of wishes, some evident and visible in their effect, some invisible in their influence. Hence the importance of wishes in the ancient fairy tales.

Cambridge, 1952

Magic is permutation of facts by Reality.

Cambridge, 1952

In a picture there is first of all, the approximate harmony, then there is the harmony, and finally there is the ultimate harmony.

A great many pictures are only based on approximate harmony, and most pictures today have only harmony. But the pictures that will live, and to which one can return again and again, have ultimate harmony, that is the harmony, the colours have been developed to their ultimate co-ordination.

A bad picture is one in which the picture destroys the subject, or where the subject destroys the picture. A great many of the pictures of the first forty years of the twentieth century are bad because they have destroyed the subject, this is a kind of arrogance of the grammatical elements, a lack of reverence for life and for things. It is clearly manifest in Cubism, which finally succeeded in destroying the human Image. When an age has nothing to say, it talks grammar, this is only another form of emptiness. A true picture affirms the subject. In a bad picture the subject is only an excuse.

Cambridge, April 1953

A truth dies as soon as it is born. But life itself begins as soon as it is born. Hence the eternal living quality of Art, and the quick crystallisations of Truth into forms without breath, empty, fossils of death.

Rationalism is the suburbia of the universe.

August 1953, Cambridge

Contrast is illumination.
The illumination of the moment.

Life is more important than Truth
Because Life is deeper than Truth.

Formula is only Truth
when it has been destroyed by life.

Renounce existence for the sake of life.

About orthodox religion,
there is no greater lie than the
one and only Truth.

Reason, analysis separates us
from life, whereas even the mistakes
we make in life unite us with it
more than the correctness of Truth.

Only life is accurate.

Reality is to be preferred to truth,
Truth always becomes orthodox.

Real Art is an interruption of
causality by metaphysical forces.

December 1955

The Artist in Society

A study and interpretation of the problems of modern painting

I WANT you to consider art as a manifestation of energy; that each age expresses its attitude towards life in the character of its energy. Before I come to discuss the art of our own time I must first speak about what I have come to call the poetic evidence of history. There are two great psychological types of artist, from which spring the two main energies in the history of art. First, let us look at this simple drawing. This is a [geometric] diagram which represents some elementary form combinations, the beauty of that curve against that triangle, the endeavour to find an objective standard of beauty by different formulas for proportion. Here, for instance, is a formula, three to five, and five to seven. The beauty of the relationship between three to five and five to seven. This type of artist uses form for its own sake, for the beauty in itself, trying to find an objective absolute of beauty. This type of artist I call Apollonian, and the clearest example of this type of art is Greek. Here is a Greek Temple: you see objective beauty, love of form for its own sake. You see in this the very nature of stone—solid, massive, resting on the ground. Now let us look at the other psychological type.

The word 'art' is capitalised throughout the typescript. It is changed to lower case here since the capital offers no clarification or precision to the multiple denotations the author intends—works *of* art, artistic movements and periods, art as more or less synonymous with culture, art as the operative habit of the mind, even art as a quasi-psychological/spiritual function.

This simple scribble [showing vigorous pencil strokes with profile head emerging at top—by artist] is first and foremost an expression of energy, of feeling. It is urgent in its need to release itself as soon as possible. Now this type of artist uses form to express emotion or states of being, and not form for its own sake. This type I call the Dionysian, who lives for emotion and to lose himself in ecstasy. The ecstasy, or the emotion, is more important than the form, or even the nature of the material. Here is an example of Dionysian art [a Gothic cathedral]. This is an expression of sheer transcendental emotion. This stone has been drawn out and up into the sky, until it is quite thin, un-stonelike. I call this Romantic art. The other I call Classical art, and the history of art is formed by the struggle between these two great psychological types, sometimes between individual artists, sometimes between schools, and sometimes within the nature of a single artist. Classical art belongs to the realm of the conscious, the conscious rational constructing of beauty. Romantic art belongs to the realm of the unconscious. I want you to remember these two attitudes because they are one of the great keys that is going to help us to understand the complex art of our own time. What happens to these different energies as they near and surround us in our own time?

In the eighteenth century the Apollonian art dominated because it was a rational age, materialistic and formal, right through everyday life. This formed a hard, materialistic crust of the love of form and logic and formula over everything. But soon there were signs, and voices of warning. The deep energies of the unconscious began to manifest themselves. One voice, in France, began to be heard—the voice of Rousseau. A super-sensitive, neurotic man, one of the first modern men—he was a romantic, he freed the emotional life of the eighteenth century from its formal restraint. He released an energy which helped to explode in that total collapse of an age, which we call the French Revolution.

In England there appeared a tremendous sign, which in spirit dealt a real death-blow to eighteenth-century rationalism, and classical art. This was the painter and poet, William Blake, whose significance was so little recognised in his own time. He was a real voice crying in the wilderness, full of warning of what was coming. He felt already 'the dark satanic mills' of the industrial era. His voice of creative affirmation reaches over a hundred years to take its place in the front line of our modern painters. At the same time, almost everywhere, the prison of intellectual order imposed by the eighteenth century upon society was being broken down by the rising revolution of romantic energy. In music, Beethoven destroyed the classical forms and ideas. Later, in France, the conflict was carried on between the artists Ingres and Delacroix. In Ingres we find the expression of form for its own sake, the supreme intellectual order of classical psychology. This was opposed by the fiery creative energy of Delacroix, who felt that this order was deadly.

Living at the same time as Delacroix, and fighting for the same cause, was the great French poet, Baudelaire, who was one of the first real modern poets; one of the first real modern men. He had no illusions about the way civilisation was going, and his sayings, from his intimate journals and other writings, are remarkable for their penetration and prophecy. It is no wonder that he is thought so highly of by the Surrealists.

The romantic energy was to receive its greatest setback at the appearance in the world of a very terrifying phenomenon called industrialism. Industrialism developed and strengthened itself with the new rationalism of science. A great part of this, when stripped of its pseudo-idealism, was the scientific organisation of man's criminal faculties, in order to make money more efficiently. The romantic, poetic faculty, wilted, or struggled to preserve itself in the Pre-Raphaelites, a movement which had a great deal of good in it. In France, just as it did many years before, between Ingres and Delacroix, the issue again arose between two artists. One was Cézanne, and the other Van Gogh. Both were to have a tremendous influence on the art of our own century. Cézanne was a classical painter, and his ideas of society were of a conventional order. But in painting he was a revolutionary. He sought to try and make painting return to the fundamental elements of form. He analyzed the subtle, abstract structure of a landscape. He said, the thing to do is 'to paint Poussin over again from nature'. The fundamental forms, as you all know, are the circle and the square. These forms appear in nature as a compound and variation. These Cézanne used again according to their bare structural value.

Living at the same time with the complete opposite vision of life and art, was the romantic energy of Van Gogh, who used form and colour as a means of expressing emotion. He wanted to change society. He was restless and felt the mechanical civilisation growing more and more. He re-affirmed human sensibility, and really lived, knowing and experiencing the suffering of poverty and ill-health. Between these two was Gauguin—another romantic—but he, too, saw what a terrible machine modern civilisation was growing into.

After the turn of the century there grew up another movement, which renounced the colour, atmosphere and vagueness of the Impressionists, and cried, back to form, back to the fundamentals of form! This was Cubism, which grew out of Cézanne's discoveries. Cubism stripped painting of its vagueness and created works based on those fundamental forms, the circle and the square, thus restoring the structural sense in pictures. They produced a series of austere works. In the middle of this movement came the first horrible manifestation of our so-called civilisation—the Great War of 1914–18. During those four years, what happened to the creative energy and sensibility of the artist?

Cubism emerged as a definite, accepted language, and survived. It was an intellectual, classical art, using form for its own sake. It made painting into a series of problems to be solved. Picasso, Braque and Juan Gris all used this language. Many artists, like Léger, made it their final language, and never used any other. This was the classical Apollonian art, and produced many fine works. But what happened to the sensitive, romantic energy which we have been tracing? It emerged in almost universal dissillusionment, in deep disgust at civilised life.

During the war, Zurich became an important centre for the streams of thought of the time. Refugees from all the warring nations gathered there, and formed a movement to which they gave the quaint title of Dada. This movement, born out of a deep disgust, was an expression of complete negation and renunciation of all art. After the war, about 1920, artists of the Dada movement organised themselves in Paris saying, why commit suicide, join us. It was a movement of organised nonsense. Each exhibition was attended by a storm. They said to society, you want art. You don't deserve it. This is the kind of art that the level of society you have created, deserves. And so, a Dadaist named Kurt Schwitters used to go round old rubbish bins picking out bits of fish bones, and odds and ends, making pictures from them. The atmosphere got more and more intense. Dadaist demonstrations took place in many parts of Europe. In Cologne there was an exhibition where, in order to get to it, you had to enter through a public lavatory. You were given an axe, to cut down the pictures with. There was a choir up the chimney, singing, and a young girl, dressed in white for her first communion, recited obscene poetry.

To give a history of Surrealism would require a whole lecture to itself, but what of its significance? Dadaism, making fun of everything, had done a certain amount of dissolving, but the artists and poets, in which the Surrealist spirit was beginning to appear, saw there was no hope and turned from the external world to the interior world. This turning away marks one of the most important points in the history of modern art. It was not just an artistic movement. It coincided with the appearance of a science called psychology, and with the discoveries of a thinker called Freud. This turning inward was really the beginning of a search for new values. But the period of renunciation was far from over. Surrealism renounced both art and culture. Why? I will try to explain.

The strongest section of society is also the most ignorant and prejudiced in matters of human understanding. That section is called bourgeois. I do not mean bourgeois in the purely economic sense. I mean the kind of mentality that hates spiritual adventure, which tries to keep society from growing, by endeavouring to preserve the status quo, by making a system of habits which are really a machine for making money and preserving comfort. The bourgeois persecutes anyone who questions that reality, either by organised force, like the police, or in England, by indifference. This class of people have always existed in one form or another, but since the industrial revolution put a powerful weapon in their hands, they have become stronger and more organised. It is they who have contempt for culture, or a secret inferiority complex about it. It is they who have created that vulgar institution, the Royal Academy, which represents their idea of culture. It was they who ignored Blake, who starved Chatterton, who burned books of wisdom and poetry all over the world, who exiled Shelley and D. H. Lawrence, persecuted Rimbaud and Verlaine, made bestial noises at the appearance of Schoenberg's music, threw stones at Jean Jacques Rousseau. It is they who crucified Christ, and hundreds of years later, crucified anybody who did not believe in Christ. Their habitual comfort of mind is based on intolerance and subconscious fear, and they have tried to crush every new manifestation of the spirit. They include people in all walks of life, from clergymen to bankers, from grocers to artists, and they exist in all nations.

Surrealism at once attacked this mentality—its outlook, its morals, its ideas, at the same time proceeded with its research into the psychology of man. In the complex activities of Surrealism there are three main fields of action—they can be roughly called first, therapeutic, second, militant, and third, poetic. The first, therapeutic, deals with the health-giving qualities of drawing and painting. It is a fact that if we have devils or neuroses, to give them their modern name, we can project the image of that devil onto paper—then the devil is in our power. He is on paper. And we can now kick him around the room. He has become conscious, familiar property, common property and we can tear him in pieces. Thus he loses a great deal of his power. Primitive people do this. They make magic images of the devils or negative images that obsess them.

Next, let us consider the militant side of Surrealism. This attacked, with paintings, exhibitions, films and demonstrations, the bourgeois world. The two most important militant surrealist artists working in this way are René Magritte and Salvador Dali. René Magritte, a Belgian, takes the world of the habits of the bourgeois mind and turns it upside down, rendering it absurd. The important thing to remember is that he uses a technique that the bourgeois can understand—a nose always looks like a nose. All forms are recognisable, but the world is no longer habitable.

Salvador Dali, a young Spanish painter, who is now only about 37 years of age, is an astonishing phenomena in modern art. He has been in the fore of the stormy history of Surrealism. He has a ferocious imagination. He uses the same method as Magritte, but it is far more penetrating and intelligent. He penetrates beneath the crust and façade of good fellowship, the hail-fellow-well-met common-sense of our nice rational society, and shows our secret repressed images and distorted wishes, our masochism, the sexual lusts of sadism, under our respectable fetishes and taboos. All this is expressed with a terrible and ruthless Romanticism. His method is to give us a dose of the poison that we hide, in order to bring it to the surface and make us sick, thus throwing it out of our system. This remarkable man is the Jesuit of Surrealism, clinically revealing our sins. His is one of the most diabolical minds in Surrealism. Again, the important thing is that his pictures are painted with a Victorian photographic 'realism', a technique everybody can understand. He is, incidently, probably the finest minature painter in the world today. The irony is that he can paint and draw better than the academicians.

Let us now consider the third section, the poetic imagination, which is a kind of healing of the wound made by the astringent operations of the other sections of Surrealism. These represent an historical attempt to free the subconscious mind of man so that it can naturally play its part of enriching everyday life. It is an attempt to establish again the romantic energy.

Paul Klee's art, for instance, is a natural, immediate, poetic expression, at once wise, direct and highly sophisticated, with the torture of sensitive expression. It is human expression, which, unlike moral or political conceptions, will endure. It is an abstract, ironic land of faery, made of peculiar, nervous geometry. It is related to Oriental art, for Klee brought back to European art the idea of the profundity of the intimate. Our civilisation is obsessed with the colossal. We identify profundity with sheer physical size.

We see in the history of art how the outer world is a reflection of the inner world of man, of his inner attitude. Thus, how right those surrealist paintings were—done many years ago—in that they are accurate descriptions of the outer world we have created from the falseness of our inner attitude. Pictures of ruined houses; half a piano, with a corset bulging out of its inside; a chair on a chimney; machinery in bits, with various parts of the human body sticking out of them. These pictures, by the Surrealists, have become reality to us during the last year, when in bombed towns the dead, and the remains of the dead, are carried away in motor cars. The dance of death, which we are experiencing, was prophesied in many a surrealist painting. Is it surprising that art, the sensitive instrument of our race, should be affected by all these tremendous happenings? Did the Royal Academy ever express the realities of our age?

We are living in a transitional age, thus we express ourselves in a transitional art, an art of unfixed forms, ever-changing, mobile. We are witnessing the death of an epoch, and the endeavour to bring about a new cycle of existence. Great forces are being released. The crisis and issue of our time is this. Through being dominated by the bourgeois mentality, which grew stronger by using that scientific rationalism which tends to crush the natural creative imagination of man, civilisation grew more and more into a rational machine. In this situation the best type of man to develop is the extrovert or useful person, who has no power to reflect upon his own condition, or situation (reflection being an introvert faculty). He can be exploited more easily either for political or economic ends.

The bourgeois phenomenon, together with the two main reactionary forces against it, Fascism and Communism, are at bottom the same phenomenon. They can only really work when man is completely rationalised and extrovert. Irrationality causes variation and disturbance. This is proved if you study Fascist or Communist education, which is fundamentally aimed at creating the extrovert man, or useful person. Although both are called political movements, I believe at bottom they are biological. If you want to see either Fascism or Communism, both working completely successfully, there is one place in this world to look. You must study the world of the ant, specially the white ant. The ant is completely rational. There is the ideal working state. There are no individuals, no critics, no abnormalities, no sick ants, each ant works all day for the state, without question. It is a highly organised system, and they have rationalised all individuality or variation out of existence so successfully 'that in some types the brain is hardly there at all, the wings are done away with, the eyes are destroyed, or are just forms, there is no sex life, particular or general, the sexual organs exist very imperfectly and do not function, they are completely sterile. These insects achieve communism, where all individuality is successfully destroyed for the welfare of the community.' You see, it actually works and this is the price you have to pay for Communism and Fascism. It is the only way it could work, because Communism and Fascism, to be efficient, must first destroy individual particulars, because these are variations and uncertainties, unknown potentialities that will not fit in with the general norm of usefulness, thus destroying the efficiency of the state or community.

See 'Social life of insects', *Encyclopedia Brittanica*.

Surrealism is nothing more or less than the poetic imagination of man organised with its back against the wall of a brutal, mechanised age. We have created an objective civilisation, and an objective civilisation decays through non-contemplation of its own nature. Thus it follows that the contemplation of its own nature, which is the process by which it grows, is only possible through its members, in other words, its individuals. The salvation and growth of man is through the consciousness of the individual. When we grow in ourselves, humanity grows also, because we are adding to the amount of growth in the world. When collective, social energy dominates the conscience of the individual with a theoretical abstract norm decay sets in through hypocrisy, because people will try to live their real lives under the theoretical one. Get away from the individual and you get away from reality into abstractions, like the state. Society realises itself in the individual, evolves through the individual, and degenerates through the individual. All barbarians are against the individual just as all creative peoples are for the individual, because they realise that to crush the consciousness of the individual is to stop this evolution. The League of Nations failed because it was only an abstract idea. There was no personal unity in the nations, because there was no personal unity in the persons who represented those nations. And where there is no personal unity there is no creative power. You cannot create a peaceful, unified society out of disharmonious individuals, no matter if you do use the police force. World peace is based on personal peace. You can talk at dozens of Peace Meetings and be a member of the League of Nations but as long as you are a bad-tempered, ill-willed man, easily angered, without kindness, you are helping to destroy the cause of peace in this world.

I say all this to show that the issue of modern life relies on the personal consciousness of the individual. It all comes down to attitude. The miracle today is how art has attained such a sensitive degree of manifestation as it has in an age in which there is such a mechanised, brutal drive against the creative spirit in man. When the general life of our civilisation is so cheap and vulgar, the environment on all sides contriving to deaden our sensibilities, not only by the thousand inane vacancies called social life, but also by perhaps the most deadly of all to our inner growth, all those cheap, pseudo-scientific catch-words which have a worse effect on a person's creative powers than many a primitive superstition. We have created a society sterilised by objectivity, frozen by the vanity of [rationalised] knowledge.

Within the body of this society is the decay of its official religion. The

Christian Church is a temporal power and profession obeying the laws and conceptions of the State, trying to give itself a place in the society of the human being by casuistry, sentimentality, good fellowship, or an embarrassing athletic spiritual optimism whose hearty blows on our wounds arouse inevitable disgust. The Church tries to hitch and adapt itself to every vital, contemporary idea in a pathetic attempt to keep alive. The Church, which recently had its last historical chance to prove its reality, failed, and showed itself to be just a huge theological vacuum, out of touch with the blood, the sweat, and the mysterious pleasures of human life. Proof of this is the atmosphere of a church, empty, decaying like a tomb. The God of Life is not there, and the instinct of people is to know it, and no amount of theological argument, cajoling or sentiment, can hide this, or convince a human being demanding the bread of life. Thus the Church occupies merely an academic place in the spiritual life of man. We are witnessing, I think, the end of the Christian era. The Church is dying, obeying the cycle of birth and decay, which works in religions as it does in nature. The real sign of the end is the usual characteristics: the spectacle of the Church, degraded and deformed, frozen into a thousand institutions, all babbling and quarrelling over parochial, theological matters, while human society is dying around them for the breath of life.

Then there is the official art created by this same society. The Royal Academy is a commercial market-place of the dull, mechanical aping of nature, sentimental, hard-hearted, unintelligent pictures, completely out of touch with the realities of our time, and in fact, an expression of nice sterility. This same society, where people called critics make a living out of selling their opinions on art, does not know what art is, and is therefore content to have the matter settled by leaving it in the hands of these critics. This is a society that regards science with uncritical awe, whose members vaguely accept the scientific view of the universe, but who, deep in their unconscious self, are dissatisfied, because the natural, creative poetry of the human heart can find no expression, and very little foothold in such a sterile, hygienic universe. Our society is based on frustration. Beneath the rational, cardboard façade of modern life lives the monster of unfulfilled essential desires. The deep frustration of fecundity breeds underground cruelty, soon to manifest itself in intolerance, and the universal disease of war. What we call the ill-constituted and the abnormal is nothing more than the world as it has been created by what is 'average' to us. We *are* the ill-constituted and the abnormal.

It is often asked by men of finance—the present princes of culture—

what use is the artist to us? And the answer is, no use. In a society where the purpose of education is to enable us to live and be a success in the jungle of a commercial civilisation, art is a luxury, and culture is something which is bought and sold, not created. The ordinary man in the street creates no culture. His main function is to be useful ('Heaven protect me from useful people', said Baudelaire). He sits in the cinema, he listens to the radio, he is completely passive, and makes no creative act. Consider the poverty of such a life, and how it leads finally to apathy and complete mechanisation, how it is gradually falling into the life of the ant.

It was against such a society that Surrealism made its imaginative revolution. Exhibitions were held in different parts of the world. In a Foreword to the International Surrealist Exhibition held in London 1936, the eminent English writer on art, Mr. Herbert Read, said, 'do not judge this movement kindly, it's not just another stunt. It is the desperate act of men, too profoundly convinced of the rottenness of our civilisation to wish to save a shred of its respectability.' Jacques Maritain, the great neo-thomist philosopher of France has said, 'Modern art is flagellating itself'. With Surrealism art became the avenger, the destroyer. The outraged, poetic imagination of man, the creative God in him, frustrated by our society, became the God of destruction. Life in our modern society had frozen into a thousand meaningless institutions. The old-world era held tight to its universe of habits, which had no longer any creative use in the world. Surrealism worked to destroy the old-world consciousness, with ruthless exposure of natural indignation, it showed up the diseases which are undereneath its rational structure. All this was done with a terrifying romanticism. William Blake said—'the tigers of wrath are wiser than the horses of instruction.' Surrealism was a psychic wrath directed against the sleep of our apathy.

If we consider the history of art we shall see that any new appearance of the creative spirit of life is announced first by the explosion of the old forms into which life has hardened itself. It must melt down this material in order to create new forms. Frozen forms at the end of an epoch must be melted down, and that melting, which in our time is Surrealism, hurts. Better the living chaos of life than the dead order of doctrine. The torment and hideous imagery of frustrated, creative instinct, which menaces us from many a modern work of art, is 'the tiger of wrath', which makes us stop and consider the question of our whole attitude to life. Artists are the sensitive instruments through which an age can recognise and realise itself. Art is a form by which an age may contemplate itself.

Now we come to the question of the isolation of the modern artist, his essential loneliness, and his tragic, yet creative position in the society of today. We have seen that culture is something that is created, not purchased. In the Middle Ages the whole community was creative. The cathedrals were made by inspired workmen—there was a degree of inspiration in every man, and he felt that he was expressing an inspiration, each according to his ability. He could look at a cathedral and know and see his part in it. Thus a general culture was created which was the soil from which the great individual masters that came after grew. Today we have seen what has happened, how life is being taken more and more out of our hands, how society is not, as a whole, creative.

This brings us to an important point to remember, for it is the real key to explaining the artist's isolation today. The point is this. The artist is nothing more than the creative remains of society. He is what is left, one of the few cells in which a sense of beauty and of creative power still lives. He is the only means left to us by which to measure the life of our senses and imagination. He is our only link with the wonder-world of the child. So it behoves us to preserve these fragments of creativeness we call artists, for today they stand in real danger of perishing.

In that curious period following the collapse of the Roman Empire, when the Christian civilisation was trying to be born, the early fathers of the Church took the seeds of their ideas into the desert, and lived the life of hermits in order to preserve these ideas. The artist today has no physical desert to go into. He goes deep into the desert of his own self, communing there, and trying to keep alive that vital spark which has no name but which is the real seed and foundation of creative civilisation in every man, no matter who he is. That is the position. Our historical situation today is a desert of death, intolerance and vulgarity, in which the hermit-artist tries to keep alive that spark of creative life. Will he succeed in carrying this sensitive vital seed across this dark transitional period? If society no longer wants him he has two alternatives; either perish, or be a kind of hermit. But there is more to the historical picture than that.

After the Middle Ages had broken down, the Rennaisance discovered new things, fresh knowledge, the re-discovery of the Greeks and their world of thought, the analysis of the physical world. A real discovery which excited them was anatomy. See the excitement with which Michaelangelo and Leonardo da Vinci regarded the discovery of anatomy. Today we cannot pretend to be excited about anatomy as a discovery in art. We have experienced its possibilities thoroughly for some hundreds of years. But the great discovery of our age in art is the discovery of the unconscious mind, which will have a tremendous influence on the art and life of the future. The outer world has been practically explored, and the physical sciences have advanced enormously. But the inner world of man is almost unknown as a fountain of inspiration and a way to the secret of life. John Bunyan said—'God enters the soul through a wound.' The soul of modern man has been wounded by the crisis and spiritual conflict caused by the folly and vanity of the conscious, rational, attitude of mind, and that wound has opened up the unconscious mind. That wound has opened up what the intellect and reason refused to acknowledge and give a place to in our life.

Today, beside the war going on in the physical world of our planet, there is another war, equally terrible, being fought in the inner and psychological world of man. This is the conflict and suffering of growth. It is there, amongst the filth, the excrement, the perversity, the love and the hate, and the sacrifice of the human psyche, that the modern artist works, trying to get into contact with the unconscious origins of these things, trying to unmask them, and to give them signs and symbols. The future of civilisation depends upon the freedom of the individual to develop his personal consciousness; to find and to fulfil that essential self, which is unique to each one of us. It can be done by gradually stripping away the impurities, the false ideas and conceptions we have of ourselves. These are a kind of dirt on the inner glass of our psychic outlook.

Take an artist like Dali. He scrupulously expresses all his thoughts and feelings. He reveals all his lusts, for now, in this transitional period, we must not put a taboo around any image. We must have the courage to express everything without taboo. Walt Whitman said—'through me forbidden voices, voices of sexes, and lusts, voices veiled, and I remove the veil, voices indecent, by me clarified and transfigured.' There is no fresh creative vision without first the purification of dissolution. The era of the old world is dying with volcanic sighs. I can well understand Dali's clinical worship of death. This coming to the surface of the filth and refuse of the psyche is an important spiritual act of our time. This dance of death, this purification is an essential and inevitable happening, which alone will make possible the re-birth of the naked human heart, cleansed from the cult of death, which is the cult of our time. We do not love life, we could not love life and make a world like we have made today. We do not take pleasure in our own natures. We have not got that mysterious pride in being what we are, irrespective of whether we are a success or a failure. We do not love ourselves, therefore we do not love others or life. The time has come for us to re-discover life again.

One of the good things Surrealism did was to enlarge the field of art and to bring the artist and society closer together. Strangely enough it did this by denying both art and culture. There I think it was right. Art is aesthetic expression. Now aesthetic expression for civilised man is trained, specialised expression. This immediately divides men into trained and untrained artists, professional and amateur. The amateur has naturally the inferior feeling, while the professional has the snobbery of feeling superior. Surrealism aimed at destroying this distinction. Hence its greatest opponents were successful professional artists. I think it is very clear that we must return to human expression again, not necessarily 'Art' with a capital 'A'.

Every human being, because he is human, is a unique being. Thus, the dreams of a village idiot, from an ultimate, human point of view, are just as sacred as the dreams of a Michaelangelo. The work of lunatics, of children, of so-called ordinary people are again, from this same human point of view, as important as the paintings of Rembrandt. It is not art exactly, but it is the rich soil from which art can grow. I have found that the so-called ordinary person, if freed from the fear of competition and other people's opinions, and also if freed from the idea of copying nature, will create very interesting pictures. Better to have a whole society painting such pictures than just a few specialised artists. For what we really all want is more life—life abundantly.

But we cannot have life until we create it in ourselves. This would give back to the ordinary man his creative self-respect. It would give him the feeling of being a creative being, and provide the soil out of which could grow the possible foundations of a world art. We all have the unconscious inspiration in us. It is a matter of contacting it. Eric Gill said 'the artist is not a special kind of man, but every man is a special kind of artist'. When the ordinary man begins to feel this, then you are getting a creative society. What is needed, in order to experiment, is more leisure, and the creative use of leisure, to widen our ideas of beauty the better to appreciate primitive art, children's art, oriental art, etc.

We hear a lot about the education of people for use and work, but what about the education of people for leisure?—to help people to enjoy life? Work, work, is the hypocritical, money-making, psychological propaganda that we have all had enough of.

This quotation is in fact from A. K. Coomaraswamy. It was given a currency by Gill it might not otherwise have had. It first appeared in Coomaraswamy's essay 'Meister Eckhart's View of Art' in *The Transformation of Art in Nature* 1934, p.64 and refers to the operative habit of intellect that determines *how* a work *of* art is made. This 'habit' or 'art' (as it was conceived by the scholastics) stays *in* the artist, as distinct from the modern conception of art as a select category of external works giving aesthetic pleasure. In saying, in the same passage, 'we all have the unconscious inspiration in us', Collins is referring to the traditional conception.

I hold that the romantic, or surrealist attitude is one of the deepest forms of life, but except in a few individuals it has not been attained, owing to the general frustration of society. People who have never experienced this attitude seek to destroy it by what they call realism, calling it an escape from life, which really means that they themselves have lost the capacity for romantic emotion. The romantic outlook requires a lot of concentration, energy, and above all, leisure. It is said by certain critics, calling themselves realists, that the machine would kill the romantic ideas of life, but I hold that the exact opposite will be true. Ultimately, it is the machine alone that will make the romantic idea of life possible, because it alone can create the leisure upon which the romantic life is based. For it is in leisure that some of the great secrets of life were discovered. Creative leisure is the foundation of the romantic idea of life. The Romantic Movement works to liberate and enlarge the field of human expression and experience, so that all human beings can be represented, the ill-constituted as well as the well-constituted. For history is the recorded process of the attempts of the creative imagination in man to transform the gross material of the world. The desperate attempt of the Surrealists, just before this war, failed. But it was a failure only in the sense that Shelley's life was a failure. That failure was their glory, because the failure was a reflection not on them, but upon us, our world, our society.

Rationalists are very fond of saying that without reason the universe would be a mad place; but of course it is a mad place, even with reason. Any artist, or poet, or really alive person, knows it is mad. It is a horrible and terrifying place full of a bitter cruelty and obscenity. It is a place full of wonderful, profound beauty, and the tenderness of vast mysterious sacrifices. What it is not is a nice little rational puzzle that works out in the end. No, the universe of experience is a different matter. It is a deep abyss, full of voices, some whispering, some shouting, the voices of frustration, the voices of unfulfilled longings, the voices of mysterious lusts, of mystical desires that can find no place in the world, the voices of deep, buried wrongs that cry out from an abyss of world desolation, the voices of misfits, neurotics, failures, the weak, an abyss full of the ecstacy of the poet, the glow of the praise of life, full of an incomprehensible love and an incomprehensible destructiveness. All these voices are centred in man's consciousness and in order to escape from them he builds in his mind a prison of rationality, and tries by the aid of the official world, to shut them out. But those voices are the very voices of life itself, and today they are breaking that prison to pieces, to compel man to face up to the fact of their existence. These voices are the Kingdoms of Heaven and Hell, and are all focused in the human heart, and constitute for man his real universe.

It is a paradox that society evolves through the activity of anti-social types. The criminal, the artist and the saint, they all have this in common, that their activity disturbs the warm, gregarious herd-loving, sleep and inertia of social life. Either by destructive activity or by creative activity. The artist has a lot of the criminal in him, and something of the austere dedication of purpose you get in a prostitute or a saint. William James, in his book *Varieties of Religious Experience,* suggests that we call these strange people like the mystics and saints anti-social, because we can really find no place in our society for them. It is likely that our society has not evolved enough as yet, to be able to use these psychological types. This applies to the artist. We simply do not know how to experience his productions, or where to place him in society. When one hears the so-called common man saying he does not understand modern art, he is not being honest enough, for the truth is he does not understand any art, ancient or modern, because the principles of art are eternal.

The great cultures of the past expressed a collective mythology. They have all gradually died. Today we are witnessing the decay of Christian mythology, and, following it, in this transitional period, we are living temporarily on a view of the universe given us by science. This is proving too barren for the human heart with its great capacity for imaginative riches.

In the past a great deal of art was propaganda. The Church employed the artist to propagate through images its ideas, because it realised that images are universal in a way that words are not. The instruments of propaganda today are the cinema and the radio, and they are so efficient that painting cannot hope to compete with them. So it appears to superficial critics of our commercial civilisation that painting is going to die for that reason. What is there left to paint, they ask? On the contrary, this is the great historical chance for the art of painting. Liberated from the servitude of propaganda, there remains for it the great task of being the one medium for the direct expression of the mystery of human consciousness itself.

Human consciousness is one of the greatest mysteries of life, and to have a direct medium for expressing its sensations in the language of form and colour, which is universal in a way words are not, not only reveals what is important in the art of the past, both Western and Eastern, civilised and savage, but it constitutes a real hope for the future of painting. Today we have no universal mythology, but the discovery of the fact that man has unknown depths of consciousness within him. And this source already beginning to manifest itself in poetic images in each artist, constitutes a beginning. I believe that each person has his own secret mythology, his own unique creation, which represents the symbolical images by which his interior life lives, and forms the psychological structure of his whole personality. Our real unconscious self speaks to us in the poetry of images. The creation and expression of this personal mythology, first of all, is far more important than either art or culture, because it is the basis of both. Those things can come afterwards. So, in a democratic society we can have thousands of people painting their personal mythologies all different, in a rich variety, because the creative imagination of each artist leavens the general sensibility of collective society, with fresh revelations, fresh because personal. Through exhibitions, the continual rubbing together of all these mythologies, and the natural influence they will have on one another, will gradually create a general version of the mythology of the human expressions of consciousness. These images will be the music of what Jung calls the collective unconscious. There will then be an organic creation proceeding from the organic sense of life and not from the imposition of a set of intellectual ideas, trying to imprison life in a dead order. It is not order that we need today. It is the organic sense of life, and for that there is no substitute, intellectual or otherwise. Until we have the organic sense of life, there can be no creative society, and so we have come back again to the consciousness of the individual, and his attitude.

All real creation is personal, in art as in life. The mystery of personality is the basis of romantic art, as it is the basis of democracy. They are one. Democracy is the most difficult and most creative form of society known so far to man, difficult because creative, and romantic art is its natural expression. The creative chaos of democracy with all its weaknesses, hypocrisy and injustice, is much closer to the human way of making a society than the iron prison of dictatorship states, Communist or Fascist. So, the flowing empirical expression of romantic art is much nearer the actual life of the human psyche. Democratic romantic vision of civilisation puts the responsibility of life upon the individual. We cannot give our problems over to some leader, who will solve them. The democratic civilisation can be the soil in which the moulding and leavening of personal vision and of the collective unconscious mind of man will create a new world mythology of expression. The re-establishment of the creative imagination in the life of man, the working towards a world consciousness, that is, the idea of the world as one living body, constitutes the great task of the democratic attitude in art and in life, because real creative energy works through diversity.

For example, the law of growth is a universal one, and yet that law is expressed differently in the form of a rose and in an oak tree. Under the diverse expressions of different artists works the same universal creative spirit. And deep under the consciousness of man works the hidden unity of the unconscious mind of the human race. The time has come for us to affirm the fundamental unity of man, to work for that which unifies him, and not what divides him.

We are told a lot about our duty today, but it is man's duty to be free. He owes it to society, and I define freedom as the fulfillment of man's essential self. Liberty is not something that is let loose: it is something that is created. It is an achievement first in the individual man, then in the nation, then in the world community. The real measure of our civilisation is its fruits. Civilisation is created by men of good will, and not by politics. A European once showed an Indian sage a wireless and told him of the wonders of modern civilisation, to which the Indian replied—'you make battleships, but you cannot even control your thoughts, to what will that lead?' We know to our cost the answer to that.

I hold the view that art is essentially a non-moral phenomenon and that is its great significance for man. The importance of the aesthetic emotion of beauty is that it is the one emotion that is purified and sanctified from all other emotions. It can exist in them, but it stands apart from them. It is purified from both love and hate, from fear and desire, from the frustration of wish and the fulfilment of wish, it is redeemed from moral, ethical, religious and philosophical ideas. It can exist *in* them but it is not *of* them. Long after religions and morals and philosophies have passed away, we can stand in front of pictures and be deeply moved by their beauty, although the religious ideas in the pictures no longer mean anything to us. Religions and civilisations pass away, but their beauty remains, for if the truth be told artists only use religions and philosophy as an excuse, as a stimulus, like drink, to create beauty. At bottom they are really concerned with the poetic emotion of beauty, because their instinct tells them that it is the fundamental emotion.

One of the keys to the psychology of the artist is that he will take politics, social life, family, and many other things, and throw them all away if they do not stimulate his creative instinct. He throws them away if they are true or untrue, real or unreal, because truth is irrelevant if it does not stimulate his creative instinct, because creative instinct is truth, and its absence is falsehood. Small wonder then that the artist should be regarded with suspicion.

This surreal emotion of beauty is universal. It can be experienced by a criminal or a banker, by a harlot or a housewife, by members of different religions, or political parties. It is surreal emotion that transports us out of the dull, endless babble of ideas of right and wrong, good and evil. It is more important than truth or untruth because it is neither true or untrue: it is a universal quality and attribute of creative power itself. It is an emotion that can be experienced for its own sake, and this experience can heighten our understanding and reconcile us to life. It is therefore worthy of study. It cannot be defined. The artist instinctively knows how to create images, forms and textures that will arouse that emotion in people, but he cannot explain it. Of this surreal emotion of beauty, which he made his sole study, in his long novel *Remembrance of Things Past*, Marcel Proust said, 'the intelligence cannot find it'—'it is the essence of everyday things'.

The terms 'surreal emotion' and 'surreal beauty', used here and elsewhere were coined by the author to denote supra-conscious, as opposed to subconscious, levels of reference. But despite the present elaborate explanation the terms do not entirely evade clearly unintended surrealist connotations.

The Surrealists are the romantics of the twentieth century, the free-thinkers of art, and like the Romantics they believe in freed emotions—in other words, fulfilled emotions. The suppression of sensibility and the emotion of beauty spells disaster for society. Read the depressing list of works of art destroyed by a deformed psychological type like Cromwell, the man who has done such incalculable harm. The ways to the mystery of life are numberless. There is no one way. It is the mystery of life that is absolute, not the way to it. The way is relative. As Goethe so wisely says—'There is truth in everything but the whole truth is not in one thing'.

The Inquisition tortured people who did not believe in their way to God, and those people who were tortured, afterwards tortured others who did not believe in their way to God. We must feel deeply ashamed and humiliated when we read of free men like Dr. Seager who was tortured by Calvin, who wrote to Calvin asking him to put an end to his sufferings. Deep down in our unconscious being is the God of life, who, if he is unfulfilled or frustrated, becomes the God of death. The life-wish becomes the death-wish. These Calvins and Cromwells, Popes and Inquisitors hate life. Their religion, no matter under what sign of love it works, is hatred of life. Communists kill Fascists, and Fascists Communists. But the person most hated is he who believes in neither one of them, neither in their God or their Devil, their just man or their scapegoat. For the artist is the eternal advocate of life. Fanaticism and intolerance, no matter for what cause, is a disease and blight upon human activity. The artist is the direct expression of the genius of life, and the genius of life cannot live in the iron-bound society of intolerance. I am not making any extravagant claims for the artist, because I believe that the artist is in every man and woman, and it is the artist in them, that is the God in them.

Sensitive minds in all times are troubled by premonitions of the next age, and in this age of creative upheaval—a time of discord and psychic flux when under the auspices of scientific achievement, we can see the pathetic meanness of modern life—the human heart is beginning to ask for new life: and that demand will increase. Surrealism has destroyed the local consciousness, and thereby cleared the way for a world art. Now Surrealism is over. Its work is done. But the surrealist spirit lives and will live because it is eternal. Surrealist emotion exists in all works of all ages, because surreal emotion is the emotion which when experienced enables man to transcend habitual reality. The world is deeper with a hidden, eternal continuity in the light of that emotion. Unsullied by morality or philosophy, in one simultaneous act of exaltation and illumination it reveals the roots of all the worlds and sets in motion higher faculties than rational understanding alone. It is part of the very empirical structure of the movement of life itself. This emotion cannot be forced: it comes of its own will and is a form of grace. It is the very essence of the poetic principle of the imagination in man. It is the profound, flowing God in us.

To re-discover life again we must attain the human. We must give up this death cult, this liking for the negative side of our nature, for to whatever direction we orientate our life, in that direction everything will lead, drawing towards us the very ideas and emotions necessary to carry us in that direction. Thus, if we harbour death-feelings and get pleasure out of cruelty and sorrow, so we draw the vibration of these things towards us. The time has come for us to renounce the obscene image of Christ hanging and bleeding on the cross. For hundreds of years Christian propaganda has impressed this image on our consciousness. It has haunted and ruined many thousands of lives, or given a distorted and destructive consolation to others. Imagine continually impressing the sensitive and magical consciousness of a child with such an image. Imagine being asked to worship such an image as representing God. It is a blasphemy against the very spirit of life.

The time has certainly come for us to reject this worship of pain and sorrow. The world's true fruit is the creative joy of the human heart, and it is in the light of that emotion—which we will call surreal beauty—that we know that the purpose of the world is not knowledge, not wisdom, not success or failure, victory or defeat, nor truth, but that creative joy which is the God of life. Until we desire that God he will not appear. Even the word life is too abstract for me. I use the word wonder. A person is alive according to the degree of his sense of wonder. He who has no wonder is dead, no matter how clever he is, or how much knowledge he possesses. The great struggle of the modern artist is to preserve and keep alive for us and for society the sense of wonder. In other words, to preserve life itself, for the sense of wonder in a person is God.

I have brought you to the front line of art, beyond that line is the unknown. About the immediate period through which we are about to pass I have very little hope, specially in Europe and in England. The immediate result of this war will be the mutilation of a large portion of humanity, the appearance of psychological and nervous diseases in our children and, unless we have a stroke of luck, economic ruin. If we are not all to perish we have got to realise that we are all fruit growing from the same, vast unconscious root of life. In whatever we destroy we destroy ourselves, for the world is one living body. We must drive out the old Gods from their hiding places in our minds and make it fresh again to receive the spirit of life. I personally feel that the God of life is appearing in the world again, and will, with creative rays, burn away the sterile, meaningless institutions, and will pierce the suffocating vestments of the priest to find again the naked human heart. The psychic discord of our time has wounded our consciousness so deeply that it is at last moving. New horizons and new doors are opening in all directions. Discoveries in all fields of activity, new drugs and medicines, for the healing of pain and suffering. Nature is yielding up deep secrets before the patient dedicated search of the genius of science. New states of consciousness and premonitions are declaring themselves.

And this more than three decades prior to the advent of the 'Gaia hypothesis'!

The immense inner world of man has only had its surface touched by the modern life of western civilisation. This unknown inner universe of man is just beginning to be explored by artists and poets. That exploration is dangerous work. Some are lost and never return. Some penetrate and awaken deep, creative energies. Such artists and poets are the saints, hermits, and primitives of a new time, and it is upon their searching and integrity of spirit that the art of the future depends.

We are at the beginning of a new era, a new cycle of human existence, and this century will see the establishment of a world civilisation based more on the organic sense of life, rather than on intellectual conceptions. Keats said, 'ultimately life cannot be lived by precept, but only by constant awareness in itself'. That is the organic sense of life to which we shall have to return.

Society must be based upon our sense of wonder, the one experience which justifies our being alive. Art is a form of transcendental magic which is created out of that awakened sense, and returns to it. In the words of the English mystic—'the secret of life is to share the creative madness of God'. If we have never experienced this madness we can be said never to have lived. For it is the direct expression of having regained that reverence for all living things which is the only real foundation for human society. When we feel, in the words of that greatest of all surrealist artists, William Blake, 'everything that lives is holy'.

The Eternal Presence

The Reality of Poetry

How often is it said—'That is not real, it is only a myth'. But for we painters and poets, we say—it must be real because it has become a myth. Only real things become myths and legends. Christ was real because he became a myth and a legend, so were all the saints and artists, so was Beethoven, Michelangelo, Goethe, Picasso, Rilke, Blake, Shelley—all of them.

The myth and legend are strong penetrating poetical forms in which everything lives focused in its essential archetypal essence so vividly that the mysterious creative vitality of life is powerfully imprinted upon mankind's consciousness, and remains there for thousands of years. Myth and legend are a sign of creative vitality in society.

The purpose of Art is to worship and praise life through wonder and magic.

Magic properties in Art.
The Reality of Poetry.

Poetry is the realisation of the nature of life by magic. Magic is the mode by which this realisation takes place. Poetry teaches nothing, explains nothing, it does not explain life, it expresses life. And this expression of life through magic conveys realisation of life through invocation, through evoking life in its essential poetic essence, which is the only way the unknowable essence of life can be contacted, experienced and realised, and yet remain as it is unknowable in its inevitable sacred mystery. Thus Poetry and Art do not interfere with life, but sacrifice themselves to life; to take on the essence of life one expresses those essences in symbols, symbol being the only concrete mode of contact with the unknowable fire of life.

Symbols are not things representing something else, they are actual emotions of the reality of existence, realised in concrete form, that can be experienced.

The reality of life is incomprehensible. Therefore the Poet and Artist creates an incomprehensible image of life, that is life as it is. For the purpose of Art and Poetry is to express the nature of life, not to explain it.

All true art is poetry, whether it be in painting, words, or music. My paintings and poems are myths expressing what I feel to be the nature of life.

All good things are one good thing, there is no separate good, and that one good thing is creative imagination—God. Poetry, like all the acts of man, needs an absolute to relate its activity to. Some poets have made the beautiful into an absolute, some have made moral and political aim into an absolute. All these have their place. But none of them have any meaning in themselves; they must be focused in a deeper aim, in an absolute that can include and reconcile them all. And also the nature of poetry must be understood.

God is the only absolute capable of reconciling them all, the Good that includes all good. God is the Poetry that includes all poetry, the Beauty that includes all Beauty, *the Poetry*, *the Beauty*; Poetry and Beauty being attributes of God, they therefore can be a way to God, the poetry that leads to the Poetry of Poetry. God is pure Poetry, the life of life, Pure Being. Goodness is an attribute of the Supreme Good—God; good is a creative attitude which gives life and is therefore given life abundantly. It is necessary to live a good life, that is a life drawing its source from God, who is understood and experienced through His Attributes. Aesthetics by themselves have no meaning; what then is the aim of poetry?

The aim of poetry is the aim of life, and the purpose of life is to realise God within us. The intellect cannot do this, because the field it was created to cover is too narrow. God is unknowable and un-understandable, but He can be realised and experienced in the state of pure being. Therefore for us God is a state of being, pure Being, Paradise, The Kingdom of Heaven, a state of pure devotion to life where one no longer seeks to explain life, but a state in which one *is life* (we only explain life when we are not alive). This state of virginity of consciousness is given to us in childhood as a gift in order that we may know it once, and remember its characteristics. Then naturally the world slowly effaces that state of consciousness, and we gradually lose the paradise of Pure Being; we lose it in order to regain it again with greater purity and strength and humility, *we lose it in order to discover who values it*. Those who lose it and are not troubled will not receive it, simply because they do not desire it. They have other aims in life, success, being acclaimed by the masses of people, power, publicity, so they get these things.

But the recovery of this state of being called pure poetry, Grace, The Kingdom of Heaven, *is the real aim of life*, and we can obtain this state of creative innocence only by difficult inner work, not to conquer life, but *to recover it*. For the Fall of Man is true; we have fallen from a heavenly state of being down into the mere heavy repetition of chemical matter. The means of our recovery are in purification; 'Blessed are the pure in heart for they shall see God'—it is God, pure Poetry, that they, the pure in heart, shall see. So our perception of Poetry is in the degree of purity of our heart, that is the purity of the source of our emotions; so that the problem of poetry and the problem of attitude to life are one and the same thing, with one aim, to attain to a greater degree of pure being, pure poetry, creative Imagination, God. Thus poetry, whether it's the poetry of words, music, or painting, is the instrument for evoking in men and women degrees of that state of virgin consciousness which the everyday life of the world does and will obliterate and destroy in them. Poetry and Art sharpens, purifies, restores and gives back life to them through magic awakening a wonder in them which is already the beginning of the growth of God in them. The beginning of the recovery of Paradise. Thus the aim of true Poetry is religious, and the aim of all true religion is Poetry.

'Poetry, Painting & Music, the three Powers in Man of conversing With Paradise, which the flood did not Sweep away.' Blake, *A Vision of the Last Judgement.*

Thus all good things (i.e. creative things) being one thing, Poetry and attitude to life being one thing, with one aim—to realise that state of being which is pure Poetry—God, what then is the best attitude to life which provides the most creative soil for attaining this realisation. The answer is the contemplative life.

The life of action provides the experience and the material; the contemplative life provides the condition for the turning of that experience into a state of being. Thus life realises its nature in those who contemplate its nature, just as it acts its nature in those who live a life of action. But as the aim of life is to realise itself, those individuals who live the contemplative life are the instruments by which human society realises its own nature and becomes aware in what direction it is going. In action it loses itself, in contemplation it finds itself, this is a dance, a breathing throughout human society. All men cannot, or even want to, be contemplatives (the world lives by interaction of these contradictory attitudes to life), but a society in order to be creative, to be living, and not be a vast desert of machines, must allow a condition in which those of the contemplative nature can live and grow. The mass of mankind are active; from these masses are thrown up and growing out of it the contemplatives who are like receptive cells to receive the voice of life. They balance the main active mass of mankind. When this does not happen, that is when there is not enough of the contemplative nature, or when they are persecuted, condemned, or when the idea is put forward that life is only activity and work, and the idea of contemplation and the growth of human personality is condemned. Then comes a terrible disaster over the society of men.

Now the true Artist and Poet belongs to the contemplatives, and finds realisation of his work in the contemplative life. Because the work of the Poet and the Artist is to take the raw material of the world, and to transmute and distil it into its essence, and from that essence create Poetry. Then mankind can realise its essence by experiencing this Poetry although most of its life is spent in action, thus a balance is brought about.

But the Poet and the Artist both need solitude in order to carry out this highly concentrated intense work of revealing and distilling the essence of life to the world of man. By the Poet and the Artist I mean not only those who write and paint Poetry, but also all those who love Poetry, no matter what their particular work may be, they also need solitude, in which to experience Poetry. Solitude is therefore a sacred thing, a thing to be reverenced, and if the society of man is to grow and not perish in the incessant work mania of a machine-ridden insect mentality, we must bring back if not reverence, at least respect for the solitude of any human being. We must bring back the idea of solitude as an important and vital element in life, the element that makes possible the highest flowering of life, contemplation, pure being; we must bring back the sacredness of contemplation, and take away the fear of solitude. In the contemplative life the mystery of life is worshipped in its simple essential beauty, for the Poet and the Artist do not desire to explain the mystery of life, but to live it.

Life is not what is, but what is created. So what we create, that is formed with our will out of the material of life, our environment, our nature; that is life. What we create exists, lives, what exists we believe in; we create what we believe in and believe in what we create. To create is to believe, and to believe is to create. So our whole life with all its acts, and our face, is an exact and accurate picture of what we believe.

The passion of life demands [the] form [of] reticence,
The form of death demands passion.

Dullness and monotony, are part of the riches of life, but not of ART.

The thing is to combine the structural thought of the Medieval School with the holy passion of the Romantics, this Tremendous Polarity is illumination, *VISION*.

The Vision of the Fool

THE introduction which prefaces this book of reproductions of my cycle of paintings and drawings, 'The Holy Fools', is not intended in any way to be an explanation of them. Paintings and drawings cannot be explained. Like life, they are unexplainable.

At the time of writing this, presumably the artist thought of the works whose subject was the Holy Fool as a limited series. This suggests that he did not envisage a continuing pre-occupation with the theme. Subsequently, however, the Fool was to be the central symbol of his work, one whose inherent possibilities he was called upon to explore for the remainder of his career.

All Art brings a message into the world, but it is not the message of morality, or of philosophy, nor of discourse and law-giving. It is the message of life, of life itself, and this message can only be received, and understood, through the form and nature of the medium in which it is created; and not by translating it into another medium, for the message is implicit in the nature of the medium.

Art springing from essence, addresses itself to essence, and is eternal. Just as the essay written here is temporal and transitory, in that the character of the conditions it speaks of will alter either for better or for worse.

This introduction then, is rather in the nature of a series of reflections and meditations upon these drawings and paintings. I am not a philosopher, nor a teacher, nor a thinker; and cannot claim the distinction and originality of any of these gifts. Nor am I a writer, and not being used to writing, I am rather reluctant to put down in words, those things which mean much to me. And I apologise for the numerous imperfections of writing with which this essay is strewn, and hope that the reader will pardon them. Nevertheless, in this clever and disastrous Age, with its vulgar and cheap norm of the useful and respectable person, it is more than necessary for artists, at least occasionally, to speak of their attitude, and of the aims and thoughts of their work, no matter how roughly and inadequately, in order to try and make clear the issues, and the true nature of Art, in the face of the vast ignorance and half-ignorance of our epoch. Just as war exists because human conscience is universally undeveloped (conscience exists only in a few individuals), so also ugly architecture, furniture, pictures and sculpture exist, because the aesthetic conscience of mankind in most parts of the western world is in general undeveloped. When conscience is absent, then ignorance becomes active and dictates the rules of life. Thus the historical position of the artist in society has become more and more impossible, as is the position of all sensitive human beings possessing some degree of conscience about life. The gap in society is between those human beings who have a conscience about life, and those who haven't any conscience. This is the real gap and difference in society, and not the false and ridiculous division into highbrow and low-brow. And the tendencies of our Age in evidence everywhere show that the position is likely to get worse. The whole situation was stated with admirable clarity by the great French philosopher Jacques Maritain, when he said,

> But now the modern world, which had promised the artist all things, will soon scarcely leave him even the bare means of subsistence. Founded upon the two *unnatural* principles of the *fecundity of money* and the *finality of the useful*, multiplying its needs and servitudes without any possibility of there ever being a limit, ruining the leisure of the soul, withdrawing the material *factibile* from the control which proportioned it to the ends of the human being, imposing on man its puffing machinery and its speeding up of matter, the modern world is shaping human activity in a properly inhuman way, in a properly devilish direction, for the ultimate end of all this frenzy is to prevent man from remembering God. ... He must consequently, if he is to be logical, regard as useless and therefore despicable, everything which for any reasons bears the mark of the spirit.
>
> An aristocracy in the order of deeds, but a truly democratic barbarism of mind, is the portion of the time to come; the dreamer, the man of speculative mind will be able to maintain his place only at the expense of his security and comfort; jobs, success or glory will reward the versatility of the mountebank: more than ever, to a degree unknown in the Iron Age, the hero and the saint will pay for their pride in poverty and loneliness.

Jacques Maritain, *Art and Scholasticism*, tr. J.R. Scanlan, London: 1930, p.37–8. The last paragraph is a quotation from Charles Maurras.

I believe that these words were written somewhere around 1920. How true they are, and have become, is now clear to us all.

I should like to draw attention to Maritain's words, 'The finality of the useful'. Therein lies one of the roots of the evil of our time. The ideal we are all being educated to believe in, is the extrovert useful person. Why? The answer is because the extrovert useful person is the most exploitable type. You cannot exploit so easily the man who is constantly reflecting upon life, and upon his conditions; who questions existence, who is troubled by desires, which seem to the useful person, not only beyond his comprehension, but utter nonsense, to be quelled by a nice practical commonsense society, where things make sense because they are useful.

History shows that you cannot so easily exploit the artist and the poet. The artist and the poet should be an unexploitable element in society.

The artist should have the same functional rights as the priest. For example, the non-participation in the pathological activity of war. The artist's rejection of the activity of war is not done from the point of view of a pacifist philosophy, for although most artists are physically pacific, a lot of them are spiritually belligerent. No, the artist cannot take part in war because, like the priest and the monk, he is the representative of the affirmative integrity of life, and therefore cannot take sides. Why should a Raphael or Rembrandt be forced to fight in a war, and the village parson or priest not have to? The vocational rights of the priest and the scientist should be granted to the artist; he is, as they are (or should be), part of the co-ordinating creative intelligence of human society. And if that be objected to on the grounds that it is difficult for people to judge a sincere artist from an insincere one, the answer is, that that can equally apply to parsons and priests; the important point is that they are exempt from taking part in war, on the grounds of their vocation alone, and not on personal perfections or imperfections. And this brings us to the real reason for the artist being forced to fight in war in this Age; and that is that modern society does not consider that the artist has an important function in its life; they still think the priest has some sort of place, they think this from sheer inertia of habit, although actually he has even less function than the artist. For the innately materialist conception of life of contemporary society has no real place for either of these ancient vocations, nor the approach to life that they represent. Contemporary society exempts the scientist from actual fighting in war, because he is the absolute representative of modern society's view of life. To let him be destroyed would be to destroy themselves. But they do not really mind destroying the artist, for when he has gone this society could still live with pleasure without the vision of Art or of Religion.

The other thing Maritain mentions, which seems to me to be of the utmost importance, is his statement that the modern world is 'ruining the leisure of the soul'. This is one of the main reasons why the art of painting has been neglected. Because the condition of its enjoyment is leisure to look, to become receptive, to reflect, to absorb; leisure to form a connection, a communion with the painting. And it not only applies to painting; we have no leisure to form a communion with life itself. This 'leisure of the soul' in which things are absorbed and assimilated into the being of a person, is being destroyed slowly and effectively by a despicable utilitarian education, materialist in outlook, and in result, an enormous decay in spiritual fertility, a society without culture, a winter of human life.

In a respectable practical society, where everybody is useful, the poetic imagination in man is an anachronism, an irritant which disturbs the chemical sleep of habits of such a society by making it conscious of the degradation of its mechanisation, by the appearance of extraordinary desires; by overshadowing it with the supra-reality of poetry, by unsettling it with a thirst and a hunger for eternal beauty, just at the moment when this society thought that everybody was satisfied. This is the affirmation of poetic imagination, which is, and always will be, the natural activity of the poet and the artist.

See 'The Eternal Presence' herein.

We have lived to see everywhere the triumph of the enemies of the imagination, the despisers of the spirit, the philistines. We have lived to see the Church become the corpse of Christianity. The Church which believes in war in war-time, and in peace in peace-time. Seeing that this is about the most convenient position the Church could take up in this Age, the only thing that need be said is that it has nothing whatever to do with the passion of Christ, nor with His martyrs and Saints; when they lived they were crucified. No one would think to crucify the Church; there is nothing to crucify. Potency, integrity, and fertility of faith are the only things that can be crucified, because they are faith. The crucifixion of the poetic imagination in man by the Machine Age is a religious fact. And modern society has succeeded very well in rendering poetic imagination, Art, and Religion, the three magical representatives of life, an heresy; and the living symbol of that heresy is the Fool. The Fool is the poetic imagination of life, as inexplicable as the essence of life itself. This poetic life, born in all human beings, lives in them while they are children, but it is killed in them when they grow up by the abstract mechanisation of contemporary society and by the teaching of the norm of the 'ordinary man', 'the man in the street'. Today these abstract phantoms have come to tyrannise all the natural creative speculation that exists in beings that are human. This norm of the 'ordinary man' is in reality the philosophy of mediocrity, into which, with a sigh of relief, the general heavy inert mass of mankind desires to sink. This is the deadly myth of the 'little man', the law-abiding citizen who obeys all laws faithfully, no matter what the laws are. The 'little man' whose servitude makes all wars possible. No individual can make war without the consent of the mass will of the 'little man'. Wars happen, because the 'little man' carries them out, and makes them happen. The 'plain and ordinary man' has made the philosophy of mediocrity a power, and this philosophy has an army, armed with guns, bombs, gas, atomic rockets, and other effective instruments for the destruction of the human race. They will allow the artist and the poet a place in their society if he is a respectable earnest educationalist, who has reassured the populace that he really is an efficient sensible fellow, like any other dull righteous worker, and that Art, Poetry and Religion are not so difficult or important; they, too, can be made mediocre, it only needs education. Yes, this society is troubled by the inexplicable sorrows and joys of the Fool. The Saint, the artist and the poet are all one in the Fool, in him they live, in him the poetic imagination of life lives.

The greatest Fool in history was Christ. This great Fool was crucified by the commercial pharisees, by the authority of the respectable, and by the mediocre official culture of the philistines. And has not the church crucified Christ more deeply and subtly by its hypocrisy, than any pagan? This Divine Fool, whose immortal compassion and holy folly placed a light in the dark hands of the world.

Our society has rejected the Fool, not only because he cannot be exploited, not only because they judge everything by its usefulness; but they are frightened and disturbed by the Fool, because he is the child of life, and not of abstract virtue. The Fool is purity of consciousness. This purity is a cosmic folly that is utterly detached from what most of the world thinks worth doing; it is detached from the deadening edifice of clever ambitions, of power, and of the incredible vanity of knowledge, that has already dulled the capacity for the poetry of life in contemporary society. For to be a success in the mechanical jungle of the contemporary world, the Fool must not exist in men, for the Fool is interested in life, in being alive, and not in power, nor in the accumulation of knowledge, nor in the passing of examinations, nor in being clever. The Fool, because he is troubled by longings transcending the world, is a hindrance to an ambitious career. The contemporary world certainly has no use for this kind of being in its society. For even the educationalist of our society is in the racket with the utilitarian commercial view of life of our time, when by education they try to produce what is called 'a useful citizen'. In other words, a sheep that believes that work is the sole purpose of life, and is educated to believe this, and is conditioned to a mechanical servitude, that is lost without continual work. For only those who believe that work is the be-all and end-all of life can be exploited successfully in the commercial, political, non-religious conception of life of modern society. The philosophy of mediocrity, and the philosophy of technical cleverness, and mechanical efficiency, understand one another very well, and the specifically materialist irreligious mentality that dominates our time, understands them both, and uses them both; wanting by education to produce from them the complete extravert type, who finds life only in continual activity. This mentality desires in fact to breed the ant in place of the human being, and a world of paid officials directing the form of society in place of an aristocracy of the spirit and the co-ordinating power of cultural intelligence. And in that direction contemporary society is rapidly decaying. Thus is poetic imagination more and more outlawed by subtle neglect, or imprisoned by mediocrity into official forms. But poetic imagination still flowers in the irony and eternal innocence of the Fool, which is the heresy of the artist and the poet. There is the element of the insect, of the mechanical in man, which degrades men into making an abstract society without leaven, a sterile state of efficiency, whose facile justice does the greatest injustice to life, because it destroys the person in men, and the person in men is the leaven by which life fertilises society. It is the person in men that creates a society which is a living organism a society made of personal beings, whose various different degrees of growth, and radiation, leaven the organic body of civilisation. This is the exact opposite to the imprisoning of life into the insect colony of utilitarian justice. It is the element of the Fool in every man that can redeem him from this degradation, this ancient element of the eternal Adam still exists deep inside a man, the element in him that holds converse with the essence of life. Spiritual joy, that is essential joy, arises from innocence, from purity of consciousness—this is the Fool. The Fool in man is a divine debonair spirit, whose careless empirical gaiety and overflowing mercy, embraces life; but the Fool is more than this, he is the sorrow of life.

Where there is no reverence, or respect, for the creative impulse of Art or Religion, there can be no civilised society. Civilisation exists only where conscience exists. And conscience is individual; one individual with an awakened conscience towards life is civilisation; and where there are a thousand people without conscience there is no civilisation; even if they are all very clever scientists who can make aeroplanes that can fly to the moon, or produce bombs that can destroy whole nations. A spiritual betrayal is on—

it is the betrayal of the love and worship of life by the dominance of the scientific technical view of life in practically all the fields of human experience, including a large part of education. And education itself is becoming a substitute for Religion, and is regarded with almost superstitious respect, as the only solution for modern society.

Where a real civilisation exists there also exists some degree of reverence for the Fool in men, and an understanding of the vocation of the Fool, by allowing him to love and move through society, clad in the ironic beauty of his devotion and compassion to the heart of man. But the ideal of our education, and of our society, is the clever scientific technician, his human emotions data laden, and atrophied by objective technicality. This ideal is becoming realised, and holds more and more power over society; dominating the education of mankind with the scientific technical view of life; yes, the tyranny of this one method of approaching existence, dominates all other approaches to the mystery of life, including those ancient and eternal ways of perception, Art and Religion. So that the meaning of the life work of the artist has fallen into the background of society, as something odd, not quite to be accounted for, which at best is a kind of almost extinct and uneasy amusement. A society moving along this line of direction will have no use or need for Art, and still less for Religion. Were there a real need for these things it would mean that the main direction of thought and attitude to life had already begun to alter. A society that has lost its reverence for poetic imagination has in reality lost its creative pride in life; with this gone, it has dropped into the universal welter of a vulgar search for mechanical pleasures of an incredible stupidity, and has forgotten the immortal goal of life. Soon everything will be cancelled out. Our disillusionment will be complete. And from complete disillusionment there can come only two things; final decay and death, or the birth of a faith.

Modern society rejects the Fool because of his faith in the essential holiness of life itself; contemporary society has mutilated the holiness of life by concentrating upon almost everything else but that, and by its neglect of the very means by which the sense of the holiness of existence is developed, namely Religion and Art.

The artist is a Fool, and Art is a cosmic folly by which purity of consciousness can be attained. For the Fool, the artist, and the priest, are the victims of the radiance of life. The true priest is a Fool whose purity of spirit is the folly by which the world grows and becomes enlightened. But modern society, by its concentration upon Science to the point where it threatens to sterilise the growth and life of the human psyche, has outlawed the priest, the artist and the Fool; and has consequently outlawed an entire field of human vision. Proof of this is the condition of society, which in spite of scientific efficiency and of the scientific outlook and education, is bankrupt and full of faces that were once human. Now people living in a desert of a thousand machines and gadgets, show the huge unhappiness of emptiness. What need have they of the magical vocation of the priest and the artist, of the poet and the Fool? Do they know that they are starving, in spite of the word progress? For just as the body needs living vitamins to feed it in order to live, so, too, does the human psyche need to be fed by the mysteriously potent vitamins of Art and Religion, given through and by those illuminated instruments, the artist and the priest. The withdrawal of these vitamins, means decay at the core and the root of the culture of man.

But there always exist in society some men and women whom the Fool touches, who respond to the Fool. For the Fool awakens the Fool in others, but in many the Fool is stifled, or sleeps. There are human beings living in isolation and loneliness in the society of men who realise suddenly that they belong to the Fool, that they exist in the Fool, that in the Fool they have found their race, and their kind, to whom they belong; and that they are united in the communion of all Fools, which includes the communion of Saints, the communion of all creative souls, and the communion of the visible with the invisible. They are united in the enigmatic and universal compassion of the Fool. The Fool is near to them, and is their emblem. The Fool is the symbol of the lost ones of this world who are destined to inherit eternal life. The Fool is not a philosophy, but a quality of consciousness of life, an endless regard for human identity; all this lives in the fun of the Fool. The Fool is the essential poetic integrity of life itself, clear and naked, overflowing in cosmic fun; not the product of intellectual achievement, but a creation of the culture of the heart. A culture of the genius of life. I believe that there is in life, and in the human psyche, a certain quality, an inviolate eternal innocence, and this quality I call the Fool. It is a continuous wisdom and compassion that heals with fun and magic. It is the joy of the original Adam in men.

Society is creative when it is ruled by creative spirits, when it is directed by an aristocracy of the spirit. For the creative impulse is an aristocratic one, that is, one of quality, and not quantitative. The artist is one of the few remaining natural aristocrats left in our society. His inevitable belief in the individual personal act of creation makes him one with the tradition of the peasant and the aristocrat. And this often enough makes him an object of contempt with our society, which is largely composed of commercial technicians, who have no tradition of the aristocratic view of life. Civilisation is only sustained by the degree of wisdom in it; progress, as it is called, cannot sustain it. And wisdom is vision and perception of life, created out of quality of spirit. Wisdom has many forms; in Religion it is the development and culture of Charity in the human soul. In Art, wisdom is the passion of Beauty. The culture of Charity and the passion of Beauty are blended in the wisdom of the Fool.

In our Age, one of the greatest feast days of the whole year should be April 1st—All Fools' Day. A day that should be kept and celebrated religiously and universally. A holy day, when no work is done. A day given over to the divine fantasy of holy gaiety. A day of the giving away in unending foolish non-rational generosity, of gifts clothed in the marvels of the imagination. The entering of strangers' houses, and the placing of gifts upon their tables. A day of mystical jokes concealing deep mercy. A day when all the mercies of the year gather to manifest themselves. At night there should be fireworks, the night sky strewn with holy signs of divine fun written in streams of fire, and whirling catherine wheels that light up the dancing of all the Fools. And the golden glow of the roman candles, with their fountains of soft fire curving in the air. Then there would be the poetic absolution of the heavy abstract machine of public morals, by the charity of the Fool. For lovers this is the day in the year to celebrate Love; their patron saint is the Fool, for all lovers are one with the Fool, as they are one with the artist and the poet, they are of the same race. Eros and Psyche live within the protection of the Fool. All Fools' Day should be celebrated everywhere by everyone; some with dancing, some with feasts, some with fasting. A day when all the failures in life, the misfits, the deformed ones, the simple-minded ones, should be revered by all men with awe, and to them should be given gifts, gifts piled at their doors in the morning, gifts given all day. They would be celebrated as one of the mysteries of life. Yes, this would be the one day in the year during which all human beings could dissolve the cruel monotony of the utilitarian principle of work and respectability, that with the plausible teeth of its mechanism, tries to destroy the mysterious wonders of life. A day when all men, the successful, the failures, the Saints, misfits, heroes, weaklings, businessmen, artists, poets, are united in the mystical charity of the Fool. The Fool who, wearing his fantastic garments of love, makes his wild painful gestures of tenderness before the suffering of all the living ones in the Universe. A day when all men share the Fool's joy in the entertainment of strong mercy. The day of the compassionate irony of the Fool, clad in the debonair clothes of subtle joy, his face full of the gaiety of the wine of life, drawing its lights from the source of tears and sharp sorrow; the Fool, who in an ecstacy of happiness bows down with his gay garments, down into the dust, with a humility that touches the bottom of the abyss of life.

It is a rudimentary type of mind that believes that the problems of human society can be solved by politics. Politics are abstract, they can never be a way of life. The idea of uniting the nations, and of the unity of mankind has not worked, because it is only an abstract rational idea; the idea of unity is abstract, in life things don't unite for the sake of unity itself; they unite because in doing so they fulfil a higher idea than themselves; the unity is only an element in that higher idea. Thus if the nations of the world unite in God, and for the sake of honouring and glorifying Him, they are united in a concrete reality, and become a living body united to fulfil a purpose higher than themselves. This applies to everything. Being abstract, politics are incapable of creating a culture, and are therefore sterile. Thus the human being and the artist must reject all politics, for the artist is essentially concrete in his view of life, and he rejects that which is sterile. It is better that there should slowly grow in society a larger and larger body of people who are neutral to politics; neutral, in order to slow up the headlong rush into the abstract solutions of politics. Once the facile outlook of this perpetual activity has been slowed up, it may be possible to create in society a contemplative condition by which society can realise its state of being, becoming more spiritually alert and detached from politics. This realisation would make the life of contemporary society more sensitive to the existence of God, and thus to a conception of life, higher than itself. This contemplative condition would prepare society and make it viable and more receptive to the only meaning that life can have, that is, union with God. The only hope is to increase the contemplative condition in society; and this can only be done by putting before society the idea of the contemplative life; a life that is more living than the life of action. The hope is for contemporary society to become more deep in its perception, and the way to make it deeper is to slow it up.

In our Age one of the great tasks for Art and Religion is the strong reaffirmation of the supreme holiness of all human identity, above all generalisations and abstractions like state, class, politics; the person in every living being, whether useful or useless, is the reality of life. Because the person in us is the mystery of existence itself. Above all ideas exists the person. The reality and significance of the Fool, and of the poetic imagination of Art, is that it is the principle of personalising life, of individualising life; as against the most active principle of our time, which is the depersonalising, deindividualising of all life, and its destruction by the abstraction of mechanisation.

What place is there then for the artist, for the Fool, the poet, or for any human being, in a society based on the principle of the depersonalisation of life by the ideal of mechanical efficiency, and the success of publicity values? There is no place, the human and the creative are in danger of dying out. From the standpoint of life, the principle of poetic imagination, of which the Fool, the artist, and the priest are the vocational representatives, is a compensation by the creative powers of life to balance such a society, to repersonalise it and thus to satisfy the universal human hunger for a poetic consciousness of life. The poet, the artist, the Saint and the Fool are outlawed by this society because they desire the unknown, the marvellous, the poetic. Because they desire with passion those elements in the universe which they know to be among the most magnetic attributes of God. The Saint finds the marvellous, the unknown, the poetic, under the aspect of Charity. The artist finds these attributes under the aspect of Beauty. The Fool finds them in the virginity of spirit. All these three attributes are enfolded in the principle of poetic imagination.

Today this great principle in Art and life is being crucified by the triumph and dictatorship of the norm of a commonplace mediocre mentality, its flattery, and the placing in authority of its view of life. But death is the planting of the seed of birth. For the mechanised society of modern life, with its vanity of knowledge, its cruel respectability, and its inhuman rejection of poetic consciousness, has defeated its own ends. It has collapsed in the violence of its own sterile brutality, showing clearly the fact that a society cannot exist by such a view of life. If you don't believe in a reality higher than man, or the society of men, the result you get is the modern world. Now that the civilised world has almost been destroyed by the illness of uncontrolled, merciless animal forces at work in most of mankind; now that the abstraction, utilitarianism, and the mechanisation have brought forth death and sterility, the ruins of society may yet prove more fertile than the barren days of its so-called progress and splendour. For we understand life not through knowledge, but through humiliation. The hour of humility is the victory of poetic imagination, when there can be born with fresh and wounded signs, a new poetic consciousness of life. It can be born when the hard crust of the habitual reality of modern society is melted, and its materialistic factuality becomes a great emptiness. Then can the world's horizon widen with the signs of a new time. For poetic imagination is only born when mankind is ready for it, ready to receive it, when men are hungry for its gifts, when they reach the supreme point of realising that they are actually starving in spirit, and are empty. It is then they realise truly the nature and substance of that of which they are starved. For a living truth shows its reality through its absence. And soon mankind will become so empty and desolate, so remote from the sap of life, that we shall be ready to say, 'Veni Sancte Spiritus' [Come Holy Spirit]. It is then that poetic imagination will enter into this world, it is then that the Fool will appear among us, to be received and reverenced in all men, and the nature of freedom understood; for liberty is the control of life by Faith, Hope and Charity. Freedom is the sense of the privacy and holiness of all human identity. Liberty is the wisdom of Art, and it is then that human society will desire to drink of its poetry and to eat of its wisdom. But until that moment, society will continue to disfigure the gifts of life. Meanwhile, now and in the immediate future, in spite of the optimistic plans of idealists, we face the degradation of mankind, unless by a miracle of creative effort we can bring about a universal awakening of conscience towards life. The old world having passed away, no other world will be possible to us; we shall have no world at all, unless we change fundamentally our attitude towards life. Before a new world can be made, first the conditions of spiritual fertility must be created in society. And one of the most important of these conditions of spiritual fertility is 'the leisure of the soul', without which there can be no flowering of life, without which no civilisation can be built.

I do not believe in surrealism, precisely because I do believe in a surreality, universal and eternal, above and beyond the world of the intellect and the senses; but not beyond the reach of the humility and hunger of the human heart. And the human heart will find no meaning in life until it returns to eat of the source from which it came; and that source is the Eternal Person of all persons—God. For there is no meaning in life or art excepting that which springs from the immortal surreality of that Eternal Person.

The Saint, the artist, the poet, and the Fool, are one. They are the eternal virginity of spirit, which in the dark winter of the world, continually proclaims the existence of a new life, gives faithful promise of the spring of an invisible Kingdom, and the coming of light.

Art and Modern Man

My theme is art and modern man and I am going to try and speak of the situation of art in its relation to society at the present time. This will mean discussing the question of communication and the instrumental use of the symbol. I am not a philosopher or thinker and I cannot claim the distinction of any of these professions: rather I want to speak to you as a professional artist who has practised the art of painting for some years. During the course of this period I have reflected much on the implications of the creative experience and on the nature of art as it has revealed itself to me, and it is of these implications that I shall try to speak, rather than of the creative experience itself, which cannot be described. Like most artists, I have a mistrust of descriptions, proofs and over-crystallisation of the fluid nature of experience and I am rather sceptical about verbalism when it deals with the visual arts. Artists are notoriously indifferent to writings upon art and I think with some justice; for unless you have experienced the creation of a work of art from within you are writing about it from hearsay, second-hand, at a safe distance. Artists also know that it is easy to write about it, and very difficult to do it. They know that between the darkness, the frustration, the mysterious joy of creativity, and writing or talking about it, there is a very wide gap, an area open to many misunderstandings. Among too many people, especially in England today, there is the idea that when we have discussed and talked about art we have in some mysterious way settled the matter and there is no need to do anything else about it. Indeed, speaking as a practising artist, it has been my experience that where there is the most talking about art, there is the least buying of pictures; and on the operative plane of culture it is the acquiring of works of art, putting them in our rooms, which makes them part of our living environment. Each one of us can easily test this by thinking of our own house or home at the present moment and see how many original works of art, especially of our own culture, we have there to live with; and then think of how many art books we have on our shelves. I am venturing to speak to you about a very difficult and mysterious experience; for when we speak of art we speak of a vision, and a vision is not something to talk and argue about. It is something to be lived.

We only explain in as much as we do not live; when we live we do not explain. Vision is life itself on the wing and we must fly with it. Vision is something to be accepted or rejected; neutrality in the face of vision too often wears the mask of mediocrity. That is why the very pleasant, sad and devitalised atmosphere of England is too often tainted with so much mediocrity of attitude towards the facts of culture. Neutrality is fatal to the creative faculty. When we speak of vision we speak of man's nature as a whole, the meaning of his life and how this is manifested in art. It is necessary to understand what the wholeness of man's nature means. It means among other things that man has an inner nature as well as an exterior one, and that this inner nature must be awakened, nourished, developed and expanded so that he grows. Man's inner nature must have a world and an environment to live in as well as his exterior nature, and art is an instrument for building that world for his inner nature, for building his archetypal home. The highest cultural achievement of man in the great civilisations has been when the inner and outer man have lived in the same world: that is, at those times when man's outer, civilised environment was a manifestation of his inner nature, and everywhere he looked was an image and symbol perpetually reminding him of his inner nature and the meaning of his life. These civilisations understood how easily we forget and become exterior and lost in a thousand manifold activities, losing the original unity of our being. With this in mind we can see today how so-called civilisation has degenerated into a technological organisation, and how culture has decayed into a shoddy civilisation with a policy of quick returns. There have been some attempts today to escape from the problem of culture, one of these is the so-called anti-art or anti-cultural movement. But seeing that we are at the present time in a state of little or no culture, this movement has no meaning except as an expression of inferiority or rationalisation of the condition of cultural inertia which exists around us.

Another escape is so-called 'pop art' which, while technically squeezing the last few drops from the corpse of Dadaism, uses the optical tricks of that movement without its bitterness and vitality; for a marked feature of pop art is its self-satisfaction and smugness, and in its English version its cosy commercialism. Pop art attempts to make pretty the rubbish heap of mass man in his cheap suburban and commercial environment. Pop art is the same thing in visual terms as pulp journalism and pop records. But in spite of being tricked out with aesthetic gimmicks, rubbish is rubbish, and what we contemplate we become; if we contemplate rubbish we become rubbish. We may then view the present situation with grave misgiving for it is obvious that no real living culture can be based on such a lack of foundations and unless we can recover a metaphysical basis for our civilisation it has no future; it is touch and go whether our civilisation will survive. It seems to me like this: the ancient metaphysical civilisations looked on the universe, the sun, the stars, trees, waters, animals and man himself, as the creation of a god or gods, a kind of vast poem written in colour and form such as we find in Boehme's 'Signature of All Things'. Very much later on in history another faculty in man began to develop, the faculty of measurement and analysis, the examining of weight, size and process, so that the universe—signature of the god—began to be analyzed as process. This was considered as something interesting in itself, and from this arose the philosophy of the thing in itself, the natural sciences or what I shall call process knowledge, or how-it-works knowledge. Process knowledge developed in Europe more and more, accelerating especially in the seventeenth and eighteenth centuries, eventually bursting into the final domination of human thought in the nineteenth and twentieth centuries and reaching its great crisis and perhaps climax now in our own time. Where the environment of man is predominantly made by the natural sciences it is an exterior environment and therefore empty of the life of man's being and does not reflect the feelings and response to life of man's inner nature. This environment is therefore a debased one preventing the whole man from participating in his environment, preventing the life of the psyche from permeating and creating a response to environment, preventing the psyche from forming a whole relationship with environment.

Hence this state of alienation, this feeling of emptiness, of nothingness, so frequent in modern cities. Also the enormous predominance of process knowledge in our education leaves man's inner nature unloved and dead, concentrating to train him to be an exterior machine subject to the constant pressure of scientific efficiency, with no questioning of what life is to be really lived for, leaving the rich complexity of his nature unfulfilled.

The vitality and truth of our culture depends among other things upon our recovering three equations, the equation between man and woman, the equation between youth and maturity, the equation between knowledge and wisdom. If we consider this question of education a little further I believe within the near future a great part of factual knowledge will be taught by electronic machines; but the significance of facts—i.e. reality, can only be taught by human experience, and human experience is the result of maturity. This means the mature man will have to return to his place in education and culture as the norm; whereas our present society idolises adolescents and immaturity and seeks to escape from the reality of growth and development in human nature. In a vital culture there is an equation between youth and maturity, between energy and experience, between the force of life and wisdom, and this equation is the miracle that signifies a great and human culture; for this equation is an aspect of the unity of life, the need for communion between all stages and states of life. But the fact remains man cannot live by process knowledge alone. Ours is the only civilisation I know of in the whole history of man which has a purely exterior environment. In the metaphysical civilisations, the environment was created entirely by artists so that the human spirit through the human hand was imprinted directly upon the material objects surrounding man.

In our civilisation most men are no longer required to be artists in their work, informing matter, giving it the direct imprint of their inner spirit. They are mostly doing jobs, a great many of which machines will soon do for them. In the future it appears that they will have the pleasant slavery of watching machines and exercising their creative faculties in what our more optimistic educationalists call creative spare time. I think one of the reasons the so-called man in the street does not understand art is because he is no longer required by society to be an artist himself: the inner experience is missing from his making of things. The artist has always been the manifester of man's inner life. If we go to our art galleries and museums we will see there the inner life of man over a period of thousands of years.° What would we know of the inner nature of these great civilisations of the past if it were not for the artist? Practically nothing.

'We are proud of our museums where we display the damning evidence of a way of living that we have made impossible.' A. K. Coomaraswamy, *The Bugbear of Literacy*, London: 1947 p.8.

Many people seem to assume that there is only one kind of knowledge. This is a tragic misunderstanding. I believe there are different kinds of knowledge just as there are different states of consciousness and each has its own language. Natural science is one kind of knowledge with its language, the language of 'how' knowledge or process knowledge derived from and limited to those fields of life accessible to description and therefore to measurement and analysis. We know today the effects, both good and bad, resulting from the exclusive use of this range of knowledge: one of them is the dark shadow of the mutilation and destruction of our civilisation and perhaps of our planet.

To an artist, what is it that is so unsatisfying about 'how' or process knowledge? The universe as analyzed by natural science [is] at first view so very exciting, eventually—for me I must confess, dare I whisper it—[it] is fundamentally uninteresting because the scientific universe is meaningless, that is, it is without significance and therefore without [intelligible] reality. And it is no use telling me that the universe is run by a lot of electric energies; I cannot form a qualitative and living relationship with electrical energies; I cannot love or hate them; I cannot worship or adore them. My heart as a human being cannot find any response in them for, as the Spanish writer Unamuno so truly says, 'Love personalises'. Indeed, we can go further and say that love personifies.

There has been much loose talk about the artist being like the scientist because they are both subject to intuitions and both are interested in pattern, but it can be clearly seen that in their fundamental attitudes and activities they are exactly opposite and complementary. The artist is concerned to personify experience, to reveal the identity, the nuance, the being of things, the presence. He is interested in transforming the thing in the spontaneous creative moment, the unexpected moment of eternity, the moment of freedom; unexpected, because the unexpected moment is the unpossessed moment. This is perhaps one of the deepest insights of the creative experience; whereas in process knowledge intellectual possession is the essential condition prior to analysis. Therefore art is a kind of redemption of consciousness and environment. Thus for the artist an environment made entirely by 'how' knowledge is not life, it is anatomical environment without identity.

Are we not, as human beings, concerned with significance, with meaning? I do not find it very interesting to know that the sun is 93 million miles from this desk, or that it is a ball of gas, any more than I find it interesting to be told that a man or woman is some pounds of water pumped up in the atmosphere, or that a medical description of my best friend *is* my best friend. These are specialised descriptions of certain instrumental processes analyzed within the range of a certain faculty. But, as an artist, I am interested in the whole man, the real man, the real woman, the human being.

We cannot form a relationship with a specialised description of a process isolated from the whole of nature, nor do we need to know all this to form a deep creative relationship; 'how' or process knowledge is meaningless unless it has a context. Now the context of 'how' knowledge is 'why' knowledge. 'Why' knowledge is concerned with the significance of things, the meaning; and the first thing that 'why' knowledge reveals is that 'how' knowledge is purely instrumental, that the whole universe is an instrumental phenomenon, that man is an instrument. An instrument of what? Of consciousness; for the meaning of life is within consciousness itself. 'Why' knowledge is concerned with consciousness itself and with its use of instrumental knowledge. 'How' knowledge is concerned with values that can be measured, 'why' knowledge is concerned with qualitative values, with being, and this is outside description, it is beyond measurement and analysis. 'Why' knowledge cannot really be translated into 'how' knowledge, because in 'how' knowledge there is no nuance—nuance comes from being, and a great deal of 'why' knowledge is known only through nuance of consciousness. Transformation of consciousness cannot be known or be brought about by thinking, by description, by measurement or analysis. It can only be known by inner nuance, rapport and sensitivity to the vibrations and rays of that livingness which is at the heart of things. It is the fruit of sensitivity.

The higher worlds are inaccessible to the insensitive; they cannot be reached by knowledge of them, but only by rapport with those worlds. For like answers to like and creates actualisation, that which belongs returns. The instrument of art helps to sensitise the interior nature and to continually re-sensitise it when it grows stale and dull in the world of mere existence—the world of repetition. The language of 'how' knowledge is concerned with communication of information; 'why' knowledge is not concerned with communication, but with communion and vision. This is why one of the basic languages of 'why' knowledge is art and the symbol.

The underlying doctrine here, that like is known by like, is stated by Plotinus: 'Never did eye see the sun unless it had first become sunlike and never can the soul have vision of the First Beauty unless itself be beautiful.' I.vi.9.

'Why' knowledge is concerned with the mystery of consciousness itself and with its transformation, for transformation is freedom, the real desire of every human heart. It does not matter how clever or brilliant we are in 'how' knowledge if we are content to remain on the level of 'how' knowledge—that is knowledge without context—we remain in the state of mere existence not of consciousness; computing machines have no consciousness, they are dead.

To make contact with the source of life we have to shift the accent from the events of consciousness to consciousness itself. This is the crux of the matter, consciousness itself freed from the world of repetition and mere existence. Other differences are that 'why' knowledge is direct; in process knowledge we know, in 'why' knowledge we realise. The knowledge is the realisation. Art is a realisation of what is and not of what appears to be, art is therefore an instrument of man's inner nature and it enables him to manifest in the phenomena of matter the nuance and living quality of his inner life so that his environment is no longer neutral or alien; a rapport is established.

As our consciousness becomes transformed we become more sensitive to a wider range of nuance and vibration, we have a deeper rapport with the earth, trees, rocks, the elements, the answer comes back to us from within them. Art enables us to experience what the French poet René Char calls 'the friendship of created things'. In other words, with the transformation of consciousness our experience of matter undergoes a change, it becomes qualitative, we have communion with it, it is consecrated and is now sacramental. Sacramental! what a word! One would hesitate to apply it to our civilisation where matter is something to be analyzed and exploited and then thrown aside without friendship. Real civilisation is a manifestation of being in environment and not an empty technological organisation made by process knowledge. If one accepts this organisation as representing civilisation then the artist today has no real function and is no longer fundamentally needed.

The predominance of process knowledge in environment inevitably means alienation and split and what is that but neurosis? So now we come to the question of environment not as mere existence but environment as consciousness; this is what real creativity means. We have to consider the problem of how to unite process knowledge with 'why' knowledge, how to place one within the context of the other. What is it that can link these two [kinds of] knowledge? It will be found I think that this missing link is psychology, but unfortunately this proves to be our weakest link for a very great deal of modern psychology is on a low level of awareness, concerned in the main with the pathology of man and not with the psychology of creativity. Indeed, for the most part modern psychology is simply man's pathological condition trying to rationalise itself—to justify itself. The cure and the disease, the patient and the doctor, are the same phenomenon. I have found so much of modern psychology lacking in understanding and wisdom in that it does not seem even to begin to consider the vital importance of orientation in consciousness, or what orientation really means. If it did one would immediately ask—orientation towards what? On the contrary it seems to offer the inadequate, naïve and superficial idea of adjustment. Is not adjustment to the environment and the condition we have been talking about a far worse neurosis than revolt against it? Too often in psychology adjustment is passivity.

We need now to change man's environment by an action from within man's being. This is where the artist can come in to help, not as someone called in to decorate, to make pretty and sweet that empty and mechanical desert we call modern civilisation. There are already, I believe, the beginnings of a realisation of this. There is interest in the idea of process of matter being seen in the light of psychology; there is a consideration of the existence of an extra range of faculties or instruments in man. The next state, I believe, will be psychology seen in the light of metaphysics—in the light of a transphysical and transpsychical reality.

We are, I believe, approaching a period in history when the metaphysical world of eternity will begin to reappear in human thought and it will not be so very long before process knowledge will begin to be more and more interrupted by it. Sooner or later science will be forced to find a solution to its basic problem in the metaphysical. If it does not do this it will be doomed to an endless repetition of half-solutions needing to be proved and re-proved again and again in different forms, acquiring more and more factual knowledge which without the wisdom of a unifying principle becomes a huge burden and finally a disaster. We can only really understand a process in the light of its function: the machinery of a motor car only has meaning in the light of its purpose. So we must ask modern psychology what is the purpose of man and if it does not know the answer how can it understand the psychic process at work in him? It is more than likely that illness and neurosis and the psychology that is supposed to cure them are indeed one and the same thing and that both arise from the fact that man does not know who he is or what his purpose is, for how can we live and create if we have no contact with our real self? Perhaps there is no neurosis but only the absence of our real self.

Is not the answer to be found in transformation of consciousness, and that this transformation begins when we have re-established contact with our centre—the centre of our being? When we are not in a state of enquiring what is—but when we are what is.

Man's real happiness comes to him when he fulfils his nature as a whole and when his personal and social life is permeated by the living quality and atmosphere of his cosmic response.

It is significant that up to at least the thirteenth century man's art and culture was a cosmic phenomenon. During the following centuries man became more and more social and political and self-engrossed in the small ego; but formerly culture was concerned with the orientation of man's consciousness towards the centre of the universe.

Now we have reached a point when we can only speak of experience as vision—illumination—realisation; and we ought really to read poetry, listen to music, look at pictures because art is the language of transformation.

We have to contact the centre of our being because there we have contact with the centre of the universe. Because we are cut off from our centre and from the centre of the universe we feel, and are, exiles imprisoned in the world of multiplicity and mere existence, longing to awake and journey back to the centre which is our heart and our home. This longing is one of the great themes of art, this feeling which Mircea Eliade so rightly calls 'nostalgia for Paradise'. We will find it in most of the great cultures and in many primitive communities, for the truth is that the secret desire of our heart is for the lost Paradise.

It is the motive impulse behind our searching in things and experiences on every level, in friendship, in beauty, in art, even in the smallest lust, even in the smallest love. It is the lost paradise that we really are seeking.

The great energies and vibrations flow down from the centre of the universe into all the worlds returning again transforming all the worlds through love, death and transfiguration.

For the artist and the poet there exists a great zone of consciousness into which this cosmic drama is transmitted and reflected and enacted. This is the archetypal world to which the human psyche has access. This eternal archetypal world of original essence is again reflected into the world of time and space in works of art and culture and in moments of transformation of consciousness in the spontaneous experience of living, or during the canonic and ritual participation of religion.

The world of time and space is the world of contraction of consciousness; space-time is embryonic consciousness. In our present state we are embryos of consciousness and one of the major problems of the artist and the poet is how to transmit the nuance of the archetypal world into the field of contraction and orientate consciousness towards the centre of life; for art is remembrance of the source of life. Because of our endless forgetfulness we need this beautiful gift—this voice of remembrance. The quality and nuance of being which we call beauty comes from the higher worlds and enters our dimension in fragments. As Goethe says 'Beauty is an archetypal phenomenon'.

We have seen that the key is in transformation of consciousness: reality transforms. When we remain untransformed we are unreal. As Erhard Kaestner says about the Greeks, 'The Greeks who invented the Myth have always thought, and still believe, that Hades stands for all that is shadowy and unfulfilled, and out of contact with the real self. It signifies the unreal, the grey vacuity in fact which threatens us all the time, yesterday, today and tomorrow. THE SHADES.' [*Mount Athos—The Call From Sleep*, 1961.]

In other words Kaestner means the world of mere existence. Art comes to make war upon the mortal, upon the world of the dead. Art exists to help awaken man's real eternal self, for in art there is an indestructible instinct for freedom, for eternity. Art is a point of interpenetration between worlds, a marriage of the known with the unknown, for it is the unknown that freshens our life, without it we grow stale and mortal.

In the great cultures of the past contact with the archetypal world was made by agreed canonic ritual. Today, having no canonic culture, isolated among the fragments of a transitional period we can only have lyrical contact with the archetypal world, for ours is the period of the free flowing non-canonic non-localised universal creative spirit of life. We have the possibility of a great new culture, a world culture, a culture of the naked god found everywhere, accessible to all men if they choose. For beneath the tyranny and captivity of the mediocre culture of political dictatorships and their mechanical systems, and beneath our own commercial travellers' civilisation, there still flows the living river of human consciousness within which is concentrated in continuity the life of the kingdoms of life, animals, plants, stars, the earth and the sea, the life of our ancestors, the flowing generation of men and women as they flower in their brief and often tragic beauty. And the artist is one of the vehicles of the continuity of that life; he is its guardian, and his instrument is the myth and the archetypal image, his language the symbol.

We have, I think, to remember that symbols are not concerned to answer questions, nor with mysteries and their solutions. Symbols are imprints of being, actualisations of states and transformations of being. A symbol is a state of being contained for contemplation and participation in the station or vehicle of the picture.

Profound states of being can be mirrored in the symbol. In contemplation all these symbols have to be returned to our being and dipped into its profound depths and thus be reborn again. It is then that the symbol has the potency, the magical archetypal qualities of realisation and expansion of consciousness.

Artists practice a vocation which goes back some thirty-five thousand years of man's history; thus art is much older than process knowledge; and yet here we are at last in a civilisation which does not yet know how to use the artist who stands well within the possibility of extinction as a fundamental vocation in society.

I seem to remember that the ancients had an idea that right in the centre of the universe the god sat on a throne and within the god was His Heart, a Great Fire, a Furnace of Most Terrible Heat and Intensity which was death to all that was not itself. Around the god there were the cherubim; they were all eyes, they searched the universe, nothing escaped their gaze down to the smallest atom: they were the knowledge of the god. Then there were the seraphim; they were blind and winged but it was they who with a movement of utter love flew straight into the Heart of the God.

I like to think of the seraphim as an image of the true poet and man as one who ceaselessly is searching among the many for the heart of the one, and then with the creative desire of his whole inner nature flies like an arrow straight into the centre of life.

From the psychological and cultural vision of life a purely political and scientific civilisation is a debased one and it is very likely to destroy itself, because it does not answer to the whole man, because it does not face the fact that man's nature is both deeper and more complex than the political and scientific view of him and richer in its possibilities.

We artists and poets know one thing for certain, that the life within man's inner nature must be kept alive and transmitted and carried through this tragic transitional period of history. This is crucial. We must reject the prison of political civilisation. Man is a metaphysical being with a hunger for life which no political or scientific solution can satisfy.

The modern technological world has the real possibility of poisoning in us those inner instruments by which we contact the very source of life, and if we desire transformation we must act upon this fact.

For we all—each one—have within us a fountain of life—and contact with it is our real hope. We carry this fountain within the secret recesses of our own hearts—this fountain—which our civilisation has forgotten as it speeds on its way towards the abyss.

The Artist in the New Age

I AM not a philosopher or a thinker, I am speaking as a professional creative artist and I want to try and offer you a few observations on this subject which is a very difficult one. Because of the immense capacity of human beings for self-deception I think it would be wise for us not to underrate the gravity and seriousness of the situation we find our civilisation in at the present time, or to underrate the extent of the problem facing us. In many ways there is a new kind of complacency about in some quarters which one can only call a kind of technological complacency.

Science of course, being the dominant mode of thought, and the dominant attitude today, we are more and more conditioned to think that our situation is a matter for technological solution, or scientific solution. Science has quite naturally impressed us with its immense achievement: especially appealing to a certain type of mind is its technical exploitation of nature. Science and technology gives us an accurate picture of man's outer nature, and that today is a great [pragmatic] success. But art gives an accurate picture of man's inner nature and that today is a very different picture and gives no cause for complacency. Our civilisation has a brilliant technological surface to it, but beneath that surface there is Hell, there is madness, loneliness; but more important than all these things, unfulfillment. All over the civilised world, as we know, mental illness is on the increase, the mental hospitals are full, not to mention the prisons, drug-taking is on the increase, especially among young people, and I think we must not forget it is only twenty years since we witnessed, right in the centre of European civilisation, a mutilation and defilement of man carried out with scientific accuracy, a defilement unknown to any previous age.

The Russian writer, and idealist Alexander Herzen [1812–70] said once 'you can only work on men's minds by dreaming their dreams more clearly than they can dream them themselves, not by demonstrating their ideas to them as geometric theorems are demonstrated.' Now the artist is as accurate as the scientist, and he is accurate in a field in which it is very difficult to be accurate, a field which cannot be measured or analyzed. That is the field of qualitative non-conceptual states of consciousness. Hence the profound observation of Herzen. The artist does precisely this, he enters into the dreams of man, as he dreams those dreams. It is no good studying those dreams and analyzing them because already part of the dream is over, and the conscious mind already begins to interfere. You have to have immediate experience of the dream. The only difference is that the artist dreams the dreams of man and remains awake at the same time. Therefore the artist, by dreaming the dreams of man—because the artist does not speak for himself—he speaks for all men, by dreaming the dreams of man he then begins to change man's dreams from within. This is the most important point of all. The artist has to suffer Hell, made by human imagination, before the process of human transformation can take place, because you cannot reach Paradise without passing through Hell and Purgatory first, as Paradise can receive nothing less pure than itself.

Now besides being an artist I am also a teacher of art in the leading London college, the Central School, and part of my job is to examine the work of students from all over England seeking entry into the School. And I and my colleagues have been deeply disturbed by what we have experienced during the last three years. We have witnessed what can only be called the death of the creative imagination. The students use mechanical formulas, images mostly drawn from advertisements and television, usually of a cheap or sexual kind, a cheap sexuality. All this is put together rather coldly and mechanically. These students say they wish to be artists and to join the fine art department. A great number of them add this to the fact that they want to be artists; they have no wish to be taught, or as they call it to be influenced. When it is pointed out to them that they are already influenced by a great many bad things they seem surprised. What this demonstrates is that they are in fact completely conditioned by the immense pressure brought to bear upon them from the vast technological industry of films, television and records, by people who make a lot of money out of the young by keeping them immature for as long as possible. The work of these students reflects an unbelievable spiritual torpidtude. But of course this torpidtude is not isolated, it is part of a general torpidtude.

One of the first things I have found in my students is that they do not know how to relate to what is great. I find that in many of them it gives them a sense of inferiority, and I always quote Goethe to them. Goethe said there is only one solution to the problem of greatness and that is to love it. If you love it it will become part of you, you will assimilate it. Now great men, great artists are really us, but focussed in a more intense way on all that we think and feel. Blake went as far as to say God manifests himself as great men of history. Now the other thing that strikes me is this. One of the great problems is, whether we know it or not, we are always ruled by an élite, and if it is not an inherited élite, then it is a disinherited élite. It is part of our democratic self-deception and sentimentality that we vaguely assume we are without an élite, when in fact it is quite clear that we are ruled today by the élite of scientific technocrats and politicians who are quite clearly spiritually and culturally illiterate. They represent a low level of awareness and consciousness; they have no philosophy of life other than the exploitation of nature and of man, and the making of money. This is the same thing actually. You can see this in the manufacture of insecticides and the devitalisation of food. All this is purposely done by these people, at vast chemical institutions. They know perfectly well about all this, but they still go on. So we have an agreed hypocrisy, and it is well known in psychology that hypocrisy leads to mental disease. But I do not think this is the root of our unfulfillment; there are other things. Why I brought this up is that we, here, and small groups everywhere, are faced with a task, because we are to a degree more sensitive and aware. How are we going to change this élite who hold all the instruments of power; the radio, the television to mention two. And it seems to me that before we can begin to talk of a new man or a new age we have first to set about putting our own house in order, because we cannot avoid that responsibility. I have felt these things, I have experienced these things, but I also know as an artist what it is to bring one's vision up against these conditions.

I want to come back to these instruments of power. What we feed on we become, if we feed on advertisements, feed on television and so on, we become this. And if you were to take a sort of statistical view of things coming over the television, or of the books that are read, you would be horrified. Now I think the unfulfillment I mentioned earlier is partly due to the fact that our civilisation does not represent the whole man, it represents a small part of his nature, because we have forgotten that science is only one form of knowledge, that there are other forms of knowledge. Now art is one of these other forms of knowledge, and by means of art we can complete this wholeness which we need. To lack wholeness is to lack fulfillment, it means to be unhealthy. Our civilisation is really thoroughly unhealthy because it lacks wholeness, it does not answer to the whole man. I shall come back to this problem in a moment.

The word patron, for example, means father to the work. In the great civilisations the father to the work was as important almost as the artist. The artist today has no real father to his work. The only patrons we have today are the élite of scientific technologists, and business men. And what fathers are they: no wonder they breed illegitimate children.

I want to speak a bit about this situation not only for myself, but for many of my colleagues. We have a vision. In our inner nature we paint this vision, we paint many of these visions. What happens to them in modern civilisation? Well, you may have heard that modern art is a form of investment, business does not buy because it is waiting to be moved by the real inner nature. Oh no; they look at the angel you have painted and they think now, what is he worth? The art world is like a huge brothel at the present moment, and in case you think I am exaggerating, on the back of the French paper *Le Monde*, you will see artists' names quoted on the Stock Exchange, with prices quoted after them. In other words the vision in man's heart is an artificially stimulated value to be bought and sold. It is quite clear that no real living culture can be based on such a hollow foundation. The reasons why all this has evolved are too complex for me to explain in a short talk, but this is the situation in which the culture of our time is found.

The author is alluding, here and elsewhere, to the traditional conception stated with admirable clarity by A. K. Coomaraswamy, 'It is the business of the artist to *know how things ought to be made* and to be able accordingly, as it is the business of the patron to know *what things ought to be made*, and of the consumer to know what things *have been well and truly made* and to be able to use them after their kind.' *Selected Papers 1*, Princeton University Press: 1977 p.80.

For example, in science millions of pounds are given for research. Scientists are given laboratories and solitude to work, but the artist is at the mercy of the market-place. He has to put his vision into a market entirely stimulated by fashion and trend; against this cheap environment he places this vision. Van Gogh for example, who could not sell anything, threw his pictures over the hedge and finally killed himself. This man's pictures are now so valued that Governments exchange them instead of money. There is a great deal of lip-service paid to art today. Many committees meet and talk, but there are very few patrons, very few fathers to the work. Talking is easy. In fact I have found as a practising artist that where there is the most talk there is the least buying of pictures. I am sorry to have brought this conference down to the practical level but actually the practical thing is also a mystical thing.

In considering a normal civilisation—that is a metaphysical one—one I believe will come in the new age, it is necessary for us to understand what a metaphysical civilisation is. It means that the environment is created by artists in every field, not just painters, it means that a table, that clothes bear the direct imprint of the inner creativity of a human being. This means that the life of the human spirit is enacted through images, through the human hand and directly imprinted on the material objects surrounding man, so that these objects function on different levels of consciousness simultaneously. That is, they are symbolic, the word symbol meaning that which connects. But we live in a world of objects, in other words a world of mere existence. Our architecture shows it. In London we are witnessing the destruction of a great city—every great architect admits it. Ruthlessly torn down are the most beautiful eighteenth-century houses and in their places are put up battery-hen boxes, machines simply to make money in offices, so that London is fast becoming one of the most mediocre cities in Europe architecturally and where there is neither civic nor spiritual pride.

English 'symbol' ultimately derives from the Greek *sumballien*, to put together, to compare. Hence, here 'symbol' is an image that joins or connects visible and invisible levels of reference.

The great buildings of a civilisation mirror the chief objects of man's spirit. I think of the fact that Chartres cathedral was made by a town of eleven hundred people! What of our great buildings; insurance—and very significant is insurance—chewing gum, underwear, these are the enormous buildings of our civilisation. They mirror what we are really concerned with. To live as we do in a non-symbolic environment, [in a world of mere objects, of mere existence], is to live a disconnected life; and a disconnected life is a life lost.

I want to explain, as an artist, something about the symbolic image. The symbolic image principally re-connects man to the original generative ideas known as archetypes. These archetypes were, in the great civilisations, imprinted everywhere to remind man of his real purpose, so that he was never allowed to forget. And because it is man's tendency to forget, all art is a form of remembrance of that which was lost. I would remind you that art is essentially the Greek word nostalgia, which means first desire, and longing to return, and the other part of the word means suffering, the suffering of the longing to return. Now the situation today is completely different, the artist at the present time has no agreed language with which to communicate. In the great civilisations of the past this language, being essentially religious, was a canonic language, it was given to him, handed on to him. His patron called forth from him what was required and he gave it, and he knew he would find happiness of service, which is very different from self-expression. Today the artist has to create his own language, be his own patron, explain *why* he is a patron. On him alone falls the responsibility that should be shared by the whole of civilisation.

This passage is problematic as it stands in so far as it implies an etymological connection between the words 'art' and 'nostalgia'. No such connection exists. However, the English word nostalgia has two Greek components; *nostos*—a desire to return home, and *algos*—suffering, distress. In which case it seems likely that the author is making the more general point that works of art quicken our awareness of the loss or departure from our original spiritual condition.

At the moment, in the wake of Picasso, there is a great crisis in art. Picasso is one of the great artists of the twentieth century. He has ransacked the whole of aesthetic history for his art, like a huge magpie, exploring so many cultures in order to have a visual language with which to communicate. He is the first emergence of a new exploratory consciousness. Yet he finds himself, as all modern artists have found themselves, alone. After Picasso, the young generation of painters—whom Picasso overshadowed so strongly —could find no way out but to repudiate him, and they were right. They therefore changed completely to investigate pure imagery. They eradicated the image completely, and it is not the first time in history that art has been without the image. This emergence of a completely abstract art was therefore a very pure move, having two aspects. First the wiping clean of the slate, and secondly, the desire to touch on pure experience. For example, it has become impossible for any of us to paint using canonic, religious images because in a strange way these images are used up. At the present moment there are two valid aspects to the state of modern art, one is the wiping out of the language of canonic, religious imagery. The other is an open sensibility and awareness for anything to come—a poised awareness.

As an artist and as a teacher my instinct about this situation is that this poised awareness is a preparation for re-contact with the world of archetypes. The repression of the world of archetypes by the mechanical, logical and over-rationalised organisation of our society has lead to their re-appearing in precisely the place where you would expect to find them reappear, in the realm of psychology, in the zone of the unconscious mind. Usually, and this is significant, in the form of illnesses, of neurosis. A great deal of the art of our time has been to uncover and project the inner world of man, so that he may first face up to the life in that submerged world, the first condition for the transformation of which brings us back to Herzen's profound observation of 'the necessity of the artist to live the dreams of man'.

The denial of this unconscious world is a death, and part of this death which we now suffer and which is reflected in a great deal of modern art, is our alienation, our lack of relationship with the experience we call nature. We have been conditioned by science to too small a field of consciousness, one limited to those areas accessible to measurement and analysis alone. So we are left with a diagrammatic, abstract conception of nature. We are in fact left with matter and energy, which are the same thing; but we cannot, as human beings, form a relationship with matter and energy.

Our civilisation is essentially a masculine civilisation. Science is masculine, it has made a specialised, impersonal environment which leaves both the artist and the woman unsatisfied. Because the artist, like the woman, has a genius for and demands relationship, asks for environment, for life relationship. We can have no relationship with a set of electrical energies. We cannot have relationship with a mechanical description of the universe.

Now what science has done for us is to desacramentalise matter, in a sense it has desecrated it; matter no longer has any identity or being for us, and that is why we can no longer have relationship, no longer have connection with higher worlds of consciousness, matter merely exists as energy. Thus we suffer a rupture in our relationship, a sense of unfulfillment, we get no answer from desacramentalised matter. Like plastic, that terrible material which cannot live because it cannot die, such matter is dead. As energy it has no identity. It is relationship and realisation that reveal identity, not energy. We as humans have spirit and grace, and with spirit and grace we can form a relationship, we can unite. But with energy and matter we are separate and alone, therefore as it stands a purely political and scientific civilisation lacks wholeness and does not give us any satisfaction. It is therefore part of the movement into the new age that the artist be allowed to re-consecrate our experience of matter, this is the task of art, to give back to man that wonderful experience which the French poet René Char has called 'the friendship of created things'.

When we have this friendship of created things our experience of matter undergoes a change; it becomes qualitative; we have communion with it; it becomes consecrated and it is sacramental. Sacramental, what a word! I think we would hesitate to use it to describe our civilisation, where matter is something to be analysed, exploited and thrown aside without friendship. And unless we become more conscious of these issues the next step is the dehumanisation of man himself, for real civilisation is the manifestation of man's being in environment, and not in technical organisation, manifesting one form of knowledge only.

The artist does not forget. He remembers there was a time when he was employed to create and set up altars to the mysterious gods of life within their temples. We artists have never forgotten the service we once rendered in giving to humanity the deepest experience of reality. That memory, believe me, still remains with us, even though we feel exiles, we do not feel at home in technological society. We may currently be filled with a discontent, but this is a creative discontent. There are two main types of artist; one is the cathartic artist, the wounder who gives help, the purifier. And there is the artist who is the consoler, the bringer of Paradise. Before the bringer of Paradise can come, first there must come the wounder. And we are living through the period of the wound. That is the function of much modern art and culture.

Looking at the present situation we see a fluidity of consciousness in contemporary art. This condition did not exist in the past. In the seventeenth century, for instance, artists living in England would not have known very much about the art of the other great civilisations. This focussed their attention with great intensity on what was local. But today an artist can stay in his studio and see civilisations throughout the whole of history. The simultaneous impact of all these civilisations at once presents a formidable problem of assimilation. Students of art stagger under this extraordinary burden which presents problems that cannot be solved for at least a hundred years, may be more. And it has lead to attempts to make a synthetic artistic language. But a synthetic language is a very repulsive language to an artist because he longs for organic experience.

I now come to this question of culture. I think we all ought to mix some culture with education. Education is not culture. Going to school and learning is not culture. Culture is intimately associated with *cultus*, cult. Culture is essentially a sacramental participation in metaphysical reality, and I would emphasise the word participation. It is not a passive listening to lectures in school; it is enactment in one's life, the metaphysical reality in every aspect of one's life, clothes, marriage, human relationships. And we suffer today from the deprivation of any real *cultus*, cult. Yet it is my belief that this *cultus* will arise sooner or later. What must emerge in our daily life is a reconnection with the archetypal world, a rediscovery and a new contact with that world as part of the organic unity of man's whole experience of life.

In the great cultures of the past contact with the archetypal world was made through canonic procedure and ritual. Our civilisation, as I have said, has no such formal, canonic culture at all. And all over the world canonic culture is dying. Buddhism, Islam, everywhere the old cultures are dying. They are dying in preparation for a new culture. We at present are undergoing the painful experience of living in a transitional period where we are surrounded by fragments of decaying culture and the non-emergence as yet of our own *cultus*. I believe that a new period of art will come not through this decaying, religious, canonic language, but through a lyrical contact with the archetypal world. By lyrical I mean immediate, spontaneous, because we are entering the period of the free-flowing, universal, creative spirit of life, the unlocalised god, accessible to all men in all places. If I may make use of a simile, the Trinity, I believe the age of the Father is over. The age of the Son is over. This is the age of Holy Spirit, this is the age of the universal principle—the open, flexible field of consciousness, the understanding of the unity of life in the multiplicity of human experience, so that we find in our culture again that hidden unity which transcends the fate of multiplicity and nemesis. As I see it this creative spirit which has entered our world is causing such disturbance that it will have to be answered by the spirit of the earth which we have denied as much as we have denied the spirits of the higher worlds. We have denied the spirit of the earth, and that spirit of the earth has to appear in woman. The meeting of the spirit of the earth and the spirit of the other world is one of the great moments that, I believe, will come in the future history of culture.

I have now to speak of what has been called pure speculation but which I prefer to call vision, as I am absolutely certain about it. We have now the possibility of this hidden unity of man's inner world at last permeating the sphere of the exterior world and transforming it. And this brings us to the big problem. Within this new open consciousness we need to recover a sacramental sense. In the past, in the great canonic formality of traditional civilisations there was of necessity a 'closed' consciousness in order to focus upon the sacred. In such civilisations this [hierarchically ordered] consciousness with its formal religious language at all times shaped man's approach to the sacramental. But we have to learn how to concentrate on the sacramental without the use of this 'closed' formality. We must have sacrament everywhere: as Blake says, 'Everything that lives is holy', if only the doors of perception would be cleansed.

Now, the outer world of science has given us communication—the possibility of uniting by means of global communication. But the inner world of art and of culture will give us a more important relationship throughout the world, a unity through human relationship. And this process is going to be very difficult indeed, and there is going to be a very narrow margin between life and death. One of the root problems of our culture is this idea of unity. The idea of uniting the nations and the unity of mankind has not worked so far because it is only a rational abstract idea. Things do not unite just for the sake of unity, we only really unite when we fulfil an ideal higher than ourselves. We can only unite *in* something. In other words our unity has to have a context. Abstract unity has no appeal to an artist because it is sterile.

This means that sooner or later we can no longer sit on the fence and talk about agnosticism. No one has ever created from such an attitude. No child, no real work of art, has ever been created out of the indecision of not knowing whether there is God or not. This reality behind culture which the past has called God is the only real thing in the universe. It has many names. The name for us in our civilisation is love—relationship. And there is no doubt that all over the civilised world, in the midst of the battlefield that is this world, a change of consciousness is being born.

We live in a time of the apocalypse, and the word apocalypse means to unveil. This is the time of unveiling, the unveiling of the atom, the opening of man's inner nature, his inner world. But there is something else that has to be opened, and that is the eye of the heart. If the eye of the heart is closed then the whole of the universe is dead, a mere turning of the wheel of existence, of mere desires. Creative art has always been concerned to touch and open the eye of the heart. We are all apt to fall asleep, spiritually, and the eye of the heart is opened by these two artists, the one with the sword, not afraid to wound the heart, make it bleed, and the other with the light. What we are asked to do in the new age is to understand what the function of art is and to give our support and collaboration to the artist, an active support, that we may share each other's creative response to life. We must understand that state of consciousness we call beauty; it is a form of knowledge. Beauty, as Goethe said, is an archetypal phenomenon.

Now, I have said most of what I have got to say, I would like to end by saying that the new age, to me, means a young age, a young age means to be imbued with the spirit of the archetypes. To feel the freshness of spring is to be in contact with the archetypes and their life-giving spirit. It is to be in contact with the impossible, the unknown, because it is the impossible that expands the possible. Without the impossible we contract, crystallise, condense and die. The Church Father Tertullian said, when questioned, 'I believe it because it is impossible'. Our civilisation asks not too much, but too little of man, too little of its culture, and that is why it asks practically nothing of the artist, because it does not believe the artist is really important. But the artist is always concerned with the impossible, he is moved by the impossible, stimulated by the impossible, haunted by the impossible.

These hopes and intuitions have brought us together in this conference. Why? Because somehow, beyond reason, beyond logic we feel there is a mysterious movement in the air. There is something hanging in the balance. I am reminded of Christ's words, 'Be ye perfect', which mean this; be whole, respond as a whole being. And for an artist the greatest happiness is to have failed at doing the perfect, and the greatest misery is never to have attempted it. I believe this is true of all human beings, whether they are creative artists or not. Once the archetype enters the mind you are haunted by a perfection. If you are haunted by a perfection, an ideal, you are unhappy, and the more unhappy you are the more alive you are. In other words you are not neutral. And remember what the angel in the Book of Revelations said: Thou are not hot or cold, therefore I spew thee out. You are not wanted in the creative process if you are trying to be neutral, and I believe that all this hangs in the balance. Although there is the dark cloud of the hydrogen bomb, with its tremendous destructive forces, yet everywhere there are small flowers of a new consciousness springing up. There is an atmosphere; it is a pure new air, perhaps of spring.

Theatre of the Soul

A conversation with the artist

B.K. *Cecil, since your visionary world embraces the innocence of virginal consciousness, it seems pertinent to begin by asking you what kind of childhood you had?*

C.C. I think you could say that it was fundamentally very happy, because in that moment was the moment I discovered the vision which lasted me my whole lifetime. You could say it was the seed experience, the discovery that Paradise is in the minutiae of life, the minute details of life, in the particulars. This formed a kind of seed vision which I have been able to carry, protect, if you like, cover, all of my life in spite of the natural, inevitable invasion of the rational mind. But that seed, as it were, carried through all that intact to manhood. I think that the initiation of passing through this dangerous period has enabled me to understand those obstacles that prevent the flowering of this inviolate purity or childlike direct perception.

Was there any specific happening or event in your childhood which you feel first made you conscious of this vision, or was it a general remembrance of a childhood Paradise?

I think a series of particular events—for the moment I can't recall individual ones except that the whole universe in those days had a very special flavour, a very special atmosphere of tenderness, of sweetness and yet of very clear formal certainty.

Was this a childhood in the town or the country or both?

In the town but on the edge of the town. I was brought up near a forest, and as I was delicate in health I didn't really go to school much and spent a great deal of time out of doors in the forest at the back of our house. It wasn't a forest by grand standards but it was a forest to me. It was a wood actually and it was there that I learnt, I suppose, the language of stones and grass and trees and especially clouds; and especially a white cloud which played a great part in my life later on. It seemed to me this cloud was a gateway into Paradise—its special whiteness. It was moments like this that came together and formed a kind of unconscious certainty that what we normally see is a very contracted and superficial view. But it wasn't just a view. It was as if there were a whole unchanging world and ordinary life was a changing of an unchanging. I found that I was interested in that world more than anything else, and that has kept me going in dark periods too.

There are a number of drawings by Palmer of white clouds. But of course at that stage you wouldn't have known Palmer's work.

No, but that only confirms from my point of view that the cloud is a possible image of Paradise. It wasn't so much a group of clouds, but a single cloud that affected me so much. I've always been fascinated by the fact that somewhere, in the scriptures I believe, God is supposed to speak out of a cloud.° Even at the age of 71 I find looking at a cloud will heal me very often of melancholy.

Possibly, Matt.17:5, 'While he yet spake, behold, a bright cloud overshadowed them: and behold a voice out of the cloud, which said, This is my beloved Son, in whom I am well pleased; hear ye him.'

I imagine that you would see some connection between the fact that you had little or no schooling and your later ability to hold on to your vision through the period of your life when the rational mind makes its incursions.

I think I was very, very lucky, actually, not to be educated. One consequence is that I really love literature and art and music. I think that's the consequence of not being educated.

Did your interest in painting and the arts follow from one of your parents?

No, my father was an engineer and it would have been incomprehensible to him. He wanted me to be an engineer too. Indeed when I got older, when I was adolescent (15) he apprenticed me to an engineer but I ran away. There was a difference between us, although I later understood that he very secretly admired my drawings. I commenced to draw very early on—not only drawing on the imaginary world—and used to get prizes for drawing objects that looked exactly like objects when I was six. My mother was more sympathetic and a very imaginative woman. My father found great difficulty with this.

You won a scholarship to the Plymouth School of Art. How did this happen?

I think some of my drawings were seen by certain people. I did a lot of imaginative drawings when I was about 14 or 15. Obviously some people thought they were valuable and took them to the local art school. I got a scholarship to go in the evenings, first of all, and there my ability to draw imaginatively was recognised, but mostly because I could draw objectively. I was given a scholarship to the day school, and from there I got a scholarship eventually to the Royal College of Art. It could be said that a lot of my life has been lived in art schools. They have been to me sanctuaries, really, where the whole world of creation was carried out. I've always loved them, and I see that they can be sanctuaries for many sensitive people today.

Can we move on a few years, to your period at the Royal College of Art in London. You were there I believe between 1927 and 1931? Did you begin to paint in your visionary style during your studentship, or was this after you'd finished your formal academic studies?

I was apparently very good at life drawing. I think I got a prize for that, but my imaginative paintings were certainly being done then. They were of course more tentative. I had many enthusiasms, for example in life drawing I had this enthusiasm for Ingres. Ingres was a master I admired very much, and there couldn't be a master more remote from my ultimate preoccupations. I also painted a great many visionary watercolours. In fact one of the celebrated teachers of the Royal College, in one of his class criticisms, said 'It's too remote a subject for watercolours'. But I certainly was already beginning to paint tentatively the world of the imagination, the lyrical world. I was very concerned with poetry—I knew a lot of poetry. My love of music was very deep and very obscure. I hadn't a chance until then to come into contact with it in a practical way. Early on in my life when I did hear a rare concert I was so moved and longed to be a musician and a composer rather than a painter. In fact music began very early on to have a very profound influence on my whole view.

Going back to what you said about your childhood, about having no education, and seeing your later development as a visionary painter one could possibly imagine that you found the formal studies at the Royal College rather irksome. Was this the case, or were you happy to align yourself with them?

Well I'm happy to say there were no formal studies. It was really more happy-go-lucky, rather bohemian. We didn't have these great bureaucratic organisations running it. It was like a studio where only artists were teaching us. When I was there—I didn't actually come in contact with him—there was Paul Nash, and Gilbert Spencer, the brother of Stanley Spencer, and a lot of artists. It was very much, if you like, bohemian. It suited me in its openness. You could be lazy, and I was very lazy also for long periods when I would not do anything. I didn't understand it then but I do now. I was very preoccupied in studying the old masters, the great masters, who endlessly fascinated me, especially their perfection. But I always have worked in spurts and I discovered that just then. Intense periods—because I can only paint a picture at a certain intensity of feeling and energy, otherwise if it drops below that I don't paint very good pictures, or at least I don't think so.

About 1933 you began to be influenced by the Surrealists, only later to reject them. Can you say why this was? Indeed, I ought to ask you why you felt, at least at the outset, that you could to some extent join them?

I think the situation in 1931, '32 and '33, when I left the College was that the art world was dominated by Roger Fry and Clive Bell, art for art's sake, a kind of weekend pleasure trip in hedonism, really. Their hold was completely dominant, and the world of the imagination, the inner life, was absent, and it was very difficult to get any attention or any response. So there was this basic loneliness in my view. Then the Surrealists burst upon the scene affirming the life of the imagination and sharing my disgust at the meaninglessness of modern technological civilisation.

This would have been French Surrealists rather than the English?

Yes, though one would see them through obscure magazines with their reproductions—one never saw the originals at that time. It was then I learnt most and met people connected with Surrealism. They saw my work and seemed very thrilled and very enthusiastic indeed about it, and Herbert Read put me in the first book on Surrealism. He included two works of mine, drawings, which I believe are now lost, and from my point of view they were quite surrealist in the sense that they seemed to appear to be directly connected with the subconscious mind. Then he invited me to participate in the International Exhibition of 1936 at New Burlington Galleries, and I showed a painting there. But this painting [*Virgin Images In the Magical Processes of Time*, 1935], already began to show the difference between my work and the Surrealists. It would be very difficult to say, about this particular painting, what the difference was because it was very close to them in many ways, but it seemed to have an obscure and hidden directional sense in it.

Herbert Read, (ed.), *Surrealism*, London: Faber 1936, reproduces Collins's *Angel Images and Negative Spectres in Conflict*, 1933 as plate 21.

What I liked about them was their rejection. But now looking back on it I must have obscurely seen that they were the last remnants of the Romantic movement gone to seed. They were the Romantic movement with its back against the wall, but I didn't criticise them for that. I am intensely a believer in Romanticism because Romanticism is one of the protections of the soul through one of the darkest rationalistic periods of the nineteenth century. People don't yet understand the significance of the Romantics—that they kept the soul alive. They affirmed it, they did not share the materialistic optimism of the nineteenth century; for that they were very valuable. Frankly, without the Romantics I don't think the soul would have made contact with the twentieth century. They are the most valuable people. But in the surrealist ideas I discerned a final explosion of this energy, a final dispersal of it. It was a sunset, although they did claim that it was a new thing.

So there was no genesis in Surrealism for you but rather a sort of death?

Yes, but I don't, like so many people, dismiss the movement. The whole situation is much more complex than that. There is certainly that decay, of course. I have written a lot about it, but it is very complex because in that decay are the signs of rebirth and without their explosion that rebirth would not be possible. There can't be a rebirth without chaos or flux. The Greek word 'chaos' implies the possibility of rebirth.

Presumably the author has in mind the Greek *khaos*, primordial or unformed matter as the latent source of things yet unborn.

Anyway, I was very young, you must remember, and unable to see intellectually my rejection clearly. But I had an exhibition in 1935 at the Bloomsbury Gallery, and a lot of people came to it, including Henry Moore, who thought a lot of it, Eric Gill, diverse people like that. And Surrealists came along. It was a great success and I seemed in a way all set to run along those lines. After that show I just retired from the scene and went into the country. I had the feeling that something had to be, not really re-thought-out, but somehow that the original direction wasn't there. And I then began to read my own pictures and to see they were not about Surrealism.

What conclusion did you reach?

I was using the word in its correct sense of surreal or over-reality or something transcending. That is where I quarrelled with them. When they used this word they did not really believe in surrealism,° they believed in sub-reality, sub-conscious reality, and the proof of that was that they were Marxists, most of them, and believed in a kind of political utopia. They were naïve, politically. They were unable to see the consequences of their own beliefs. Many differences crept out. In my life there was a turn towards studying that creative wisdom which I call tradition and vision, so I began to come into contact and to read books and to have much more solitude, which is unusual because I was a young man, not yet thirty.

° Presumably super- or supra-reality is meant here.

So initially it seemed that they opened a door to go beyond the materialist view and yet having passed through that door you discovered it to be a dead end. Instead of going to transcendent levels it ended in sub-reality.

They are symptomatic and inevitable of something which has died into crystallisation, they exploded it and that was their function. I suppose it was necessary. It is still going on. It has to go on, but what they have done in modern art is to turn up a lot of material which is not being used by more creative minds. The fact that they dismantled the world is part of it. They proved by doing this that the world is an illusion from one point of view. They were really put in a situation where people had to seek what is real, you see?

As if they are not really in earnest about the world they re-made, as if it were a game.

That's right.

Without being aware of the more cosmic connotations of illusion. Would it be fair to say that?

Yes, they weren't creatively aware of all the possibilities that were made possible by the explosion. They congealed themselves into formulas, clichés. They had a kind of psychic furniture they moved about in their pictures. It was really easy to paint a surrealist picture. You just put a boiled egg on top of a railway station, that sort of thing. It was really quite easy.

Yes, that was what I meant by it being a game, for you it wasn't in earnest enough.

It was a game which had many attractions, because after all, creativity is in a way a game in the sense that you play, in the sense of cosmic play, *Līlā*;° maybe they are doing the work of one aspect of that. But I haven't perhaps conveyed to you the fact that the atmosphere was very intoxicating. They were people who did not accept the status quo. The atmosphere was electric, and of course it showed in their pictures—ruined buildings with half a leg coming out. Six years later it was made a reality in the air raids of the World War that followed. The front page of every newspaper was a surrealist picture, so they were beaten at their own game by life itself. The concentration camps and what happened afterwards made their work look like a nursery. They prophesied and what they prophesied was greater than what they were.

Līlā, the Sanscrit word for 'play', used here in the sense of God's act of manifesting Himself as essentially a 'game' or 'sport'.

Was it about this time that Picasso and Klee influenced you?

Yes, I should say so, in the thirties.

I wouldn't normally have associated you with Picasso. I can see that at one period Klee might have interested you. Less so Picasso.

Yes, I agree with that. Picasso only interested me for his admirable courage and freedom to move about imagery.

His virtuosity, you mean?

Not his virtuosity, but his exploration and openness and lack of any of the ordinary conditioning of people I admired tremendously. It had a great effect on me. Klee I admired for his nervous finesse and his secretiveness, his connection with fairy stories and the folk mind, but used in a very sophisticated way of course. He helped me to understand how there is this undercurrent of unified being throwing up its imagery, which is rather different from just dismantling the world.

Of course the Surrealists claimed everybody from Lewis Carroll to Blake, the more the merrier, without distinguishing one from the other. Bosch they admired and quite rightly. He was dismantling, also, but then you see in Bosch there is the hint of redemption. What I have against the Surrealists is that there is no redemption, there is no context for their destruction.

There's no escape, either. It's a descent into a psychosis from which there is no escape.

That's what's wrong with Francis Bacon—incomplete in the sense that there is no context for redemption.

Do you think this was true of Klee, that he lacked the power to handle symbols that would have released the neurosis of his imagery, the minute detail and the fussiness that seem to come from a very individual, private, subconscious level?

Yes, I think that . . . it's very feminine, very introvert, self-communing, very delicate, very sophisticated and so on, but too influenced by child art, I think. But the fact that he was seeking out child art showed the need to find somewhere some connection with this world of direct perception.

The world of child art is really closed to the adult mind, in a sense, isn't it? I think your paintings actually indicate this because the only true way to go back to child art is to rediscover the world of childhood Paradise rather than thinking in terms of going back to a 'child-like' vision, which is really impossible for mature men.

It's the rediscovery of the second Paradise, that's the real discovery, which doesn't mean that you are not sophisticated in your technique.

Was Odilon Redon an influence at any time?

He must have been an influence at one time because now I am much older I see there is a connection. Again, he is more feminine. His art is very passive

In retrospect this 'hunt' for influences seems clumsy, for influences are far more complex and subtle in their operation than even the artist can be aware of. Sought too vigorously they can give a false and misleading impression of how an artist's imagination works, more especially since much, inevitably, is left out of account, as is the case here.

in many ways and subdued. Mine is very dynamic in many ways, there's a dynamic rhythm in a lot of my pictures.

1939 saw you teaching for the first time. Now teaching has always been very important to you, hasn't it? What do you see the role of the teacher to be now that the concept of art has virtually broken down completely?

I think this is a teaching age because everything has broken down. The modern bureaucratic view of education is a failure. It's not working. So far as art is concerned I think more artists should tackle the art schools, because the only people who can teach a living knowledge are those in whom that living knowledge is active. The art schools will have to be reformed, I think, because creativity is not a product that can be rationalised. And it is not concerned with products. It is concerned with unveiling or revealing something. That's the important thing about creativity. Therefore, the most important thing the future should be concerned with is first of all the student and not with drawing or painting; the way the student thinks and feels, the way the student lives, because that is what art is—not the other way around, art is not about art. The student should come first because as all creativity is the mystery of being, so the mystery of being is the first thing you should be concerned with.

I had an academic training and I used to draw from the casts for about six weeks with charcoal and bread for the highlights, and I am absolutely all for it. It is a very special discipline which is missing from the art school today. I would certainly bring the cast back for several reasons. First, the discipline in drawing from them can be a form of meditation. Secondly, because if the casts are rightly chosen they are bringing back the archetypal forms that the student should study. Contemplation of archetypal forms is one of the most important things that should come back to the art schools. Because what you contemplate you become. If you don't have these archetypes then you are laid open to a confusion of influences that you cannot sort out if you are a student. You start with basic archetypal primordial energies and understand what they imply and the art of drawing from them over long periods—like six weeks—is a very important thing. But I discovered another knowledge altogether—a knowledge that was nothing to do with objective reproduction, and that is really to do with form as energy. The drawing flows and forms itself rather than is produced as an object, whereas if you are drawing from a model very often it deteriorates into a kind of object, not a human being at all. It might be a piece of wood actually. The technique of drawing should be learnt consciously. But one creates unconsciously. Technique is then at the disposal of the unconscious because, you see, creation is always a leap into the unknown. If you have a programme in front of you you are already dead, because you then know what will happen—you prejudge the experience, but you don't have this element of the unknown. The technique though is consciously assimilated, so you have these two aspects which are really one. There's a lot I can say about teaching but it is really a bit complicated.

Are you pointing towards a future in which there is less emphasis on curriculum and more emphasis on the interrelationship between the teacher and the pupil in the teaching of art?

Yes. I see it as working in small cells, groups of cells, rotating around the teacher. And I would bring back workshop conditions again where the technique is not learned as a material thing but is taught in contact with one's own being. My own classes are highly technical. They are all about technique, but not as mechanical technique. What they are really about is the nature of creativity, what it really is, and the interpretation of form, the art of the interpretation of form and the psychology of creativity. Most psychology today is about pathology. But there is a psychology of creativity. This is not a rule of thumb thing, it's very mysterious. It's learned in direct contact where it is active in somebody and is not analyzable. The students know exactly when they have received it and you know when they have received it, and the proof of the pudding, as always, is in the eating. You can see in the students, in the colour of their skin, everything, whether that creativity is at last awakened in their inner nature. Ultimately there will be teachers of this. It demands a great deal from them. My teaching is based not on analysis—because we are dominated by analytical knowledge—but on empathy, knowledge which is an empathy. Empathic knowledge is the way I would describe my teaching. Being able to receive that gnosis through sympathy with the form. Some people think that's very vague, actually its very, very clear.

How was Rudolph Laban important to you?

Rudolf von Laban, dancer, choreographer, and ballet master, born in Bratislava in 1897. He came to England in 1938 and spent some time at Dartington Hall. He died in England in 1958.

I met him in 1940 at Dartington Hall when he had just fled from the Nazis. He opened my awareness to the many aspects of the mystery of movement, and he confirmed my deepest intuitions about movement being a form of knowledge. He was important to me in that intuition, he confirmed and freshened it because he was a man who had mastered it. He invented a language you could work from—choreographic. I see all creation as a dance really and my teaching is based on the dance too. I see the drawing as a dance and as it were the paper as a stage, over which the instrument moves. I have always been very moved by ritualised gesture, archetypal gesture. In a way a lot of my teaching and most certainly my paintings are rites.

What comes over very strongly in your work is the constant freshness of your vision, and the fact that it never seems to tire or grow stale is a testimony to its reality. You have said to me in the past that for many years you thought that your vision was wholly subjective.

I think I remember saying that, but I think perhaps you are leaving out the context. I was always told by critics and by people that my work was subjective, but in spite of this there persisted in me a strong intuition that it was universal. This is the context, and recent events have proved this to be true. People tend to dismiss it as a dream but there is a difference between a dream and a vision. A dream tends to vanish at the first touch of the cold fingers of the world. A dream has no dialectic. I believe a vision has a dialectic. In a dream one is a victim, always. In a vision one is a participant. A vision doesn't come to you unless you are willing to actively participate in it. In a dream you are pushed around. But vision nevertheless shares some characteristics of the dream in that it is freer—its combination of imagery more fluid. It has to do with spiritual energy not being fixed. Whereas fantasy is too fluid. The point of condensation makes a vision. Fantasy disperses it. Madness overfixes it. This fluid, open condensation is really against all people who want things as either/or, where it's got to be this or that, whereas it's paradoxically this *and* that *and* such, to use linguistic terms. The right condensation.

What did you mean about vision having a dialectic?

It has implications which can be discussed by the rational mind and showing how it is active in the world.

You say in the film [*The Eye of the Heart*, British Council, 1978] *that you don't enjoy painting, but it's fairly evident that you enjoy the material substance by which pictures are made.*

Yes, the question of not enjoying it—that's a very deep one. I think it is because primarily one is haunted by a perfection and one only experiences the absence of this perfection in creativity and this is very painful—it even seems futile—this absence. The animal in one, doesn't like doing futile work, because it can't see what it's plugging away at. But the soul, the inner eye of the psyche, can see the goal, and is both unhappy because it can't reach it, but happy that it can see it at all. I'm trying now to analyze this experience. But after the thing is done and recedes then even the animal, even the ego can see it. It's partly due to that. A lot of people enjoy painting all the time and do not seem to go through this experience. They enjoy a kind of self-expression, but self-expression is not creation. There is a difference.

Creation is transformation, something quite different, and no transformation takes place unless the energy is qualified and denied by limitations. For self-expressionists there are no limitations. It's just a relief, getting rid of something. But the real creative artist immediately has a vision and a perfection which is qualified by materials. You imagine something is infinite but then it has suddenly got to be in a concrete shape. The shape, the size, the whole thing resists you, and this qualification is pain, and this pain purifies the energy and transforms it.

Do you feel this qualification is something that you must pit yourself against—is that what you mean?

No. What do you come up against when you have a vision?—you come up against the problem of incarnating it in a denser way, in a material. The very fluid and open way of the world of the imagination is infinite. The problem is how is this infinity to be condensed in the material object.

But it could be said that there's a reciprocal relationship in any creative activity inasmuch as the artist determines what is to be made, yet on the other hand the materials with which the thing is to be made, inasmuch as they exist as physical substance, that has some determining influence as well, doesn't it. How does this relate to what you said about incarnating?

Oh everything, because the resultant fruit is mutual qualification. The vision immediately qualifies the material. It has got to be something higher—it has got to be more fluid. It immediately qualifies the vision so that you've got to come down in a much more condensed form. That is where the purification comes in. The energy becomes transformed through this mutual qualification, and then it's in a state of grace. There's no grace without qualification.

There's a technique which I like very much in your work and that's the layers of varnish—when you are working at that sort of technique how does it relate to what you've said about qualification and incarnation?

The technique itself is a form of meditation and gradually, because it's a slow process, it gives you time to bring the vision into relationship with the materials. The adjustment is gradual. It's really a form of marriage, you see, and gradually you find the perfect marriage. Remember what this infinite thing is—it's not an object, it's a fragrance, it's an atmosphere. And how is the miracle of that atmosphere to be permeated into a solid object you are painting? You could analyze the paints, for example, before one paints with them and analyze the painting afterwards, and chemically there is no difference between one and the other. And yet in the painting there is this fragrance present which is absent from the tubes of paint.

So the very slowness of the method is a way of giving birth to an incarnation?

It's more a perfect marriage. It doesn't follow that it cannot be done in other ways. In Chinese painting it is done immediately.

To go to the other extreme, how does this relate to your drawings where we find the single line?

I think the one influences the other. You learn an enormous amount through the slow meditative technique of the relationship between the inner fragrance and atmosphere and climate and its marriage, and the more you learn at that slow tempo it enables you to do it fast, in your drawings. We are in that area which is very difficult to talk about because for one thing there is no description of it.

In a sense, your paintings are the description.

Yes. It applies to everything. It applies certainly to icons. An icon can follow all formulas correctly and be as dead as a dodo in that it doesn't have a climate or presence of the Divine Reality. And ultimately this is the test of every work of art, and traditional works of art are no exception to it.

Henry Moore says somewhere that there's a right physical size for every idea.

I'll tell you what it is really. It's finding a physical body for the vision—the perfect physical body for the vision, and this is what aesthetics is about. To like a painting for aesthetics only is to like a woman for her toilette. But if everything is subject to this perfect physical body then aesthetics ceases to be a kind of delectation and becomes this perfume. I set everything on this perfume, and they are the words I would use—perfume, nuance, climate. And that brings us to the whole question of imagery and symbols.

I wonder if we could leave that subject for a moment, Cecil because I want to come back later and ask you about the role of the symbol. My next question relates to the period 1957–58, when there was a change of style in your work. You moved from a lyrical eloquence to a blacker, more harsh, possibly even a strident series of images, perhaps more violent in mood. Did this reflect a changed state of mind or influence of any sort?

It reflected something very important. During the late 50s I began to find a great need to expand in consciousness and gradually, about 1957 to '58 I experienced a tremendous expansion of energy. It seemed to demand a more direct, lyrical form of painting, as if a great storm had overtaken me. And I realised, not at the time, but later on, that the function of it was to enlarge the new field before I, as it were, formalised again. I usually find that's how it goes. I have lyrical periods of expansion and then condensations of formality. I move from one to the other. This was a very strong one and it lasted well into 1961. I did a series of lyrical paintings on a big scale. I did six of them in about a month, which is for me very quick, in the summer of 1960.

You say lyrical, could I ask you to qualify that word?

I mean direct, gestural, as if I were dancing it; not built up through a series of procedures but really direct, as if you were writing it down in you're handwriting. The need for direct manifestation. And by that means the energy was opened up. Otherwise I would have gone on contracting and possibly even stopped.

Turning more to the content of your art, you have referred to your imaginative vision as a 'theatre of the soul'. Can you explain what you mean by that phrase?

I mean that art is not a place but a condition where the life of the soul is re-enacted. When I say the life of the soul I mean the real life of the soul, what is happening in the life of the soul. It's a theatre because the theatre is ritual, and this is enacted in various paintings of mine to remind the spectator that art and life is a covenant made with the Divine Reality. Anyone experiencing my painting would be reminded of this covenant. Because, in general, contemporary culture is old and stale. I hold this word 'covenant' as very, very important and I see that the only hope for our art and our culture today is for it to make a new covenant with the Divine Reality.

Does this link up with what you said earlier about the dynamic of the dream?

Yes. If it is connected with the Divine Reality then it would mean that there would be a point around which the imagination circles, and that is what I mean by concentric imagination as opposed to eccentric imagination—imagination which has no point to circle round. Creative imagination circles round a hidden point, so I think of the theatre as concentric imagination, and in itself already a point of enactment. And the pilgrimage of the soul, the quest of the soul is enacted before one's eyes, and is enacted by using ritualistic and visual magic. Magic is very important. Magic is creative illusion as opposed to uncreative illusion. When I say creative I mean illusion which gives life, which is the play of life. The life-giving play, even.

'In all the great cultures there was some kind of agreement as to the nature of reality where there was a point of orientation to which, more or less, everybody turned. Today there is no point of orientation and so there is no, what I call, concentric imagination, only an eccentric one which dispenses [dispurses] itself in fantasy. We have a great need for concentric imagination; what the ancients would have called higher imagination—imagination not contaminated by the wavering changes of climate in the lower imagination.' From Cecil Collins's interview with John Lane in *Resurgence* no. 122, May–June 1987, pp.12–13.

Were you ever conscious of a need to, as it were, populate your 'theatre of the soul'.

I had no idea of having a 'theatre' and 'populating' it because it doesn't work like that with me. Everything is revealed and unfolded, gradually or suddenly, from the unknown. I don't know what's coming, and what's more, I'm not really very interested in what's coming, because then I would not get that very important surprise which is what creativity is about. I've never had a programme which I carry out. It's always something being born in me and revealed. Any kind of rationalisation would come last, not first. In fact, it has taken me many years to understand my own paintings afterwards. It is not necessary to understand in order to create but it is necessary to create in order to understand.

Can you say something about the main people, occupants, protagonists of your theatre? Obviously the first one that comes to mind are the Fools. What do they represent?

The Fool represents that innate, inviolate, primordial innocence which sees clearly, directly or perceives directly and clearly, the recovery of which constitutes for me the object of all real culture, and all real education and civilisation. It seems to me that is what life is about—the recovery of direct perception. And, after all, all the scriptures are about that—'Except that ye be as a little child you will not see the kingdom of heaven'. The Fool is not interested in success or failure, or the vanity and burden of external knowledge. He is interested in life, in the mystery of consciousness and the exploration of the mystery of consciousness and the transformation of consciousness which comes about through direct perception. He is interested, in other words, in love and its manifestation in that harmony and wholeness which we call beauty. He is therefore in a state of creative vulnerability and openness and he is easily destroyed by the world. I have painted a picture of an angel comforting a Fool [1957] who has been broken by the world. You see there is a great relationship between the Angel and the Fool and the Angel is, as it were, deeply concerned with the Fool—in fact Christ Himself says that anyone who should injure one of these little ones it would be better that a millstone were tied around his neck and he were thrown into the sea.

Yes, the Fool has always been held to be near to God, and our world is a great ignorer, if not destroyer of Fools.

Because it is not the type that can be exploited, it is not the type that makes the state work. You see in the Fool's mouth this quivering, vulnerable joy and humour and sadness and melancholy—very much the voice of truth.

Could you say something about Angels?

The angelic tradition, or the angelic intelligence is that which connects all the worlds and very often visits this world and enters into the world, into the battlefield of this world. Angels exist to help transform our consciousness, to open our awareness—and contemplation of their beauty purifies us. But some angels enter right into the war of the world and some are deeply wounded. There's a picture of mine called *The Wounded Angel* [1967], where the Angel has returned to Paradise, and is lying on the ground of Paradise, wounded, resting rather like a butterfly whose wings have been injured. Now this vision of the Angels is an expansion of our awareness where the Angels are instruments of transformation and through their flow of love they are very close to us. Angels are living at a higher speed than we are, and because they are at a higher speed we don't see them. And that's why we call them invisible. They are here as part of the transforming process of the universe, and of course the Fool and the Anima (the woman), are two instruments of this transformation. In my pictures you see them in different combinations—Woman with Angel, Fool with Angel. They are the vision of God, the winged thoughts of the divine mind. Winged because they're free in the sense that they are multi-dimensional.

Always the intermediaries between the divine and the human worlds?

Yes, absolutely. Between, to speak technically, low density and high energy.

There's another thing; one traces the Angel as an image of meaning, of visionary intention, of life. An Angel, a winged figure—you can't get a foot hold there if you're a rationalist. With the Fool you might get it, with the Anima, but the Angel, no. And that is the importance of the Angel. It allows of no compromise. The mind has to make a leap immediately, and, the Bible is quite right, the Angels are something we have to wrestle with and, significantly, there is no let-up until dawn; and dawn is a climate that plays a great part in my paintings.

What about the various heads we find in your work?

For me the head is the combination, or climax, or the flowering of the human nature. In the head is condensed and focused the whole reality of the person. That's why I think I've done so many heads. To me it's the most beautiful part of the human body. In fact you can say the head is a theatre of the soul.

And what about Oracles and Sibyls that have figured largely in both your paintings and your drawings?

'Certainly the soul suffers from isolation and forgetfulness. But the Angel is a great reminder; it is an image of freedom. The wings, for example, are made for the sky. Angels belong to the open sky of eternity. They live in the oxygen of God, the only reality which keeps us alive. They are also images of what is the highest in us. Our consciousness has to grow wings in the sense it has to transform; the wings are an image of transformation. Angels come into the world to help this transformation, they take part in this battle, and some of them get wounded and have to rest on the floor of Paradise. This is the experience of my painting *The Wounded Angel*. It is like a butterfly that has had its wings damaged. The painting, *The Angel of the Flowing Light*, also shows the world of the Angel. It appears walking on mountains, it glides over the mountains which are a symbol of the transformation of consciousness. It is dawn, the dawn light is behind this Angel and out of its side comes this flowing river of light.' Interview with John Lane, op. cit. pp.14–15.

They seem to be visions of certain functions of the feminine soul—prophetic, oracular, sometimes coming out of caves, guardians of altars, uttering prophesies. They are, as it were, the voice of the unknown or entries into the unknown land, guarded in my paintings, I think, seldom by a man but practically always, by a woman or an Angel.

Which came first in your 'theatre of the soul'—was it the Fool or the Angel?

I think the Angel came first, and then the Fool. The Fool as it were came suddenly into my consciousness and I wasn't immediately aware of its significance. This was revealed to me gradually; it unfolded itself. The Angel was the first immediate image that I recognised as coming from the unknown world. The Fool I didn't recognise right away, though I was deeply involved immediately he did arrive. In fact, some of the early Fools, like *The Sleeping Fool* [1943], deeply immersed me in the experience of the Fool, and throughout my life these images continued to evolve, unfold, and to give off their various implications.

For an account of the genesis of the Fool see Anderson, 1988, p. 52.

What period would this have been?

It would be in the late thirties—1937. There were Angels appearing in my paintings as far back as 1934.

I can't think of a Fool picture earlier than about 1940? Were you conscious of the Angel giving rise to the need for the Fool?

No, the Fool actually arrived, I would almost say, suddenly, out of the blue. A mystery, really, but a very strong image, a very potent image, and in a way I hadn't thought at the time that it would persist to reveal itself in all its possibilities. Then of course when one is young the whole vision doesn't reveal itself, right away.

Could we turn to landscapes? Would it be true to say that your landscapes are, or comprise, imaginative space?

Yes. It is the landscape of the soul. It's the land in which the soul walks about. Anything in that landscape is a state of being; is a state of consciousness.

Is this indicated in many of them by the forms and shapes and images that interrelate from figure to landscape, from rock to bird and butterfly, to the leg of a figure?

Yes. They're all interchangeable. You get a figure who can become a cloud, a tree. A tree can become a cloud. It reminds you that it is one consciousness, though multi-dimensional. There are no objects in my paintings: no objects at all. It's a kind of music. It's really a landscape in a state of music.

And this interchangeability and interrelatedness of shapes and forms indicates the unifying ground of consciousness?

Yes. It's a landscape also. The opposite would be a landscape by Cézanne, which is a kind of Aristotelian rationalisation of external forms. Although, without his knowing it, he may well have been concerned to try and mirror consciousness.

What about the reversed perspective in some of your paintings and drawings? I'm thinking in particular, of course, of the Double Portrait, The Artist and His Wife *of 1939, and the drawing* The Afternoon of the Fools, *1976.*

I use perspective for emotional reasons, not optical reasons, and if you like, spiritual reasons, where I want a certain emotional experience. I take the table and turn it round very often the opposite to an optical view of it, as in the Double Portrait. The perspectives have certain compositional functions of leading the eye from one episode to another in a painting. It's an essentially emotional and spiritual use of perspective.

Is this related to what I've heard you say about their being no such thing as spatial values, only the space of *something?*

Yes, and in this inverted perspective I very often use human figures in different sizes in a picture. There's no fixed size necessarily because the whole of the imagery is to do with being and not with some kind of observational optical relationship. A being relationship, that's the first thing that decides the form in my pictures and the relationship of one form with another is that they manifest the relationship of one being with another, and the perspective is used the same way. Also inverted perspective has the function of dissolving the so-called 'real' observational world, and making the mind able to enter into a world in which there is enacted all aspects of the spiritual life. In fact it makes the 'theatre of the soul' possible.

Would it be a mistake to attribute this inverse perspective to the fact that your vision is of the inner world, the other side of and beyond the veil of the outer world?

It wouldn't be a mistake, because as I say the perspective is often used to break the habits of the conditioned mind, and the first break is that here is a table which doesn't look like a table but is a table at the same time, because in the painting things are what they are or what they appear to be and yet they are not what they appear to be. In other words the openness of the imagery and the state of the imagery enables the mind and the consciousness to freely experience and move about the painting.

You force us to reconsider the beingness of the table, because it doesn't look like an observable table?

Yet it remains very much a table. It's like the sacraments—St. Augustine talked about sacraments. He says, I believe, 'one thing is seen but another is known'; and the table, the inverted table, makes you see that it is a table, and yet it's not a table. Another thing is known.

Can we turn to another theme, which I know is very important, not only as an image in your paintings but to the whole of your thought, the theme of the eternal feminine figure, the Anima.

Woman as soul. Very important, I think, because that's what's missing from modern education and modern civilisation, and also the feminine is the receptacle of divine mystery.

You don't think of that in specifically Christian terms—the Virgin Mary for instance?

No, this idea is very limited in Christianity, I think, because you only have the Virgin Mary, you don't have Venus, the laughing Aphrodite. On the whole it is an all-male pantheon, fortunately relieved by femininity at one stage. But it has only one aspect, the Holy Mother. We are very lucky in the West to have that.

Yes, the all male Trinity of the Christian Church, the later doctrine of the Christian Church, was something that Yeats felt he needed to find an answer to. The Father, the Son and the Holy Spirit doesn't appear to adequately explain things.

In Hinduism the divine reality is split up into many different facets of gods and goddesses, and you don't get any bloodshed. Bloodshed comes through the one god, the monotheistic, which is a male idea. The feminine is pluralistic psychology where you learn that life is really creative, it is pluralistic as well as particular. Again, in Hinduism as in other religions you get this marvellous feminine aspect all the way through. This teaches one how to qualify this deadly male preoccupation with the one and only. You could say that all quarrels come from this one and only.

What about the Anima in your paintings?

There are two aspects to the Anima, usually very contemplative and receptive, or else as Priestess—in one of my lithographs [*A Song*, 1960] she is holding the worlds, and she has a sword in one hand. She's very much a priestess in my work, or—the eternal bride. In my painting [*The Eternal Bride*, 1963], she is seen walking through the workshop of the universe, which is a world of fire and she's carrying the cup of life which is a distillation of all the experiences of life. The red background is of fire, and on the ground is the world egg. It's very much what Goethe talks about in The Mother [*die Mutter*]. Then the other aspect is this marvellous passivity, this marvellous receptivity as an image of the contemplation of the universe. Then there's this relationship with innocence, which is again the relationship between the woman and the Fool.

This is very important to the way you think in terms of the modern world, isn't it, this lack of the feminine element in the modern world itself?

I think it's due to the predominance of Aristotelian knowledge, analytical reasoning, what I call process knowledge, and the assumption—which is now almost fundamental in all modern education—that that is the only form of knowledge. We have to realise that there are other forms of knowledge, and that the feminine is another knowledge or gnosis. We are now in a state of complete disequilibrium. We have a highly specialised external world which in no way reflects the inner life of man, the psyche, so he goes through an absolutely—from the point of view of a human being—meaningless landscape. It's an environment without being. In other words a really empty environment, a series of mental diagrams, which you walk through. It produces in you this tremendous emptiness, because the soul, like everything else, needs to find its reflection in the environment, because that means that it is unified with its environment. There's an absolute split between the soul and the environment. There's no reflection. I consider modern architecture, with few honourable exceptions, one of the supreme failures of modern culture—the one big betrayal. The series of boxes, which is basic, is very masculine. Not a breast to be seen anywhere.

We have very briefly mentioned music and I know music is very important to you Cecil. I remember once we were standing in a gallery and you explained to me how a drawing of yours could be read like a musical score.

That's true. I have this great love of music, and it certainly is a very important influence in my painting, and in my life, indeed, and because in my life in my painting. The whole feeling of flow and rhythm and texture and length of phrase, pulsating rhythm—it has a very deep influence, especially on my drawings. Also music is capable of really touching and awakening that which tends to fall asleep in people—the inner sensitivity. Certainly if I ever chose again to be a creative artist I would choose to be a composer, and a performing instrumentalist, because music seems to be able to penetrate very deeply, but I'm hoping that my painting is a form of music.

There is in itself a close alliance between line and polyphony. Drawing is like chamber music, painting is like an orchestral piece—you've got the colour of the instruments, and colour is a very mysterious element—unanalyzable. It's very significant that the best theorists are the worst colourists.

In colour, you see, you've got also a kind of musicality. I think what I'm trying to say is that all great art, all real art, has a musicality which is at the very root of the matter. You can't explain music to a tone-deaf person—you can't explain religion to a person without religious sensibility. You can't convince people by arguments about reality at all—it's a question of inner sensibility, and what I call musicality is really a spiritual reality.

Has your wish to have been a musician got something to do with the fact that music is the least tangible of the arts and therefore seems to have a more direct relation to the divine?

That's right. That intangibleness which is the way I have sensed all my life to be the reality of the thing. But how to manifest that intangible quality? That's why I don't very much like the later rationalisations which we call iconography. Because what you have to do is to present this intangible quality. And coming back to your original question, musicality is the spiritual element. If there's spirituality there's music in a painting. If there's no music then the thing is no good.

Do you ever use colour in a symbolic way?

Not consciously, no.

Or gesture? In Blake's pictures—if the figure has the left foot or the right foot forward—I think it's the right foot forward the rational man, and so forth. There's nothing of this sort of symbolism in your work?

No, there's nothing of that symbolism, but there is something else. The action of the hand can be a musical action, a ritualistic action, and entirely bypass the rational mind, and can touch the heart, the knowledge of the heart, and you know immediately what it's saying. Real creation of a work of art has nothing to do with having ideas that you wish to put in action, or having a programme, no matter how grand—it is a revealing, an unveiling of the nature of reality through evocation and through climate, atmosphere, through musicality. And therefore it's always active, always alive. And that brings me to the real point about it—atheists are people who are always wanting God to be proved—it's a contradiction in terms. I don't respect a God that can be proved. I only respect a God that can't be proved, because that is really God—what you can prove is never God—so what you can prove is only a projection of your own mind. To prove God is an atheistic statement from my point of view. It's the same with a work of art, it can't be proved, it has

'Colour is the realm of intuition; colour is vibrations. As an artist I am not concerned with conscious colour symbolism, which is academic. Colour is a most beautiful and mysterious element. At the moment [1987] I tend more towards the more classical view of colour which is to reduce the harmony to a few colours and to avoid kaleidoscopic harmony. It is in this that I find the serenity and harmony that I am interested in, the harmony which contributes to the serenity of the world.' Interview with John Lane, op. cit., p.14.

to be experienced, this fragrance, this perfume and this musicality. It doesn't mean to say you are unable to write about it, but you can't explain it. The human heart doesn't respect a God that can be proved, only a God that can't be proved. The human heart is rightly suspicious of all that's proved.

Do you make preparatory studies for your paintings?

Very seldom. I made very elaborate drawings for the Double Portrait which is very unusual. I like to make a very rough sketch in pencil, usually. I have two ways of working. One is, I think about my work from within, in my imagination, and very often I think it right out to the very smallest details. Sometimes they are so elaborately thought out that I don't paint them. There doesn't seem any reason to do so. So I must leave them a little rough and unfulfilled in order to paint them at all. But I can in this case see the painting very clearly from within, right down to the minutest details, even the colour. I can pre-see these things.

The other way I work is not knowing what I am going to paint at all, but simply to get a group of colours and strike straight away at the painting. And the idea arises from the working of the paint itself. Of course what happens is that the idea or the vision is already within me in a seed form and the working of the material excites the seed and it unfolds within me. And I participate in this unfoldment, knowing when to come in, I hope, and trying to come in when it is necessary to give it a little bit of form in this way or that way, and not trying to interfere with it too much—to let it reveal itself. The whole problem is one of becoming sensitive to its intention, its unfolding. It knows perfectly well what it wants to do, and I mustn't interfere with it. On the other hand one has to control the energy, to give it form, to be participating all the time in it. It is a wonderful balance between revelation, as it were, and form. And I love the actual making of pictures—the craft of them.

You said just now that you can 'pre-see' before you paint, are you ever surprised by something that you hadn't allowed for or pre-seen?

Oh yes, even towards the end something new will come out which I hadn't thought of. To me the great delight is being able to see the thing right down to the details. But you do lose a bit of interest when the thing is already complete in the mind. There doesn't seem very much reason to paint it, that's why it's rather dangerous, because you are repeating an inner mechanical process. You know what's going to be there. The joy is to work with the unknown in flight, as it were, with wings, and to fly with this extraordinary eagle of vision and to be prepared to be taken wherever it wants to go—if it soars above the clouds into the golden light of the immortal sun—well then follow it.

In one of your etchings there's the theme of the great happiness and the little happiness that goes with it. Could you say something about these?

I think the root vision in my painting has to be understood in this way—I say this because it is very, very difficult to put into words. If I may say, roughly, there are different levels of consciousness. The lowest level one could call the small happiness, and above that you could say a small unhappiness, where one is restricted to fear of losing the small happiness—the small happiness being restricted to automatic reactions, like and dislike. Above the small unhappiness is the great unhappiness, which means that you've seen through the small happiness. I mean by that that it doesn't satisfy you, and you are unhappy in a very deep way because you know there's a great happiness, and if you cannot experience that, you reject every other form of happiness, because that is the happiness that you know to be the greatest and the most real. In the state of the great unhappiness you are unhappy because you know there's a great happiness, a perfection. Let me put it another way—you are unhappy because you can't reach it but you are very happy because you can see it. In a word, you're alive. And that I think is how we should understand the very profound melancholy of so much great music. The music of Chopin is the music of the great unhappiness, but there is more real happiness in the unhappiness of Chopin's music than in the small happiness, because the real happiness is that this melancholy comes from being able to see the great unhappiness. My painting is basically a vision of the great happiness and that is why so much of the emotion in my painting is complex—in the melancholy there is joy, in the joy there is melancholy. There is no question of either/or, it's a complex emotion, but it is because consciousness is infused by the great happiness, that is why it is in the painting, the great happiness.

Always, in other conversations, Mozart was the nominee here.

[Here, for a period, the conversation became too scrappy to warrant giving a full transcript. But following on from the subject of music's significance we spoke specifically about which composers were important to him. 'The purer aspects' of Messiaen—such works as *Vision de l'Amen*, *Vingt Regards sur l'Enfant Jesus*, Ravel and Debussy—especially *Pelléas & Mélisande* were approved. But this short list hardly did justice to his wide knowledge of music. The artist mentioned that he had taped his own improvised (but never scored) music and that he had written poetry.

Asked about Jung he claimed he had not read him; had avoided reading him, feeling that such an analytic approach was to 'pre-judge experience'. 'Better to get lost in the unknown than lost in the known.' But none the less affirmed his own 'great respect for him because of his affirmation of the necessity of finding the soul again.'

The French scholar Henry Corbin was also approved: 'Of all the writers on tradition he seems to me to be the most real in that he never defines but always evokes everything.']

Cecil, there are two artists that, inevitably, you seem to be linked with, though for very different reasons in each case. They are William Blake and David Jones. Blake's doctrine of the imagination as a world of eternity has an obvious affinity with your own vision, but you mentioned earlier the great difference between your own and Blake's work.

Anybody who has a very highly developed sense of imagination is nearly always linked with Blake. Blake seems to be the criterion, and a very good criterion too. But my work is really very, very different from his. Blake had a great problem, of course, of language. His language is very much influenced by eighteenth century rationalism—figures drawn with very anatomical knowledge, muscles etc. For example, he got his figures so much from the late Italian Renaissance, from reproductions of Michelangelo, so that he has this curious, very materialistic, sophisticated figure. You don't find this in the later works; the watercolours where this is dissolved and fused in a marvellous atmosphere of vision. Also, Blake's whole work is filled with conflict and struggle and he is very much a Romantic of the early nineteenth century.

My own work is much more concerned with earlier civilisations. If there is any influence at all it's pre-Renaissance—it goes back to the more primordial civilisations, and my work is not so rationalised in language or so concerned with the reproduction of muscles and physical features. The forms are developed as a kind of music, built up of energy flow, and this relates it to much earlier cultures. This is significant because there is in my work a kind of pristine purity of outlook, which is more in keeping with the kind of childhood of civilisations. I think that is one of the main differences. Also many writers have labelled my work Romantic, or neo-Romantic, but there is in my work a formality and a detachment, almost a classicism of form and even a serenity of form. But these labels of Romantic and Classical don't really fit in my case. I seek always in my work to reconcile or to bring into equilibrium the two opposites—the energy and flow of the Romantics with the formality of the Classical. I like always to bring together in equilibrium contrasted elements, tenderness and austerity, passion and form, so that they come together in a point of equilibrium which therefore cannot be labelled either Classical or Romantic.

You think Blake was perhaps unsuccessful in finding a language for his vision?

I wouldn't say he was unsuccessful, I would say that he had a very great problem—you get the same thing in all the artists of that day—Fuseli overcame it by extreme formal expressionism. But in certain works of Blake's there's a clinging to the form—almost a literal clinging to the anatomical form of the figures. In spite of his impediments there is this very great vision which finally came to flower in his late watercolours. There you have, I think, the vision in its purity. And it already brings him right into the nineteenth century and further, in fact. There's something oriental about those last works of his. They're pure vision. There's nothing of the eighteenth century about them. I'm thinking of the illustrations to Dante in contrast to those where he has this very heavy, fleshy, muscular figure. It's very disturbing to have a gross figure concerned with manifesting the eternal world of essence. It was a legacy from the eighteenth century, this mechanicalness of the figures. But in the other great works of his where there is beautiful pen line supported by delicate and wonderful washes of harmony, there you have the most wonderful vision.

More disturbing is the fact that as he is painting the eternal vision he's hung up in the world of human conflict. Blake is very like Beethoven. He's the Beethoven of painting at that time. I don't think it's an accident that they both lived at the same time. They both were in fierce reaction to eighteenth century rationalism. They both brought the eighteenth century to an end and both let loose the flood of Romanticism, which was based on conflict. Blake was saved by the greatness of the last works. But the whole of his work is disturbing in that it is unlike Buddhist art or the art of Byzantium, which is somehow an art of peace and serenity. He has somehow invaded the eternal world with this struggle and conflict, unresolved in himself it seems to me.

You find much more of the contemplative returning in Palmer. There you have a contemplative artist of course.

This question of conflict in the eternal world is a very difficult one. Is there conflict in the eternal world? According to the Kabbala there is. There is war in Heaven, we're told. Perhaps Blake reflects this war in Heaven? Perhaps his fight with his own times is a reflection of the war in Heaven. There must be a connection between everything. He was a very masculine artist. Very aggressive.

This spiritual conflict is the trouble with western civilisation. I think it comes from the dominant image of the Crucifixion. Probably an image which has caused a great tragedy for western civilisation. I mean by that, as a dominant image of contemplation, rather than the resurrected Christ. The hung man as a main image for a civilisation. So that Blake is in a way very western, and has mirrored this conflict in the European soul. He fits very well with the Romantics, and probably that Romanticism, that dynamism in Blake was one of the instruments for conveying the life of the soul out of the clutches of the eighteenth century. It was a kind of covering, a kind of protection of the soul. When you consider the situation he was in he couldn't be other than on the attack because he was ignored. Palmer and Calvert were obviously much more feminine and contemplative by nature. But they hadn't the dynamic range of Blake.

I was going to say they are much lesser figures, in those terms, than Blake.

Contemplation is not a state of passivity. It is a state of transformed dynamics. I think it was André Gide who said that 'if you scratch the surface of a Classicist underneath you will find a subjugated Romantic'. I think of it the other way round too, that if you scratch the surface of a true Romantic you find a subjugated Classicist.

The other artist who you are sometimes linked with is David Jones; as being the two outstanding spiritual artists of our time. It seems to me that you complement each other, since David looks outwards to the natural world and to history, transmuting it into its numinous essence, whereas you look inward to transmute the soul's world of imagination into its hidden forms—I mean that in the sense of a form being a mirror of a hidden perfection.

David works within a canonic context, or shall I say, to be more accurate, within the context of a decaying tradition. His work is full of nostalgia for the far-off days of imagined perfection, and he works within the specific world of European Christendom which gives him a form and cohesion. My own work is not within the context of any formal tradition, and is therefore very much open to a point of universality which would agree with all the traditions. This agreement is essential, I think. The relationship between my work and David's is that there is a sacramental dimension in both our works and that my experiencing of nature contains that same dimension, but in an open sense so that a Hindu, or anyone, even a person belonging to no religion could come into contact with my work, and find the eternal world is mirrored there in new combinations, new musical chords, images which could never occur at any other time that I can think of before now. Whereas the images in David's work are combined correctly within the context of a single religious perspective.

He is very much an artist of the terminal phase of the decay and disappearance of European Christendom. Would it be proper to say that in that very decay and disappearance you see a new genesis?

There's no decay in my work at all, and no nostalgia for the past in it. There's no twilight in it—there's twilight in David's work—a beautiful twilight. There is in my work predominantly the climate of dawn, of something being born, something new, and this dawn, as I sense it, is essentially to do with the unity of mankind, a universality which no localised absolute can now deal with. It's obvious that we have reached the point in the world's history when we have to unite or perish. And we have, ironically, the universal instruments of destruction—this is not an accident, this is wisdom. Man has to have fear to prompt him to realise that if he doesn't unite he's finished. Gainsborough, for example, could possibly have seen a Chinese painting, and we know that Rembrandt possibly did. But the student today can come into a room and see 25,000 years of culture simultaneously. He now has a simultaneous view of history, not a sequential one, any more. Now, what is he to do? Is he to put blinkers on and say 'this is not so'—which would be impossible, and is every culture going to do that today? If you find anything like orthodox religion alive today you will find it inevitably allied to nationalism, kept alive by nationalism—Russian Orthodox, Greek Orthodox and Arab, and that means a localised culture—it clings to a kind of tribal view of culture. And this is an absolutely basic question in discussing the difference between David and myself. I believe that the tribal view, the tribal god, is over, and this is a period of no god, which is a possibility of a god that every man must stand in the presence of, because all the arguments in religion are about dogma and not about God. They are rationalisations about God. Therefore, whatever in my painting that's at work, has this spirit of universality where the archetypal images of the world are displayed in different combinations. I am not denying the dangers of this or the difficulty, since I experience it. But I feel a sense of very great adventure working in something that is growing and not closed and finished; something that is opening and opening and opening. That is the difference between David's art and my own art. He's a very great artist, but of a dying culture. I'm only a primitive of this new sense, using the word primitive in the sense of being concerned with primary things.

I have heard you speak on other occasions about a polarity you see between yourself and Francis Bacon.

He paints Hell, and Hell is a most popular subject today because so many people are in it. Hell is very stimulating and very easy to understand. Paradise is very difficult to understand, and also, there is in Paradise a rebuke. In that Paradise there is a purity which reveals one's own sense of impurity. Bacon paints a condition of mankind which you find all over the cinemas, on the advertisement hoardings, in the police-court news, and in newspapers. People are grateful because they think it is interesting. It's profoundly uninteresting because it's beside the point. But I respect him, in the sense that he paints it uncompromisingly. He is damnation, and damnation is very important. In a way he's my brother. I'm not interested in what he says and yet I see, very clearly, that it has to be said. It's inevitable, and it's exactly the opposite to what I am concerned with.

I always link him in my own mind with Eckhart's statement that the more you blaspheme the more you praise God.

He's an inversion of the light.

You have often been accused of being too private, and therefore too obscure, in your art.

All my life I've been accused of being too subjective and too personal, but from these long years of solitude I've had this deep, obscure sense that what I was experiencing, what I was manifesting was universal and was going on in everybody. And in my late years it has been plainly confirmed, not only to myself but in all sorts of people. When people ask me 'are you satisfied?', 'what do you feel about this new recognition?', the thing that has moved me is the fact that as an artist I have been able to touch the human heart.

It seems to me, Cecil, that the 'metaphysical catastrophe'—if I may borrow a phrase from the French writer Gilbert Durand—of the West, is that because modern man has spent so long, has gazed so persistently at the outside world, gazing, searching, poking, prying at what it does, *instead of what* he is, *that he's lost the sense of the reality of the inner world, and this accounts for why he expects the material world to yield him rewards beyond its capacity. And it seems to me you have touched upon this 'catastrophe' in referring to the scientific world's destruction of the leisure of the soul. And moving on to talk again about dreams, as we talked earlier, because man no longer has this inner space for his metaphysical dreams, he becomes the passive victim of his own fictions.*

Yes, that's a very good description, but you are describing the effects—*why* does he spend so much time looking into the outer world? Why has he lost the inner sense? It's not because modern civilisation has given up religion, it's because the life in the religions themselves is dying, because civilisation depends upon religion and if the religion is dying then the effects you describe are inevitable. This inner sense has been dying for some hundreds of years, leaving the external faculties as the only ones which are active. For example, some people complain that icons are on sale in the market place, in the galleries and how terrible this is. They are admired for their beauty, but why are they on sale in the galleries? Because the energy in the religion is dying out and icons are no longer, or very seldom, commissioned by the Church. In the great spiritual days they were commissioned and there was no question of them going outside. This is all symptomatic of the dying out of the phenomenon we call religion, and it's because religion is cyclic. Religion is born as a vision and ends as a cliché—a set of reflex actions and formulas. First you have the revelation and then you have it rationalised into dogma and theology, which crystallises. And remember dogma and theology are peculiarly male preoccupations, of finding security in justification and definition. The soul of man, which is much more feminine, finds no need for definition and no need for justification. The soul is essentially concerned with relationship with the divine.

When theology and dogma crystallise into a kind of power and fortress of definition and justification inevitably you find this has to be defended by the masculine—one against the other. But the enemy is already in the camp. Crystallisation is already the beginning of the end of the original experience and the original energy. And then you are left with the outer faculties, the Aristotelian view of analyzing the thing in itself. A tree, for instance, is not a symbol, in the old sense—it is something that can be measured and analyzed. Then you get the dominance of the philosophy of the thing in itself, which has now reached its climax and is beginning to be dissolved back into the original metaphysical position by what is happening in physics, ironically, in the phenomenon called 'matter' itself. So all these things you are talking about are absolutely true and they are symptomatic and this is the important thing. I'm not going to pretend I speak with an *ex cathedra* authority, but simply from my intuitive sense, the same sense that paints the pictures. I feel that what is happening today is that the world is being reborn, because new civilisations and cultures are not created by following formulas. They are created from a rebirth from within the soul of man. I believe that this divine sun is arising upon the horizon of the world and that it's rays are melting these hard crystallisations, these mental prisons which man has built up over the centuries. That is why formulas today seem so empty.

The conditioned mind is the one big obstacle to seeing the presence of art. Today this conditioned mind of ours is being stripped of all the rotting clothes of its crystallisations, religious, social, political, so that we shall once again stand naked before the living God as we once did in Paradise. This I would describe as what is happening at this moment in history. In other words we can never find again the point of reality through argument, through discussions but through this terrible experience of life itself. We have today two aspects of this in art—the art of manifesting decay and fragmentation of the old cultures and formulas, and people delighting in that—after all it's a kind of relief to see them disappearing. The other aspect is a strange sense of expectancy, of waiting for something. A lot of people have this sense, and it's very uncomfortable. We are all feeling, as it were, old and stale, culturally. Our civilisation in spite of its brilliant, active, restlessness has this feeling of being exhausted. The true picture of our culture is not in science. It is in the art of our time that we can read its real condition, the inner condition. There is about modern art a staleness and at the same time there is also a sense of something trying to be born. I believe this birth will see ultimately a very great world civilisation, in which the feminine, the inner knowledge you speak of, will rise and bring into equilibrium the other one, the male, the scientific polarity.

I think we can go on from there. One of the consequences of what you mentioned is this question of looking on things in themselves. A lot of modern art has been based on art for art's sake and what they call 'space-values', 'form-values'. But there's no such thing really as 'space-values' or abstract space. There is a space *of* something. Space is essentially the world of the imagination, the world of the landscape of the soul. In no sense is it abstract. When we say it is abstract it means that we are unable to read the score or play the music, and the printed score of a piece of music is not the music. It only becomes the music when you can read it and perform it on the instrument of the imagination. This 'space-value' outlook has now ended in, appropriately, minimal art where there is nothing but a colour and a space, so-called. We can see now that this is simply delusion. We have to rediscover the fact that the whole inner world of man has its own space—the space of human imagination.

I suspect this is related in some way to your reluctance to have the language of your art interpreted in the light of the specific doctrines and imagery of a tradition. As you put it in one of your essays, that we can only hope to have a lyrical contact with the archetypal world. Can you define or elaborate what you mean by lyrical in this context?

I think my art in no sense denies the essence of traditional thought. But what does tradition mean? It means transmission. What is transmitted, that is the question? Is it a set of formulas, or is it, as I believe it is, a vision of creative wisdom which is in the unconscious mind of the human race always, and surfaces in times of decay and crisis, gives birth to new cultures, new forms which in themselves crystallise, enter into the winter and die and feel the need again for re-birth. I believe that the traditional vision of this ancient wisdom, this creative wisdom, is coming to the surface again but it's faced with a world of local cultures all in decay, none of whose imagery can be put before the world as the final archetypal image. The image that is arising now is an image of universality, like light, for example, and instead of having the penetration into the eternal world along certain formulas of the past we have only the attitude left of love, of openness towards the eternal world, of sensitivity towards the eternal world. Above all we are forced into a position of complete humility, not having the support of the canonic traditions. In this state of humility we have to face this divine reality in a naked way, using the language of a lyrical movement. By lyrical I mean a natural, open flow of images that seem in accord with, or answer or vibrate with one's sense of the divine.

Are you saying that one has to improvise one's path to God?

Improvising isn't exactly it. I mean simply this, that there are two main ways to God—the way of spiritual knowledge, which is extremely dangerous because you can have spiritual vanity right up to the very threshold of vision. The other way is the way of disillusionment which is the sure way, since we cannot define God. The way of disillusionment is the way of a non-canonic culture. Facing the pain of disillusionment in order to find what really is there. You can say that the whole of modern art is a process of disillusionment. That is the lyrical approach, the approach of openness.

What we've discovered today is that spiritual life doesn't depend upon religion, but that religion depends upon the spiritual life—in other words we have discovered the universality of the spiritual life. We've discovered that every one of us is in the presence of God. There are those who know it and those who don't know it. The ones who don't know it lead a certain kind of life with its consequences and those who do know it lead another kind of life. We've got nothing left but the process of exploration through disillusionment and development of spiritual sensibility. And the proof of it is that if you look at all the artists today who are trying to do something in a canonic religion it's all coming to nothing. There are no canonic works today. Otherwise you could say, if you were speaking in terms of religion, this is the age of the Holy Spirit. You can't get up in the world now and claim there is only one canonic way—it's the way of no way, to use a Chinese phrase. Remember the ancient saying—the name [Tao] that can be named is not the name. I'm not saying that it's desirable or better, or that we are more unfortunate, or that those in a canonic religion are more fortunate. But the practical fact of the matter is that very often people who write about art, especially the traditionalists, are not themselves artists and don't know what the burden of creativity is or what the problem is from within. They write theoretically, repeating old formulas. They know in other words from the outside.

Primarily, René Guénon, A. K. Coomaraswamy, Frithjof Schuon and Titus Burkhardt.

[There followed here another scrappy exchange during which I suggested that formal, canonic culture forms, in a sense, an aesthetic path to God. Collins replied that it remains a path to God only for a certain time. Eventually, it crystallises out of a desire of the rational mind to grasp and possess the truth.

This masculine need for security is then blinded to the deteriorating relationship of the soul with the divine. If the feminine were more predominant this would not happen so easily—the feminine is quick to discover how formulas can separate a relationship. The god of method disappears with the method. There is no such a thing as being metaphysically insensitive to the movement of the spirit.]

One of the things I value most about my acquaintance with you Cecil is your feeling and reverence for keeping the channels of communication open to the divine. I see this as your main significance as a painter.

It's the substance of my art. My art is obviously being fed, there's food in it. It's the feeling, the sense that life is not either/or but is some mysterious flow that goes on all the time. One must be in contact with that flow and keep the bounds between crystallisation and openness and flowingness—to know that to fix a thing permanently is to bring it to an end.

For most of your career you seem to have been a lonely figure, but in recent years much less so.

I've had a great sense of solitude, working at a vision especially through the more hedonistic epoch—art for art's sake—but I'm not lonely any more. This is the miracle, because the climate of the world has radically changed since I was a student. The books we used to read under the table, mystical or metaphysical books, are now read openly everywhere. One can discuss with young people these ideas right away. One is no longer laughed at when mentioning God. So you might say there is arriving a sense of community, a sense of sharedness, a sense that in the world there is a family of people, and a real family too, since nationalism is less and less important. The problem for us is the development of consciousness and to be able to develop this universality. I must say that now in my old age I feel much more creative and alive and related to people than in my youth, which was a time when one had to defend one's position to the very hilt with the people in the art world.

Has teaching had a beneficial influence in this respect?

I was teaching metaphysical ideas, and very often only a few students would come and would often make a tremendous row and walk out of the class or shout insulting things. But all that's over, now it's exactly the opposite way round. It's one's colleagues one's got to deal with now, not one's students.

It's obvious that your work points towards the coming of a new order of things. You've referred to this as an age of a new poetic consciousness of life. I ought to interject here the statement of Goethe's I've often heard you quote to the effect that an artist is linked to his times by his weaknesses and not by his strengths. Now would I be right in saying that your strengths are linked to the coming of this new order of things?

I've painted for forty years more or less against the tide. I sense that the tide is turning now. Painting against the tide is a special kind of experience, and now the tide is moving, there's a distant sound of the sea moving in another direction. And Goethe's remark is perfectly true. It's what the critics call being *of* your time, you must reflect your time. This is incorrect, it's a contradiction because one can never reflect one's time, time reflects us. Time is the mirror that tells you exactly where you are. If you change your state of consciousness the image in the mirror of time is different—so Goethe's quite right. It's the line of least resistance to reflect 'one's time'.

Although your work doesn't consciously represent our age yet there is the fact that it couldn't ever really have been painted at any other time.

That's true. The whole question of languages shows that. In a sense they [the paintings] are of their time, but they are not concerned with the immediacy of time but to re-affirm that which is eternal. The language in which they re-affirm that eternal life has arisen out of our time though it's not of our time. The vision is not of our time.

Going back to Goethe's statement; do you feel that you have had weaknesses which have compromised you?

I've had temptations; but I think on the whole my work is uncompromising. I could have been a very nice official Surrealist, and then I would have reflected 'my time', as so-called, and that would have been easy for me to do. But then I couldn't have done it really because you see I never paint my pictures so much as the vision in me paints the pictures, so the issue is decided already. My students are always asking me for formulas. But for me painting is a sort of birth, a kind of compelling birth. That's why I don't paint all the time. Lots of artists can paint pictures every week and get them hung. They've got a good technical formula for doing it. I'm not sufficiently interested in art in that sense. I am interested in, compelled to be interested in, this vision that flows in me periodically. So the answer is simply that the vision paints.

From all you have said it seems we have come full circle to the traditional view that works of art are supports for contemplation.

The experience of art—painting, music, poetry—it all belongs to the contemplative life, and one of the main tasks of our education and our culture is the re-educating of people in the contemplative life. Again, the feminine mode of bringing the dimension of stillness and inner space back again into life. The language of the soul and the inner life, is poetry, dance, music and silence, they are all aspects of the same language, which, in the case of the visual arts is the image-symbol.

There is a great deal of misunderstanding about the symbol which comes about from a later view, known as iconography, which in my opinion is a later rationalisation. In iconography the symbol is something that stands for something else, like a kind of code, and when you've cracked the code you've got the answer. This banality is something very repulsive to the inner life of the soul. The symbol has really nothing to do with that. The symbol doesn't exist to define anything or to represent anything or to explain anything. The symbol is an instrument of evocation—to evoke in the soul the atmosphere and climate of that hidden reality—to set in motion an articulation of the soul. The soul articulates, as it were, the mystery of its own life, and the perfume or the climate of its destiny. Thus the relationship is always a living relationship.

One last thing Cecil. It concerns the very prevalent attitude in our time, that because the Divine is concerned with metaphysical reality, a reality that is above the mundane world, it should be represented by abstract forms, and yet we never find this so in your paintings, not to my knowledge, anyway. Have you ever been conscious of rejecting abstraction as a possible expression of the Divine?

Well, I have done one or two abstract paintings in my youth, and I don't find them difficult to do. As regards representing the Divine Reality I do consciously reject abstract art. I find it leads to intellectualism. I think it was Kandinsky's delusion, thinking that you could manifest a supernatural reality in abstract form. My chief objection is that it is a form of puritanism. I believe that the Divine Reality should be reflected in the wholeness of human experience, in nature and in man himself. The other thing lacks wholeness, it's partial, and one of the great needs of our time is for wholeness. The Divine Reality should be felt everywhere—in an insect, in an ant, in a fly on the window-pane, in a speck of dust. Moreover, this abstraction, which is a mental abstraction, is very masculine, whereas the feminine feels experience through the particulars—the particulars as they come into life. This way of experiencing is vital to our civilisation. Abstraction, I think, has affected our civilisation badly. We are suffering from abstraction, suffering from living in a mental world. I don't really want something that represents, I want the Divine Reality reflected in the living wholeness of life as it is. This wholeness comes from a very human need, the human heart. Just as the human heart is not interested in a god that can be proved, so the human heart wants a wholeness of experience, and I feel the human heart can find no satisfaction in a mental abstraction representing the divine reality. It must have wholeness, because it must have something that it can relate to, that it can recognise, and the heart recognises, right away, this wholeness. My own painting is essentially of the heart.

Selected Bibliography

Anderson, William. *Cecil Collins: The Quest for the Great Happiness.* London: Barrie & Jenkins, 1988.

Collins, Cecil. *The Vision of the Fool*, London: Grey Walls Press, 1947. Reprinted with different illustrations, Chipping Norton: Anthony Kedros, 1981.

____. Notes in the catalogue of *Cecil Collins: A Retrospective Exhibition*, London: Whitechapel Art Gallery, 1959.

____. 'Art and Modern Man', in *Tomorrow: The Journal of Parapsychology, Cosmology and Traditional Studies*, Vol.12, no. 4, pp.319–26, 1964.

____. Notes in the catalogue of *Cecil Collins: A Retrospective Exhibition*, London: Hamet Gallery, 1972.

____. *In the Solitude of This Land: Poems 1940–81*, Ipswich: Golgonooza Press, 1981.

____. 'Theatre of the Soul: a conversation with Brian Keeble', in *Temenos I*, pp.59–85, London: 1981.

____. Some notes by the artist, in *A Paradise Lost: The Neo-Romantic Imagination in Britain 1935–55*, London: Barbican Art Gallery, 1987.

____. Reminiscences of 1927–31, in the catalogue *Exhibition Road*, London: Royal College of Art, 1988.

____. Foreword in *The Living Tree: Art and the Sacred* by John Lane, Hartland: Green Books, 1989.

Collins, Judith. *Cecil Collins: A Retrospective Catalogue*, London: Tate Gallery, 1989.

Comfort, Alex. Introduction to *Cecil Collins: Paintings and Drawings 1935–45*, Oxford: Counterpoint, 1946.

Fuller, Peter. *Images of God: The Consolations of Lost Illusions*, London: Chatto & Windus; The Hogarth Press, 1985 (contains 'Cecil Collins: Fallen Angels', pp.124–29).

Keeble, Brian. 'Images of the Unknown: Looking at Cecil Collins', in *Temenos II*, pp.113–28, London: 1990.

Lane, John. 'Cecil Collins: To the Gates of the Sun', an interview with Cecil Collins, in *Resurgence*, May–June, Issue 122, pp.12–15, Hartland: 1987

Morphet, Richard. *The Prints of Cecil Collins*, London: Tate Gallery, 1981.

Raine, Kathleen. 'Cecil Collins: A Platonic Painter', in *The Painter and Sculptor*, Vol. 1, no.1, pp.24–26, 1958.

____. *Cecil Collins: Painter of Paradise*, Ipswich: Golgonooza Press, 1979. Reprinted in *The Inner Journey of the Poet, and other papers*, London: Allen & Unwin, 1982 (pp.137–54).

Rothenstein, Sir John. *Modern English Painters*, Vol. 3: Wood to Hockney, London: Macdonald, 1984.

Skelton, Robin. 'The Vision of Cecil Collins' in *The Malahat Review*, no. 13, pp.56–80, British Columbia: University of Victoria, 1970.

Vann, Philip. 'The Poet's Vision, Cecil Collins', in *The Artist*, Vol. 101, no. 1, Issue 659, Tenterden: 1986.

The Plates

Measurements are given in centimetres, height, preceeding width. All works are 'private collection' unless otherwise ascribed.

Frontispiece

Bird Singing in a Tree 1944
Ink and pencil on paper 19 × 14.

Colour Plates

1 **Souls Singing in the Evening** c1933
Watercolour and ink on paper 73 × 55.3
Collection: The Yale Center for British Art, New Haven, Connecticut.

2 **The Pilgrim Fool** 1943
Oil on canvas 39.5 × 24

3 **The Secret** 1943
Oil on canvas 25.4 × 30

4 **Morning** 1943
Oil on canvas 35 × 30.5
Collection: Peter Nahum, London

5 **The Greeting** 1943
Oil on canvas 25.3 × 17.8
Collection: Peter Nahum, London

6 **The Invocation** 1944
Ink and watercolour on paper 38 × 56

7 **The Gardener** 1944
Ink and watercolour on paper 37.5 × 55.5
Collection: Derby City Art Gallery

8 **The Shepherd Fool** 1945
Ink and watercolour on paper 38 × 57

9 **Angels** 1948
Gouache 59 × 46

10 **Angel Paying Hommage to Christ** 1952
Ink and watercolour on paper 76 × 55.5

11 **The Resurrection of the Dead** 1953
Oil on board 121 × 90

12 **Landscape, Dawn** 1959
Oil on board 91 × 121

13 **Landscape of the Threshold** 1962
Oil on board 107 × 123

14 **Scene in Paradise** 1964
Tempera on board 76 × 91.5
Collection: Peter Nahum, London

15 **The Wounded Angel** 1967
Mixed media on board 75 × 90

16 **The Angel of the Flowing Light** 1968
Oil on board 122 × 106

17 **Landscape and Figure, Sunrise** 1970
Oil on board 20.5 × 30

18 **Daybreak** 1971
Mixed media on board 75 × 85
Collection: Bryce McKenzie-Smith

19 **Daybreak, Head and Tree** 1971
Oil on board 15 × 20

20 **Dawn Music** 1977
Gouache on paper 38 × 57

21 **Fool and Landscape** 1978
Mixed media on board 25.4 × 20.3

22 **The Divine Land** 1979
Gouache, watercolour and ink on paper 40.6 × 58.5
Collection: Tate Gallery

23 **By the Waters** 1980
Gouache on paper 46 × 59

24 **The Music of Dawn** 1988
Tempera on canvas 71.1 × 83

Black & White Plates

25 **The Peace of the Fool** 1942
Pencil on paper 54.6 × 36.8
Collection: Peter Nahum, London

26 **The Sybil** [The Blessing] 1942
Pencil on paper 54.6 × 36.8

27 **The Artist's Wife Lighting a Lamp** 1942
Pencil on paper 54.3 × 37.5

28 **Landscape** 1944
Pencil on paper (size unknown)

29 **Woman in Shell** 1944
Ink and watercolour on paper 38 × 53

30 **The Artist and his Wife Walking in a Landscape** 1945
Pencil on paper 38.7 × 56.5

31 **The Sun Blessing Stones** 1945
Pencil on paper 55.9 × 38.1

32 **The Gift** 1945
Watercolour on paper 76 × 55

33 **Evening** 1947
Gouache on paper (size unknown)

34 **Still Life** 1947
Watercolour on paper 61 × 49.2

35 **Nocturne** 1948
Oil on canvas 25.5 × 17.8
Collection: Peter Nahum, London

36 **The Crucifixion** 1952
Brown ink on grey paper 72 × 52.5

37 **The Resurrection** 1952
Pencil on paper 76.5 × 51

38 **The Fools** 1956
Linen fabric woven by Edinburgh Weavers

39 **A Song** 1960
Lithograph on cream paper 55.5 × 40
Collection: Tate Gallery

40 **Two pages from a sketchbook** 1972
Pencil on paper 17.8 × 12.8

41 **A Fool Praying** 1976
Pencil on paper 24 × 21.5

42 **Two Fools Dancing** 1976
Pencil on paper 27.6 × 22.9
Collection: Jonathan Stedall

43 **Landscape** 1976
Pencil on paper 11.5 × 11.5

44 **Paradise** 1976
Pencil on paper 45.8 × 42

45 **Kneeling Fool** 1977
Etching on white mould-made paper 20.1 × 13.4

46 **Fool and Bird** 1978
Etching on white mould-made paper 25 × 17.8

47 **By the Waters** 1982
Pencil on paper 100 × 157

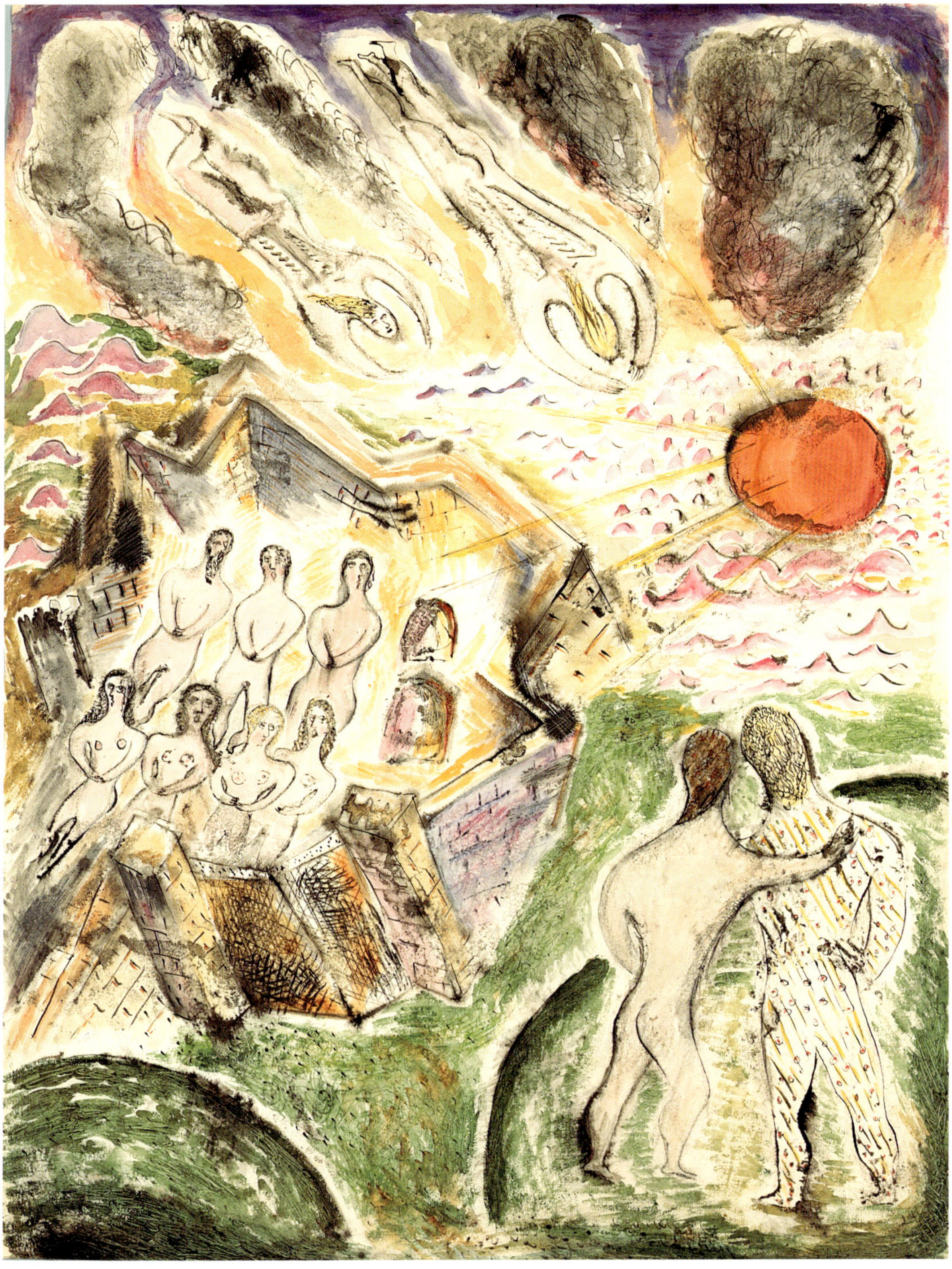

1 Souls Singing in the Evening c1933

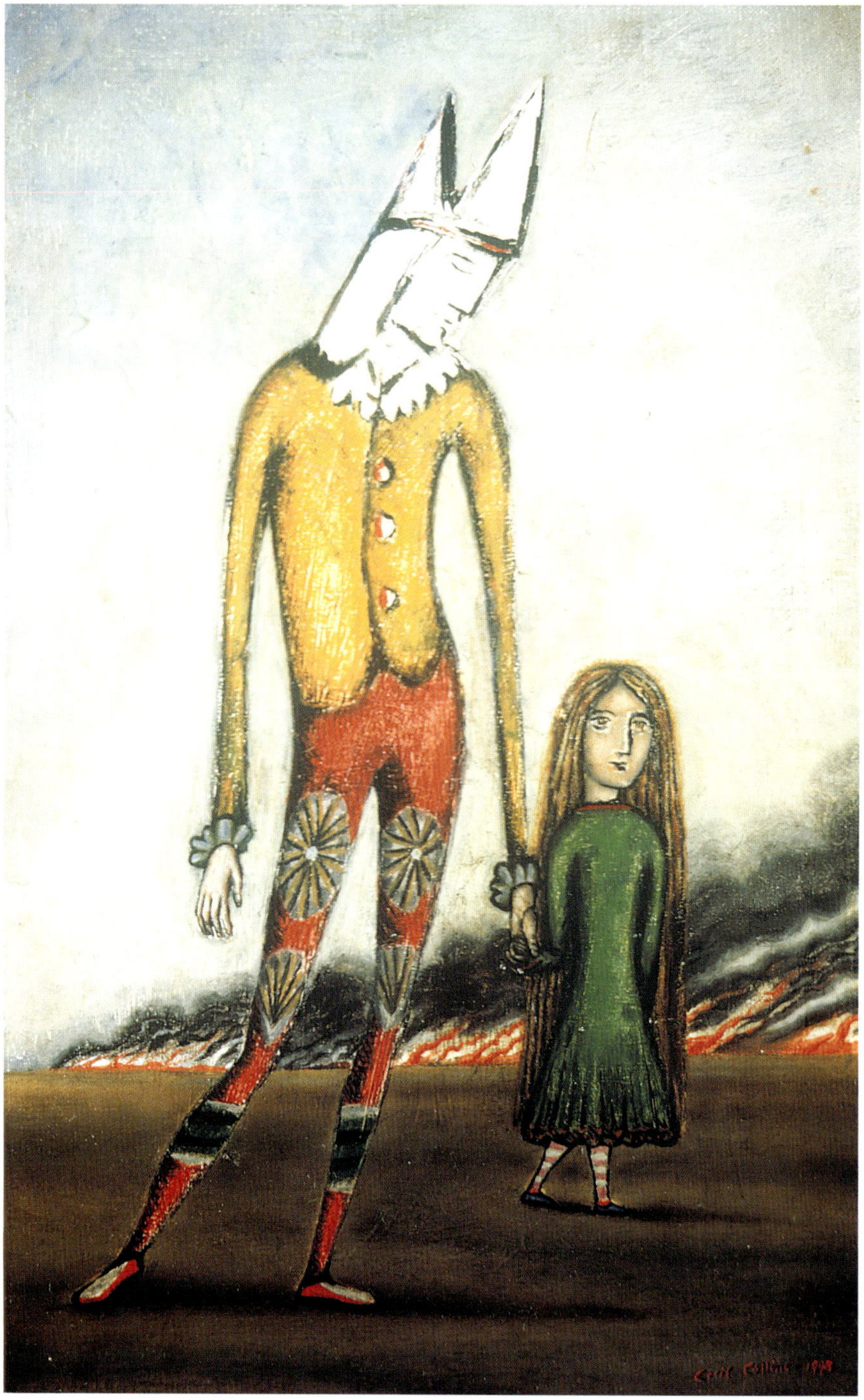

2
The Pilgrim Fool
1943

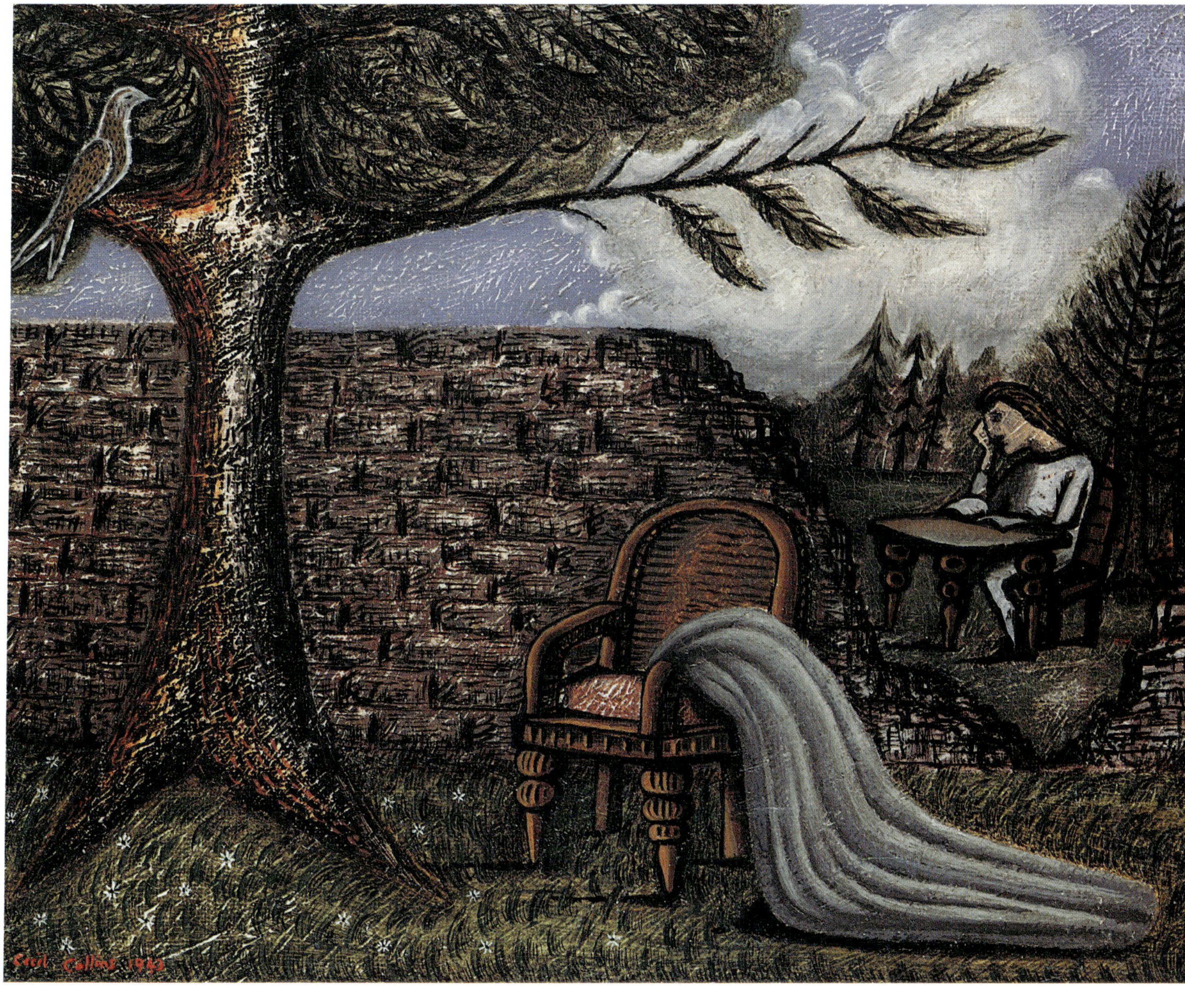

3 **The Secret** 1943

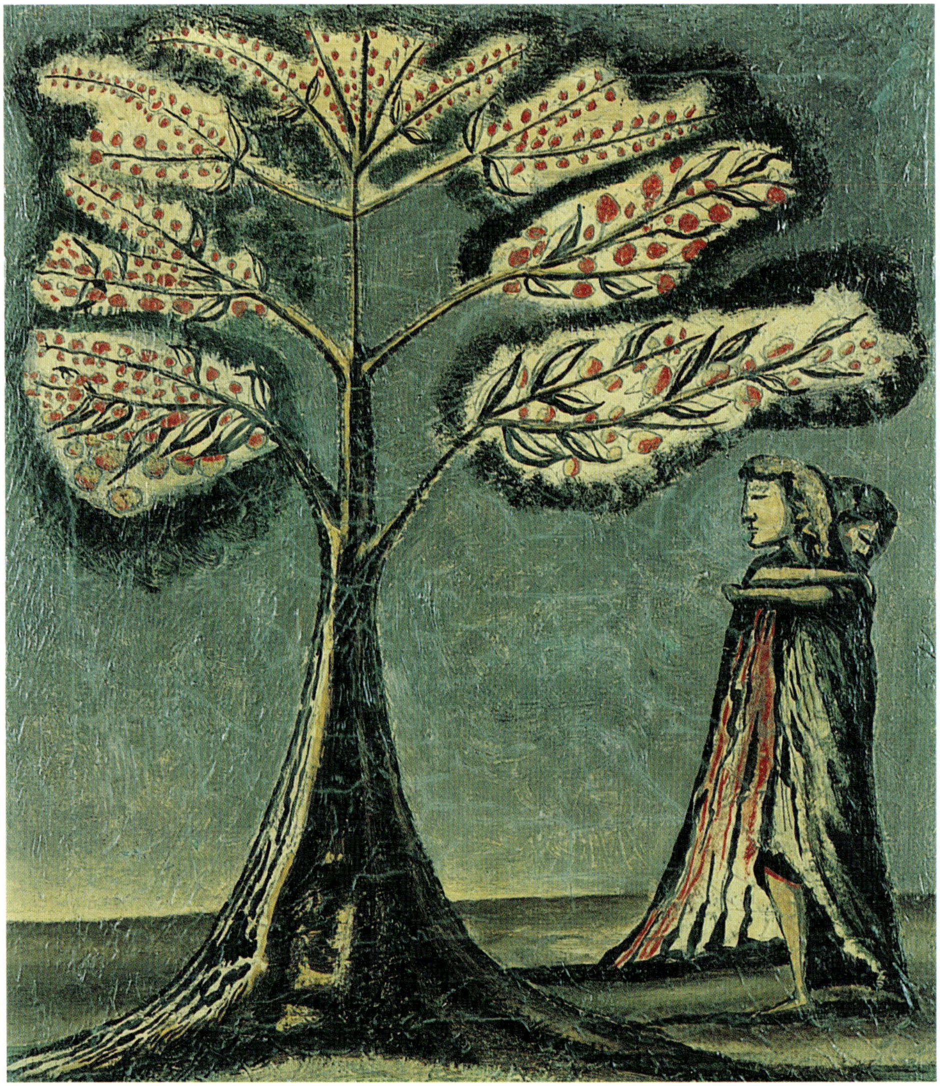

4 **Morning** 1943

RIGHT: 5 **The Greeting** 1943

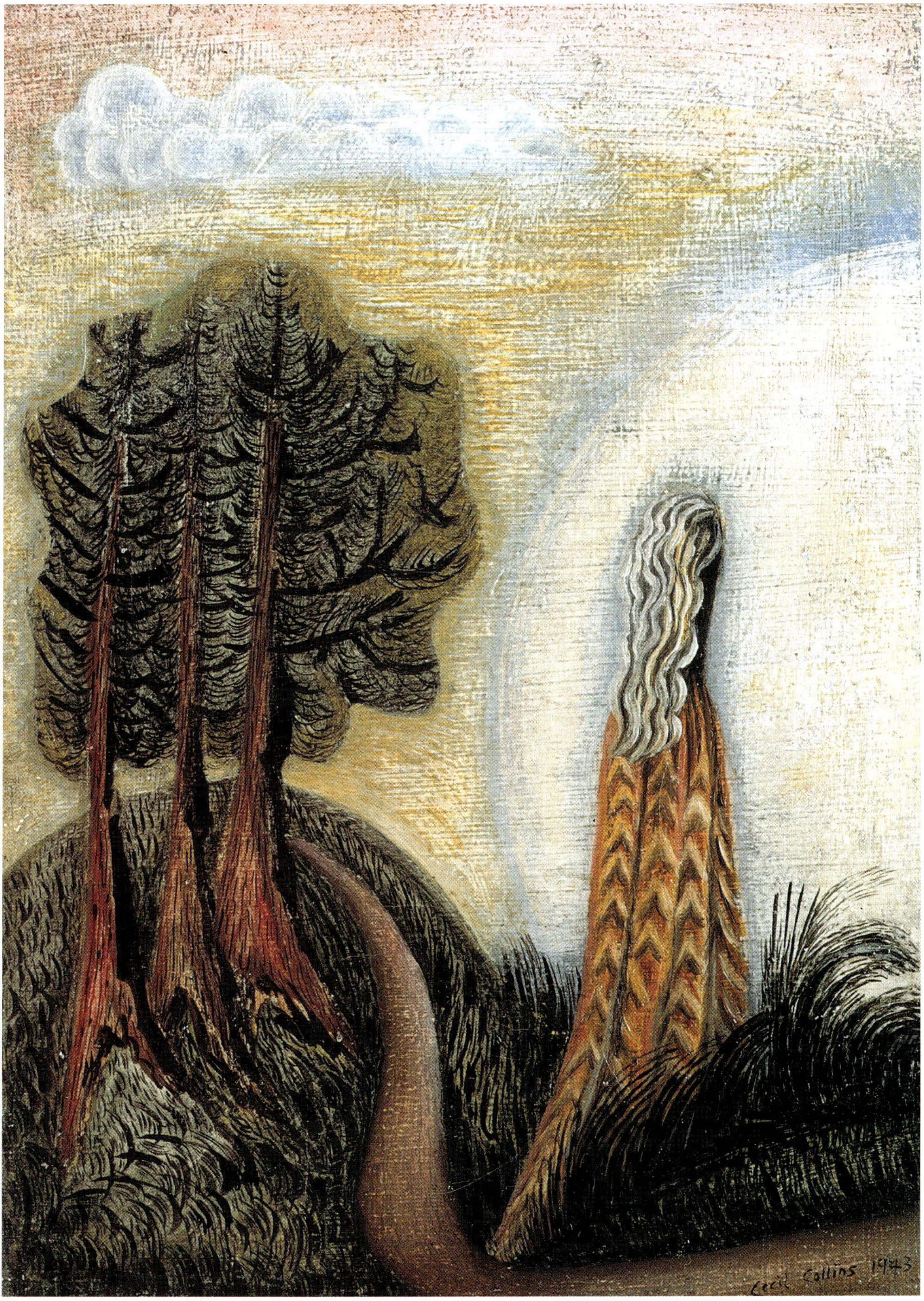
Cecil Collins 1943

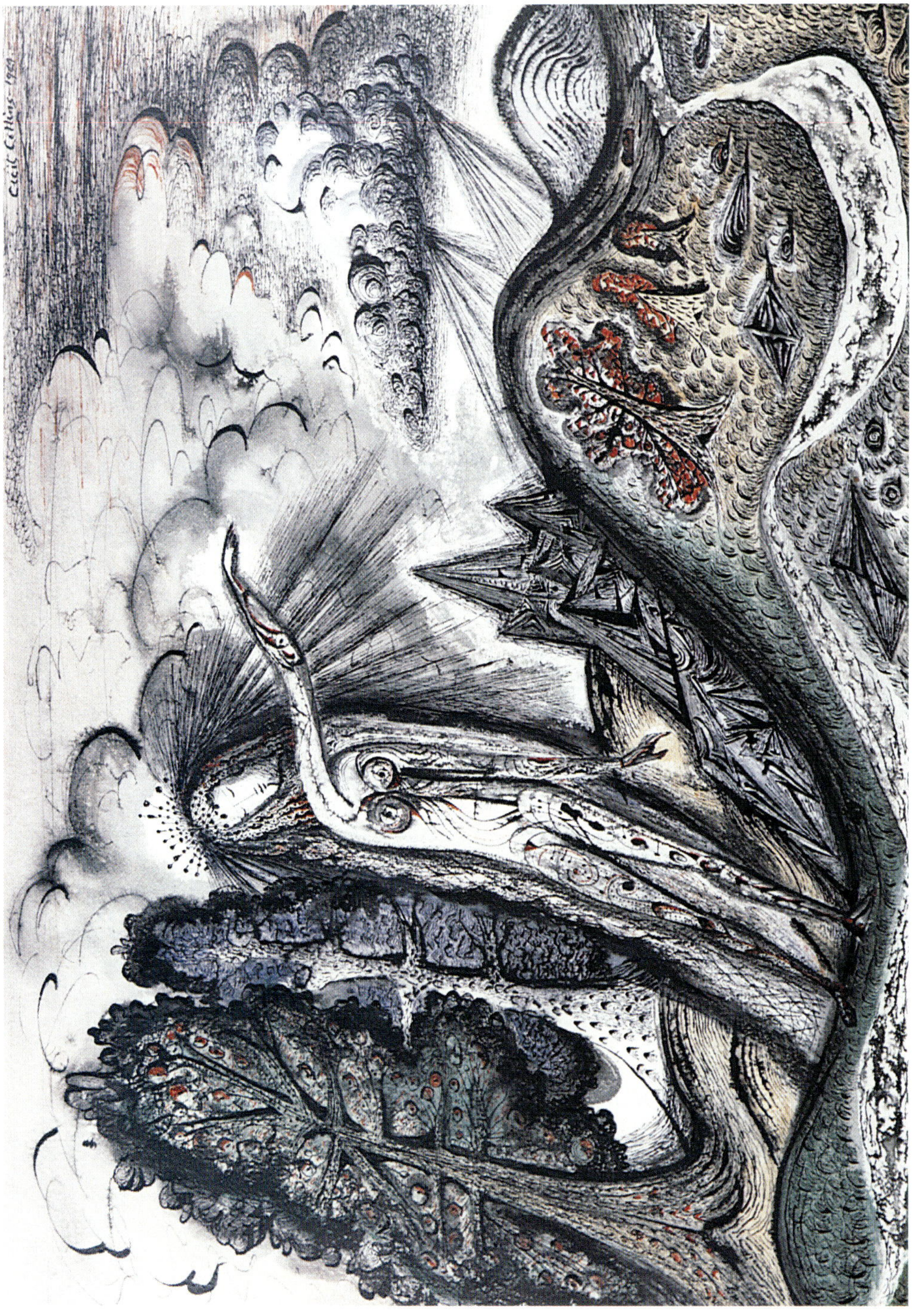

6 The Invocation 1944

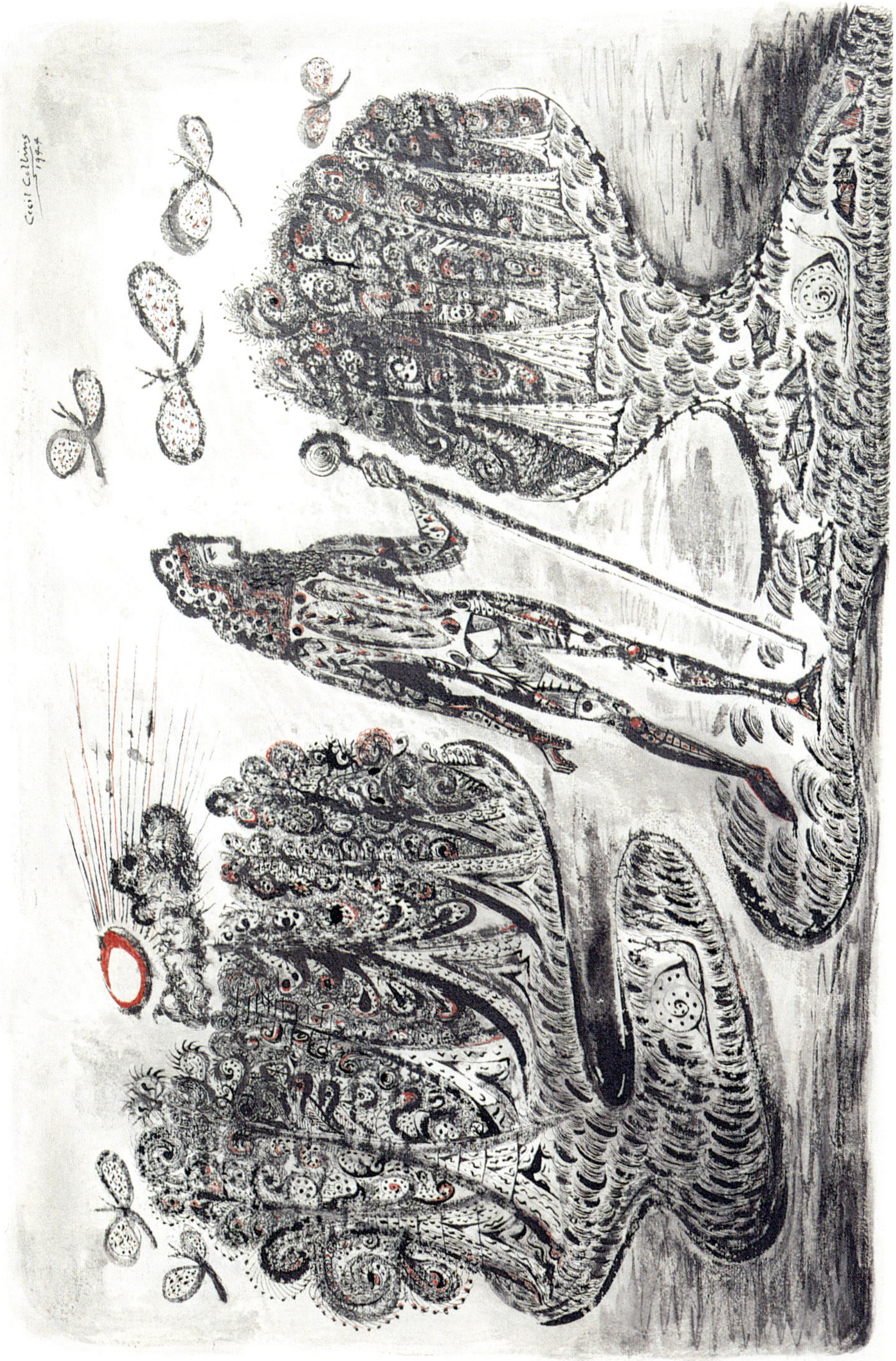

7 The Gardener 1944

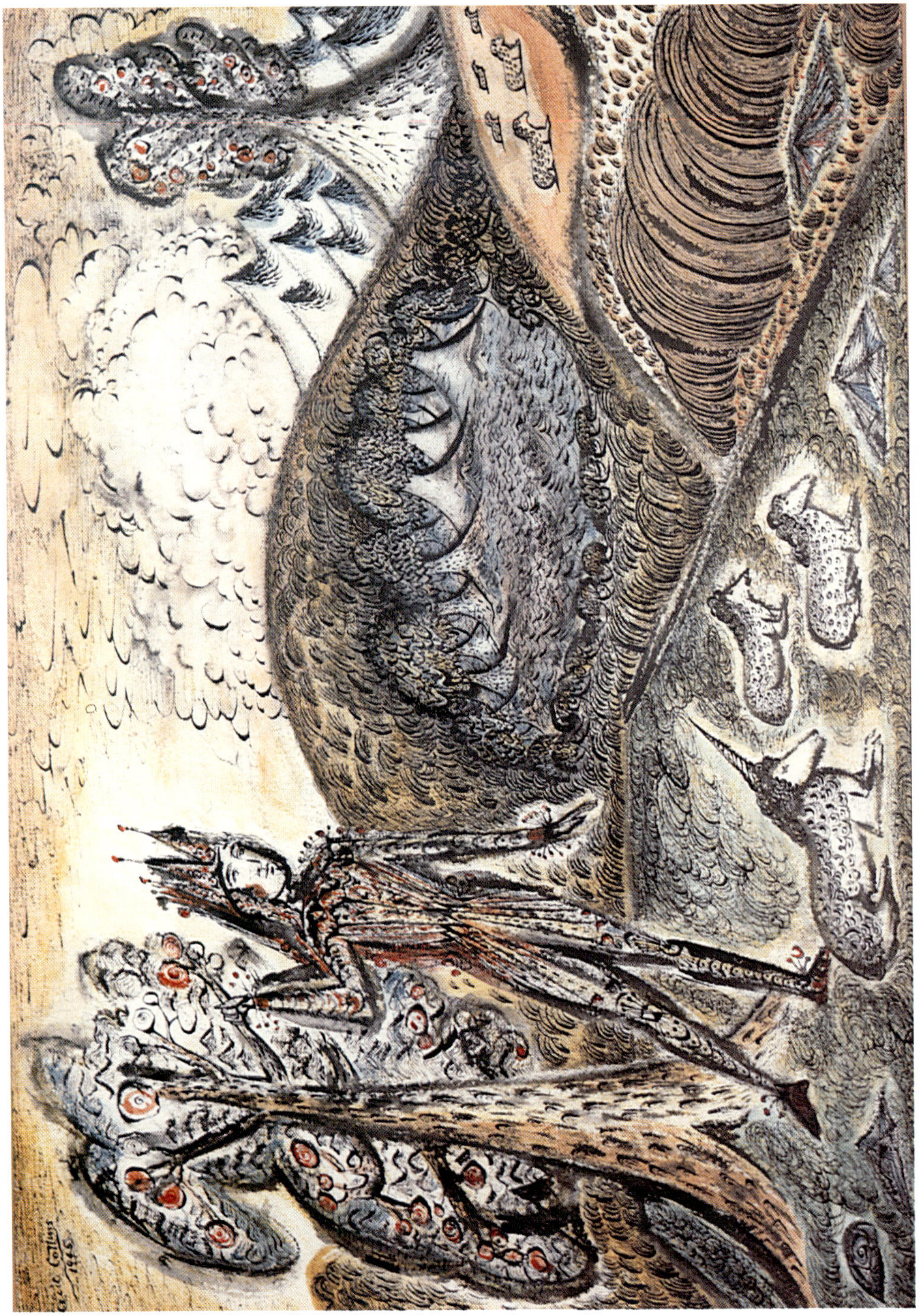

8 The Shepherd Fool 1945

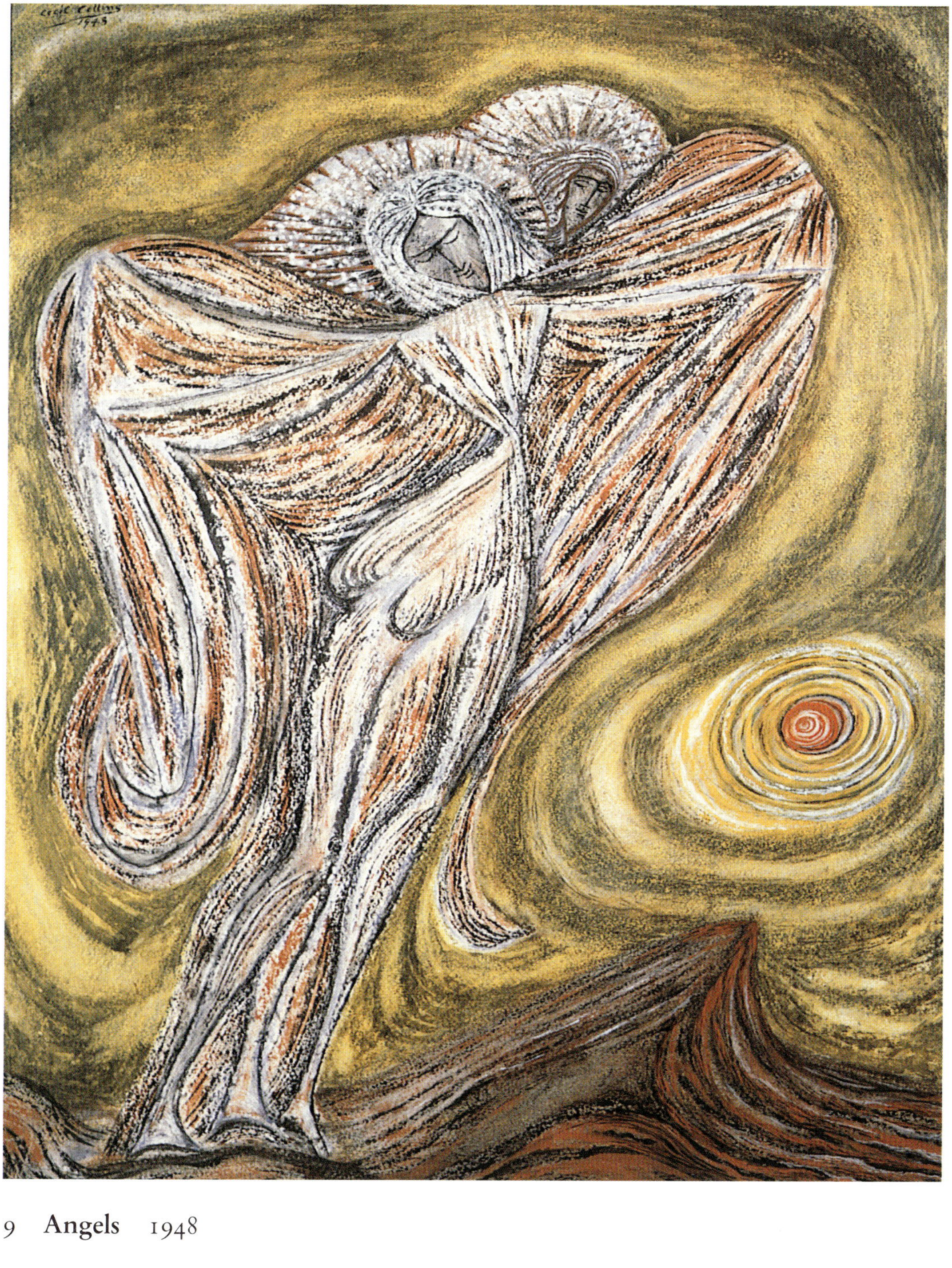

9 **Angels** 1948

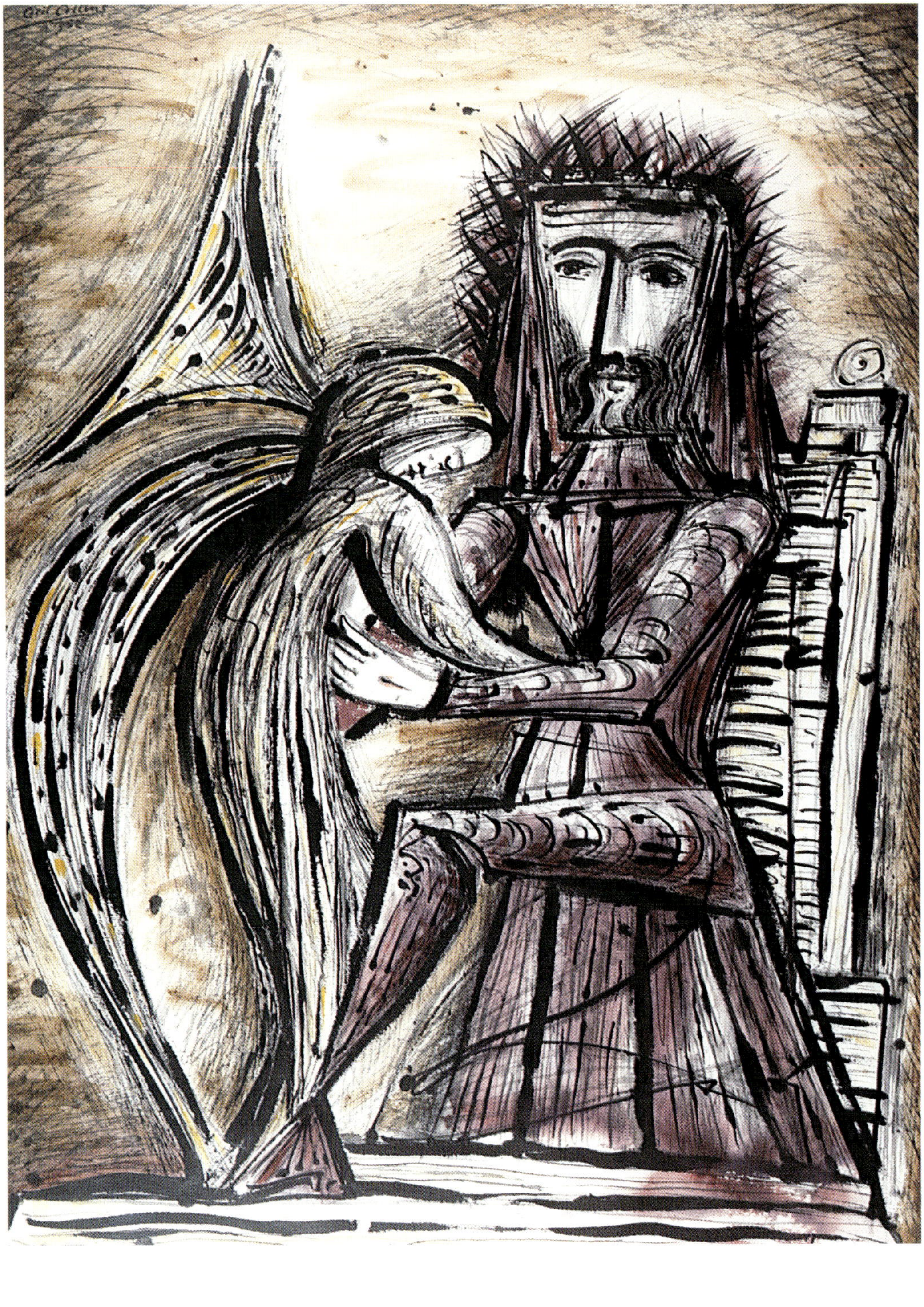

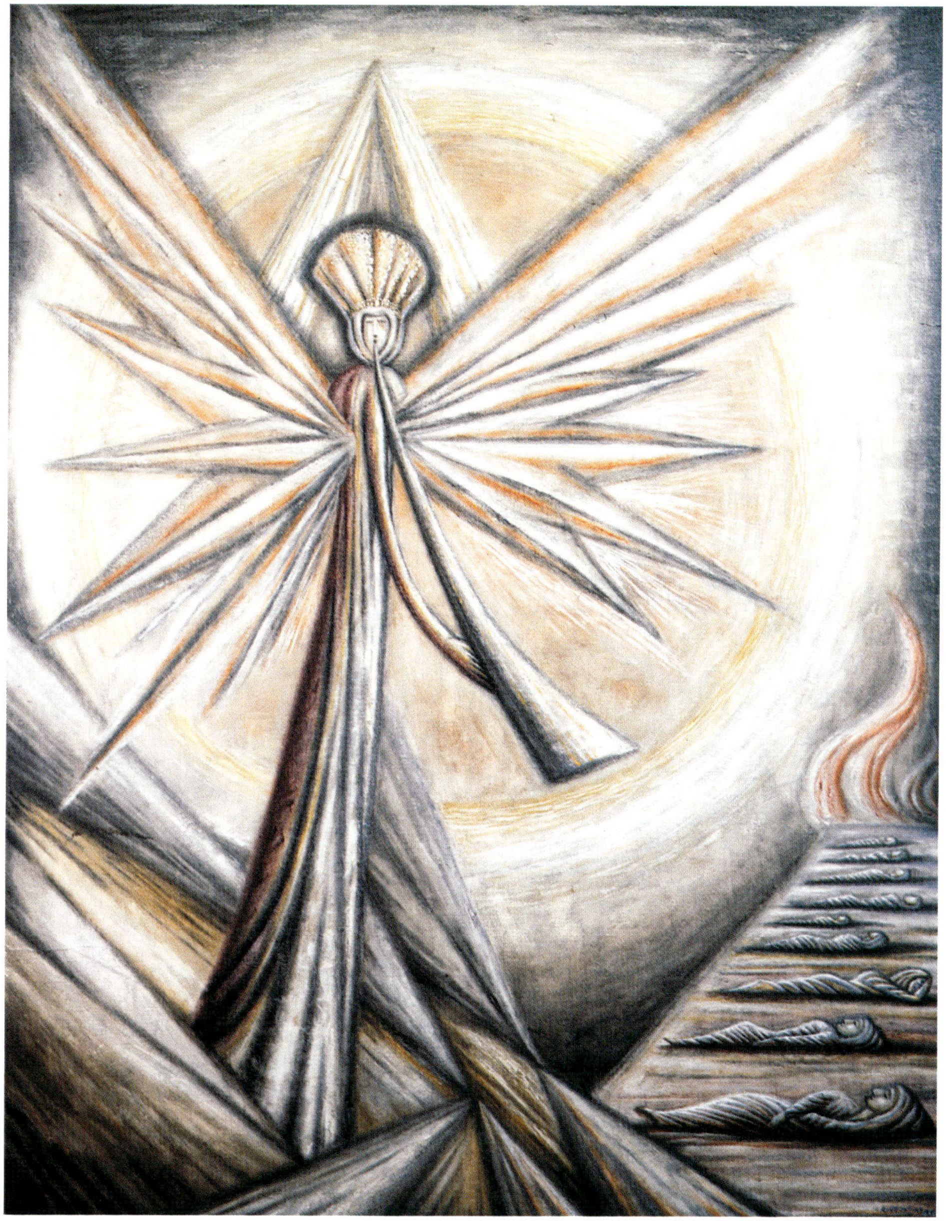

11
The Resurrection of the Dead
1953

LEFT: 10 **Angel Paying Homage to Christ** 1952

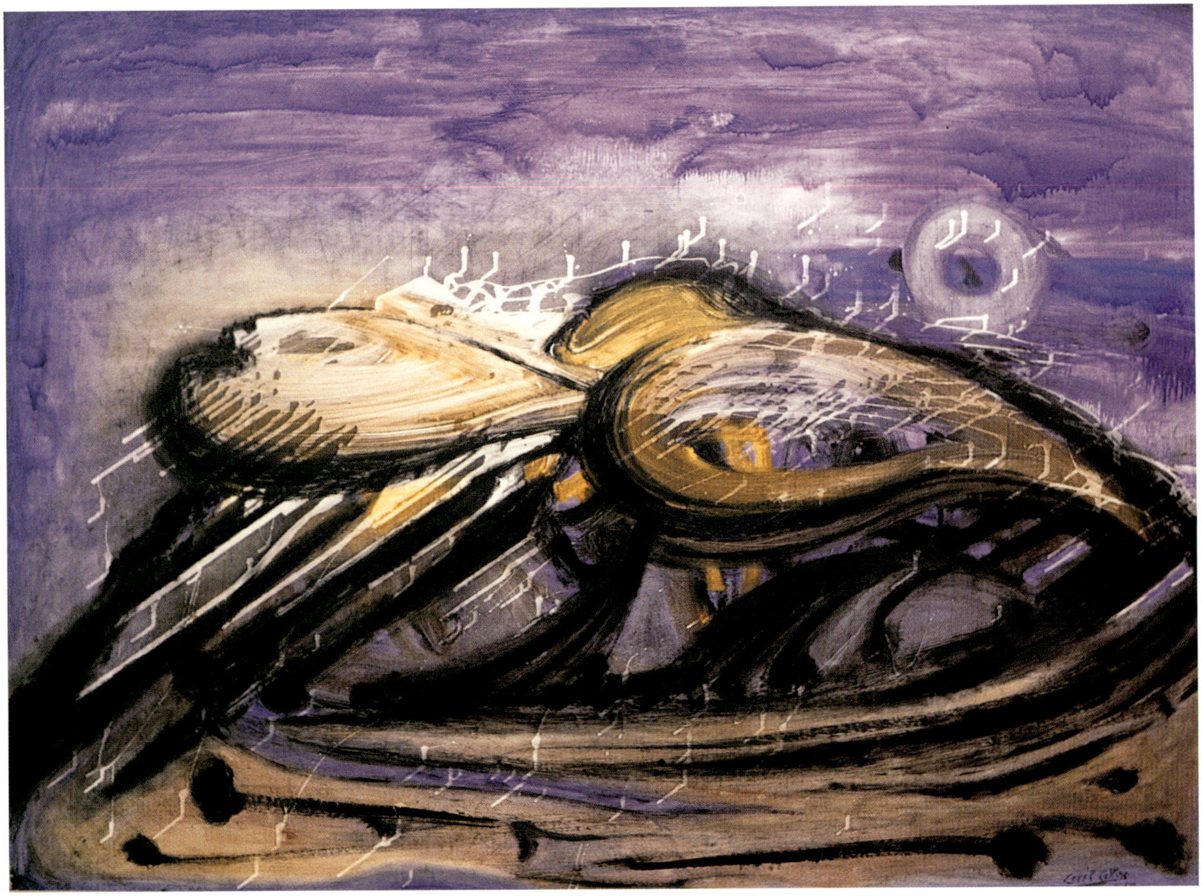

12 **Landscape, Dawn** 1959

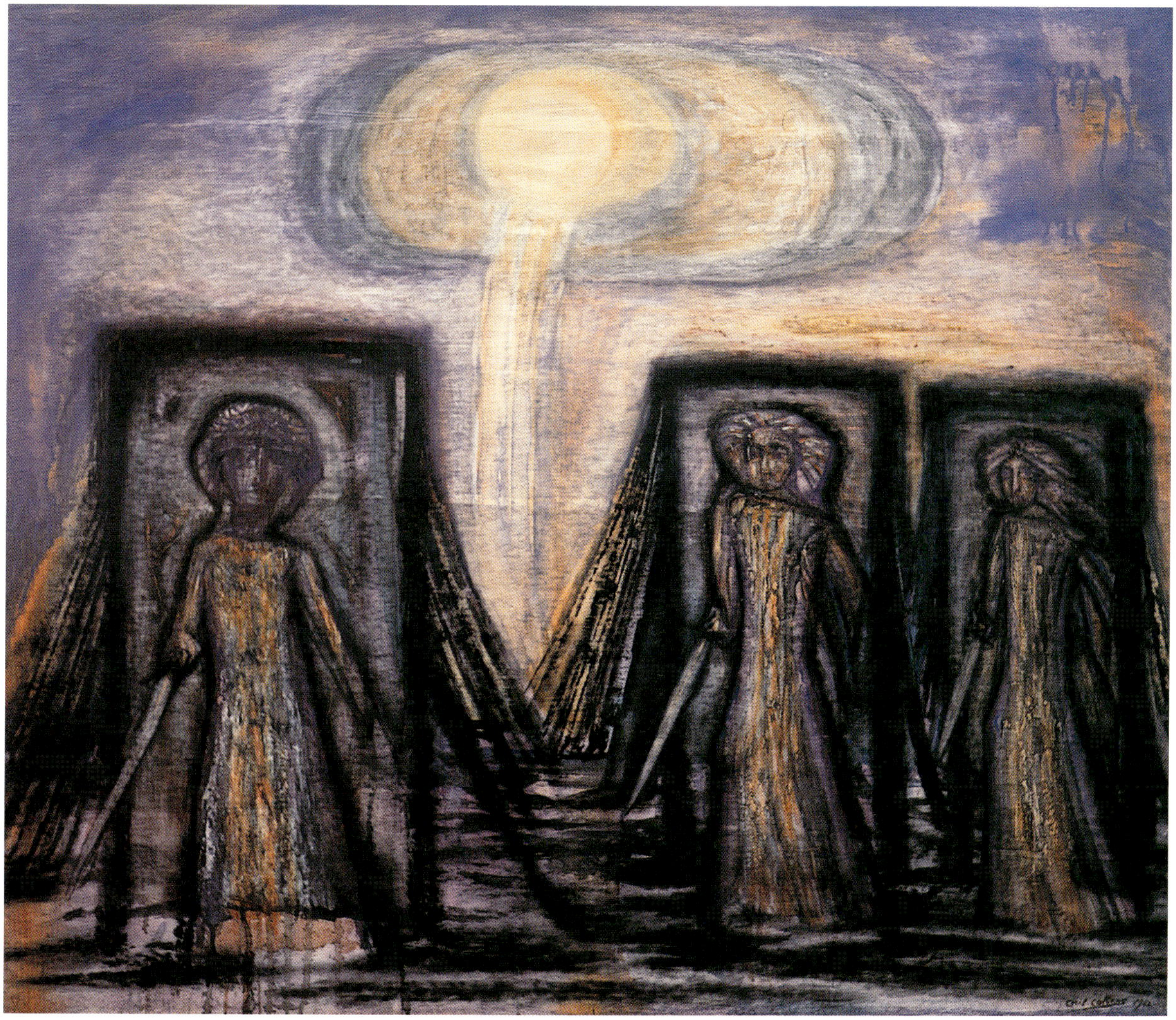

13 **Landscape of the Threshold** 1962

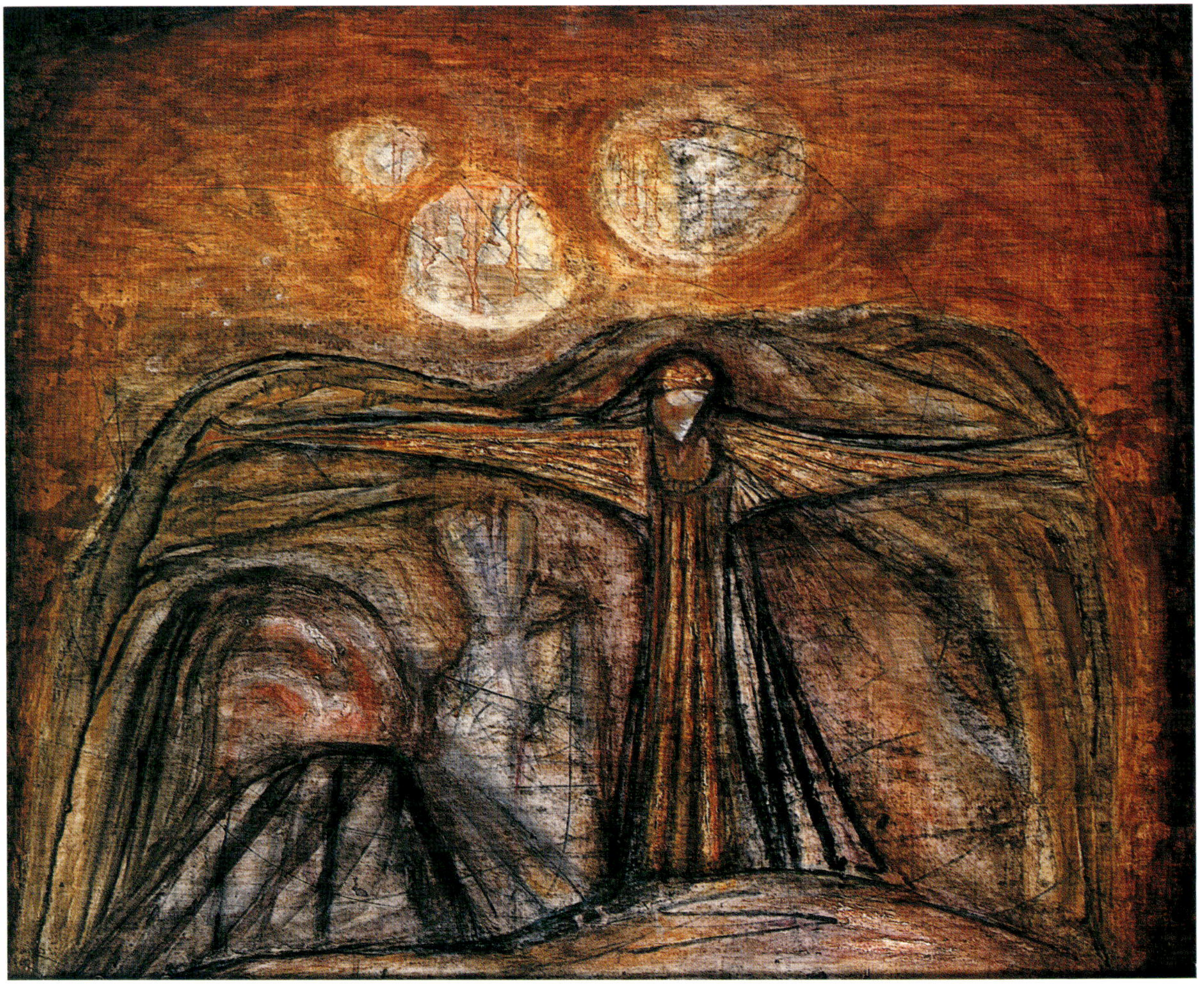

14 **Scene in Paradise** 1964

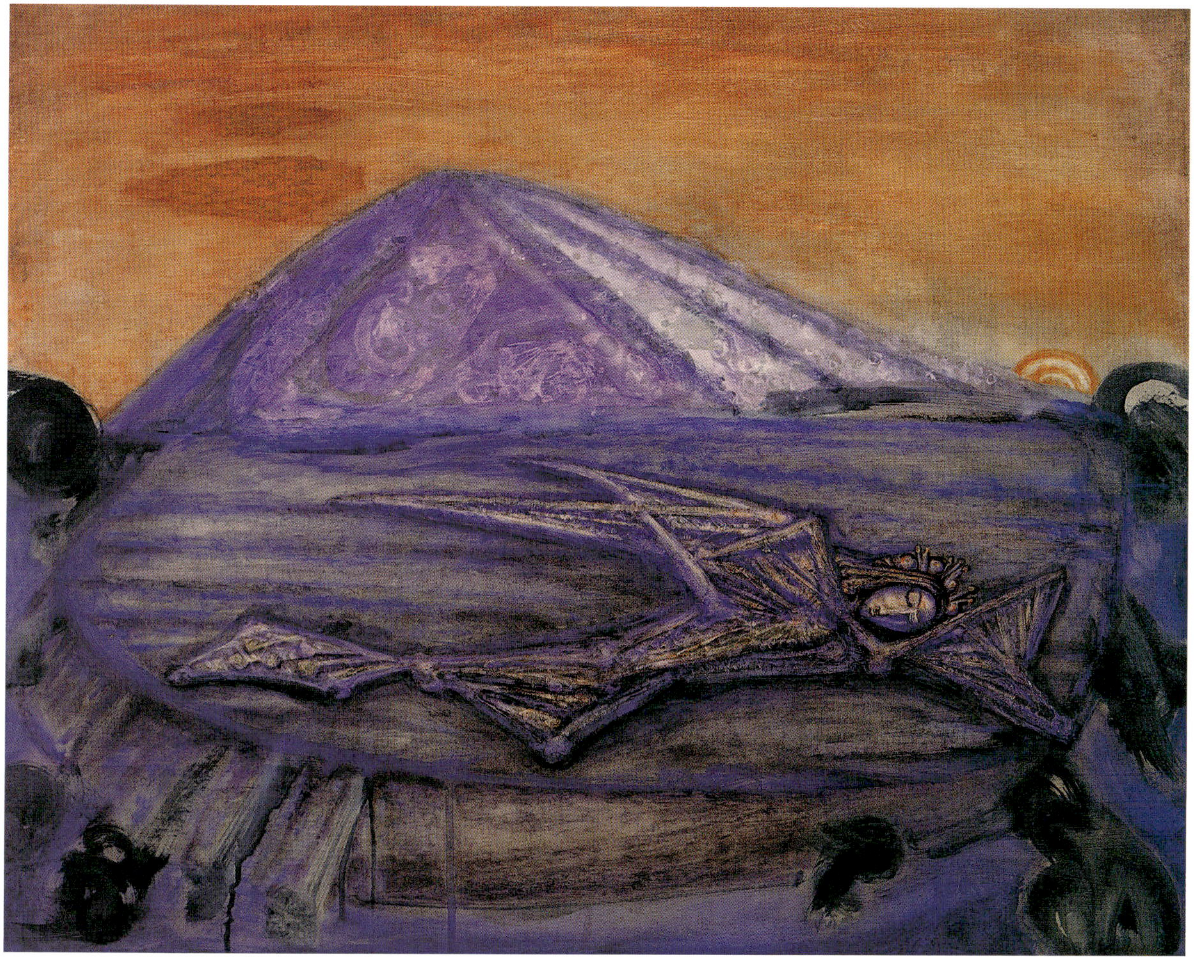

15 **The Wounded Angel** 1967

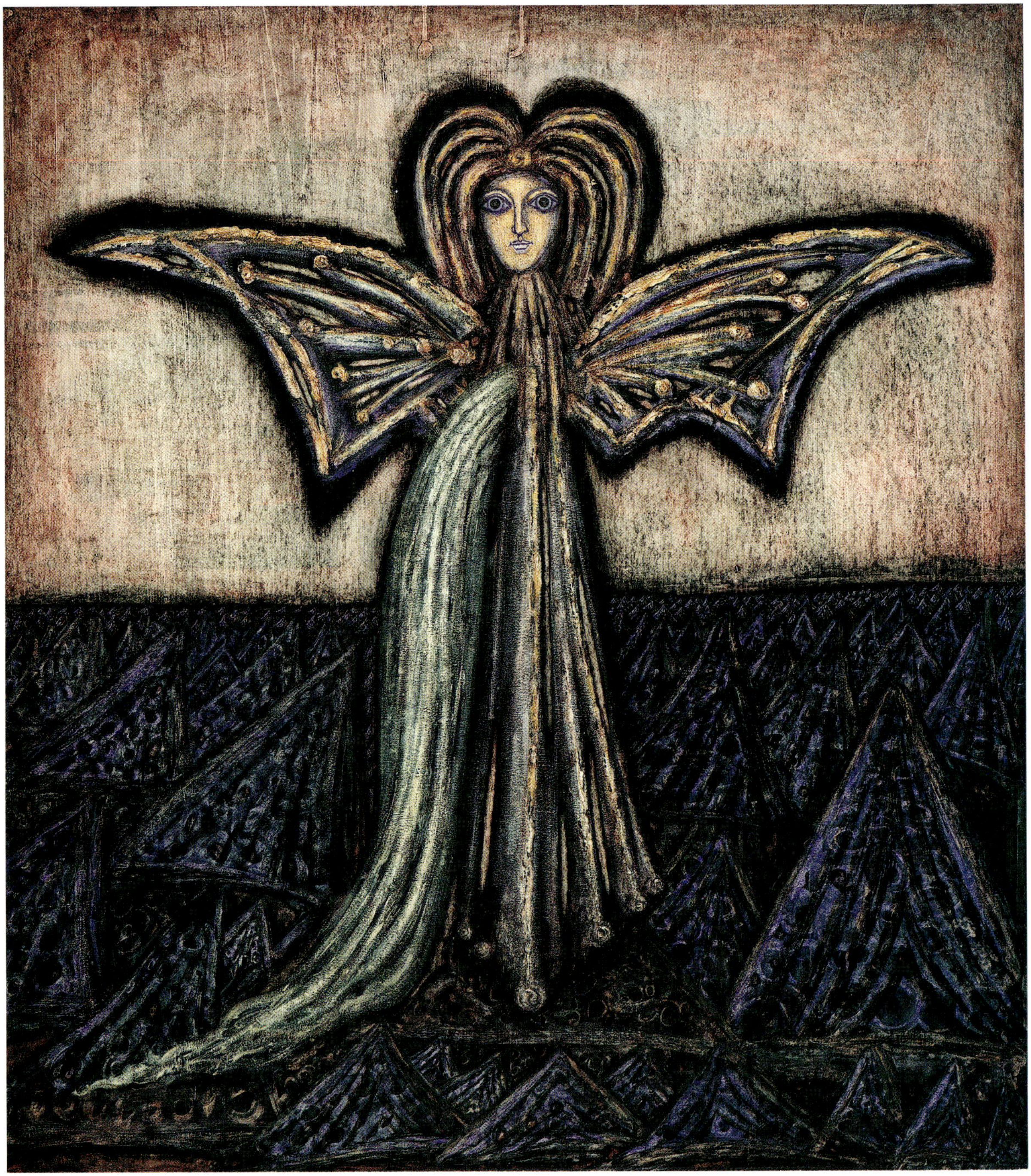

16 **The Angel of the Flowing Light** 1968

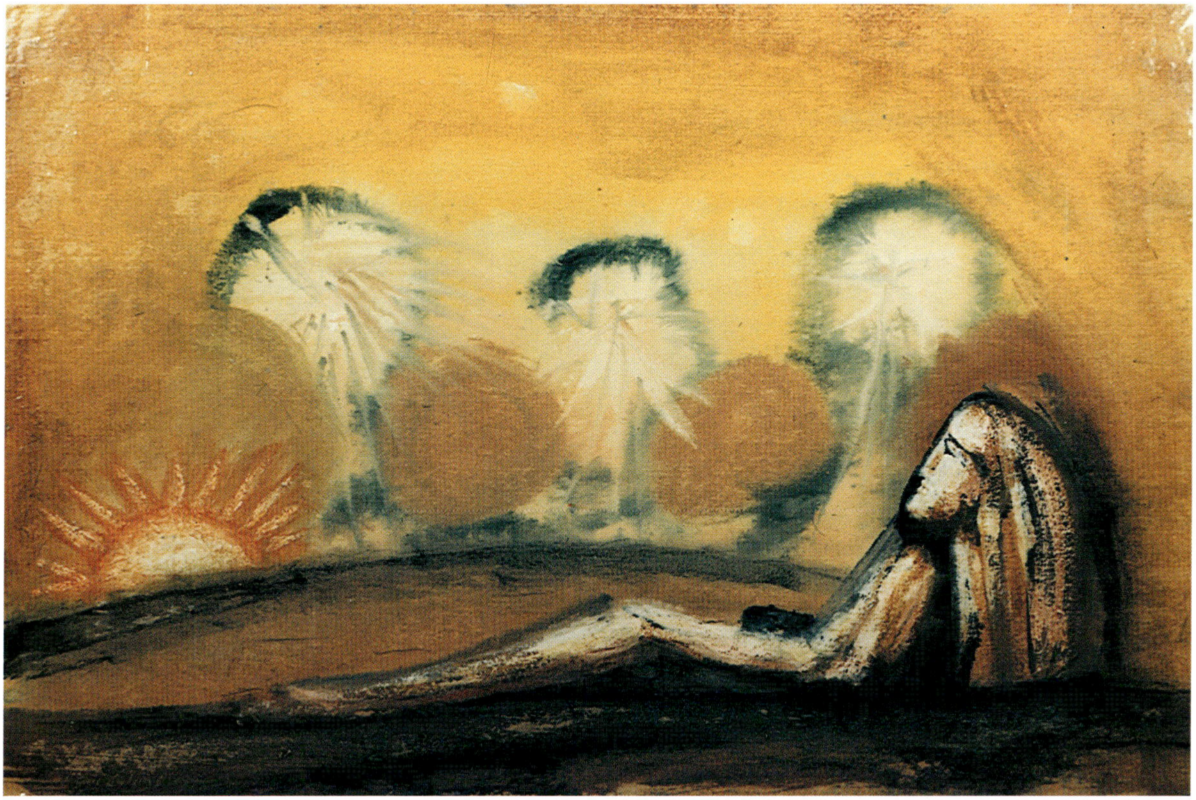

17 **Landscape and Figure, Sunrise** 1970

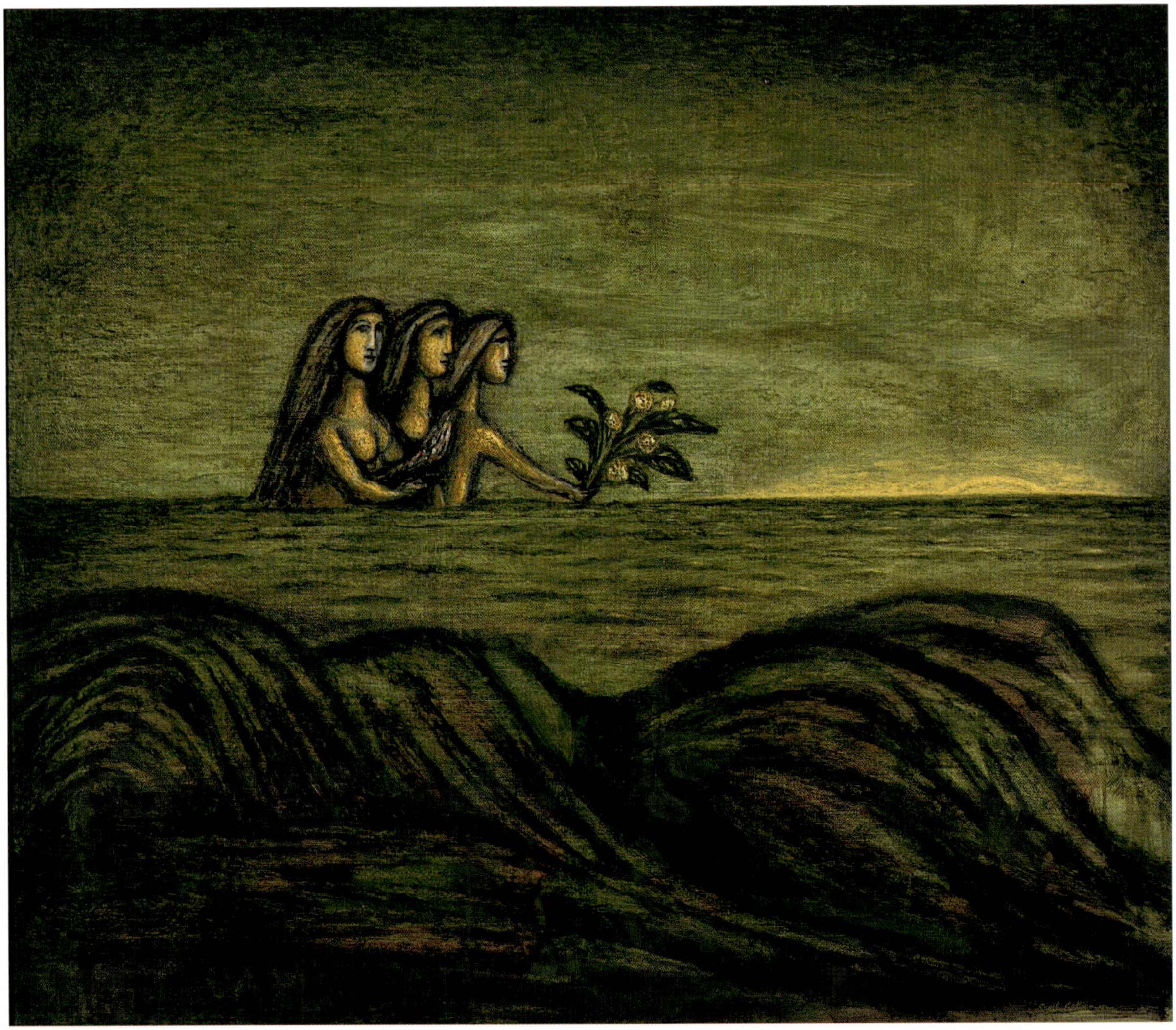

18 **Daybreak** 1971

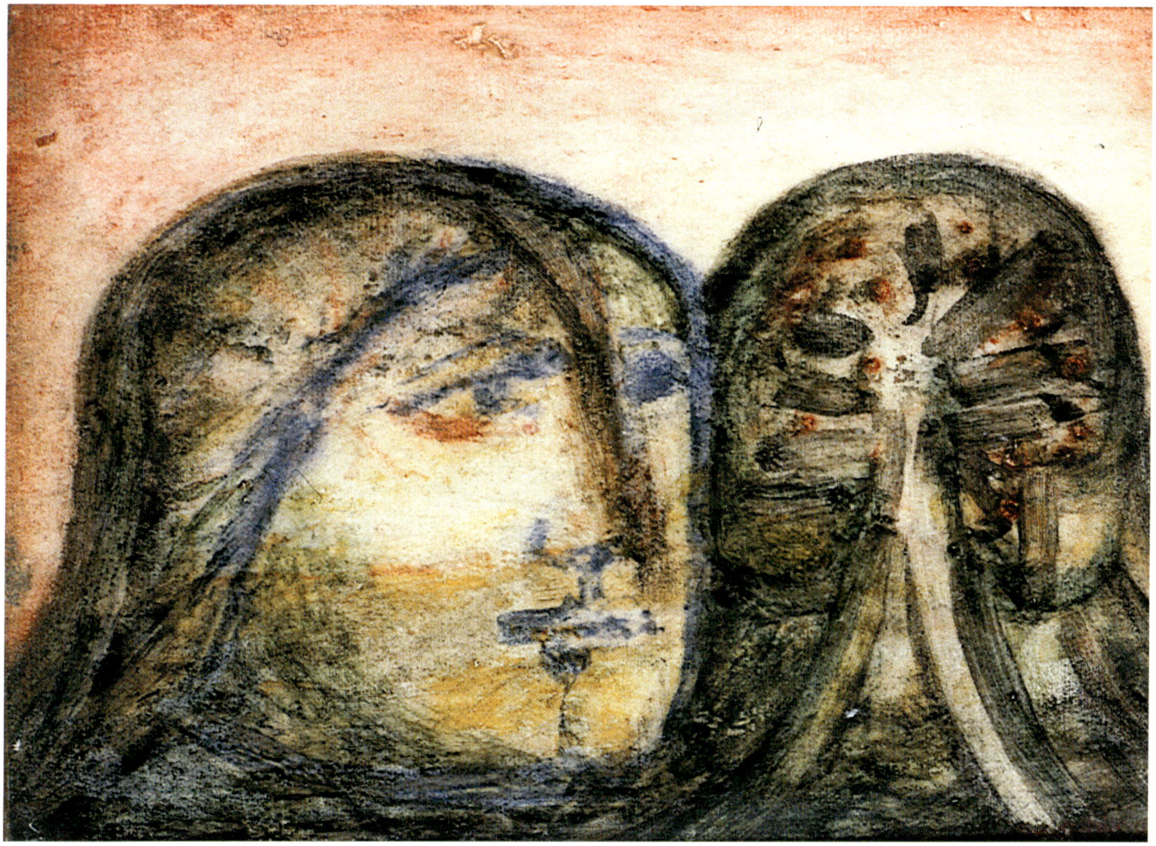

19 **Daybreak, Head and Tree** 1971

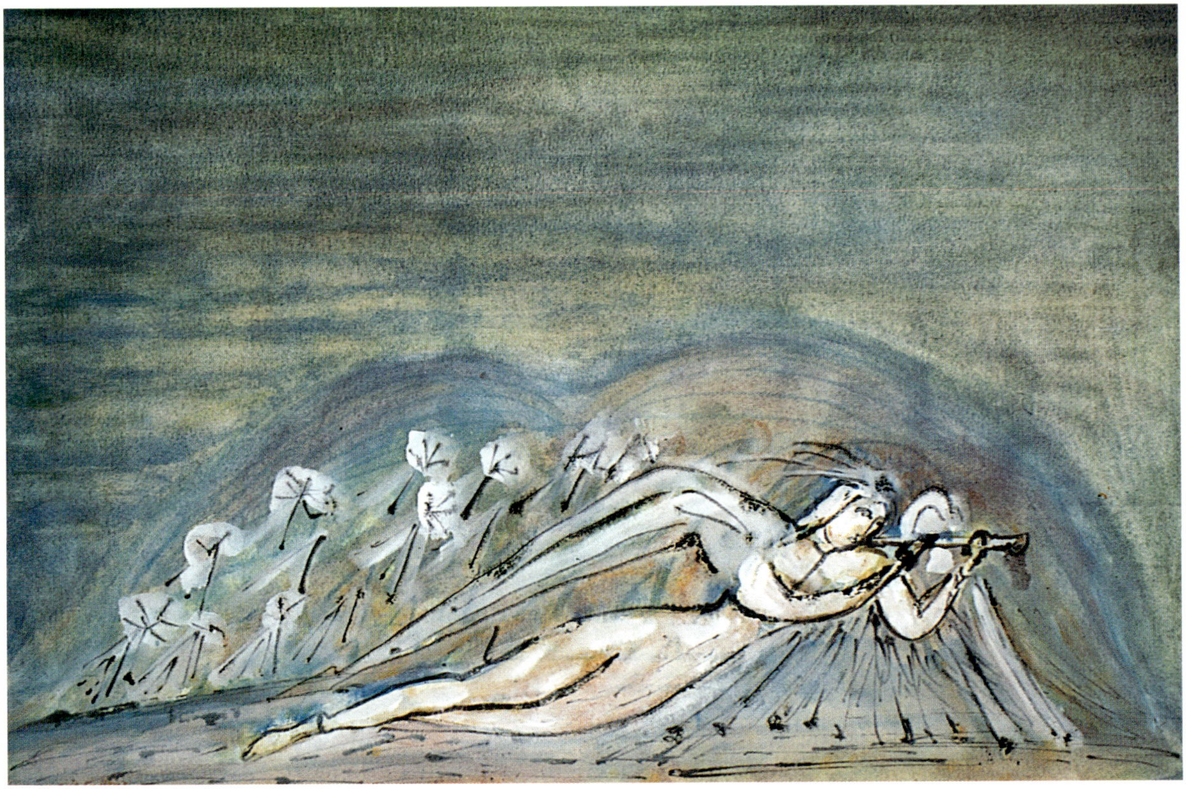

20 **Dawn Music** 1977

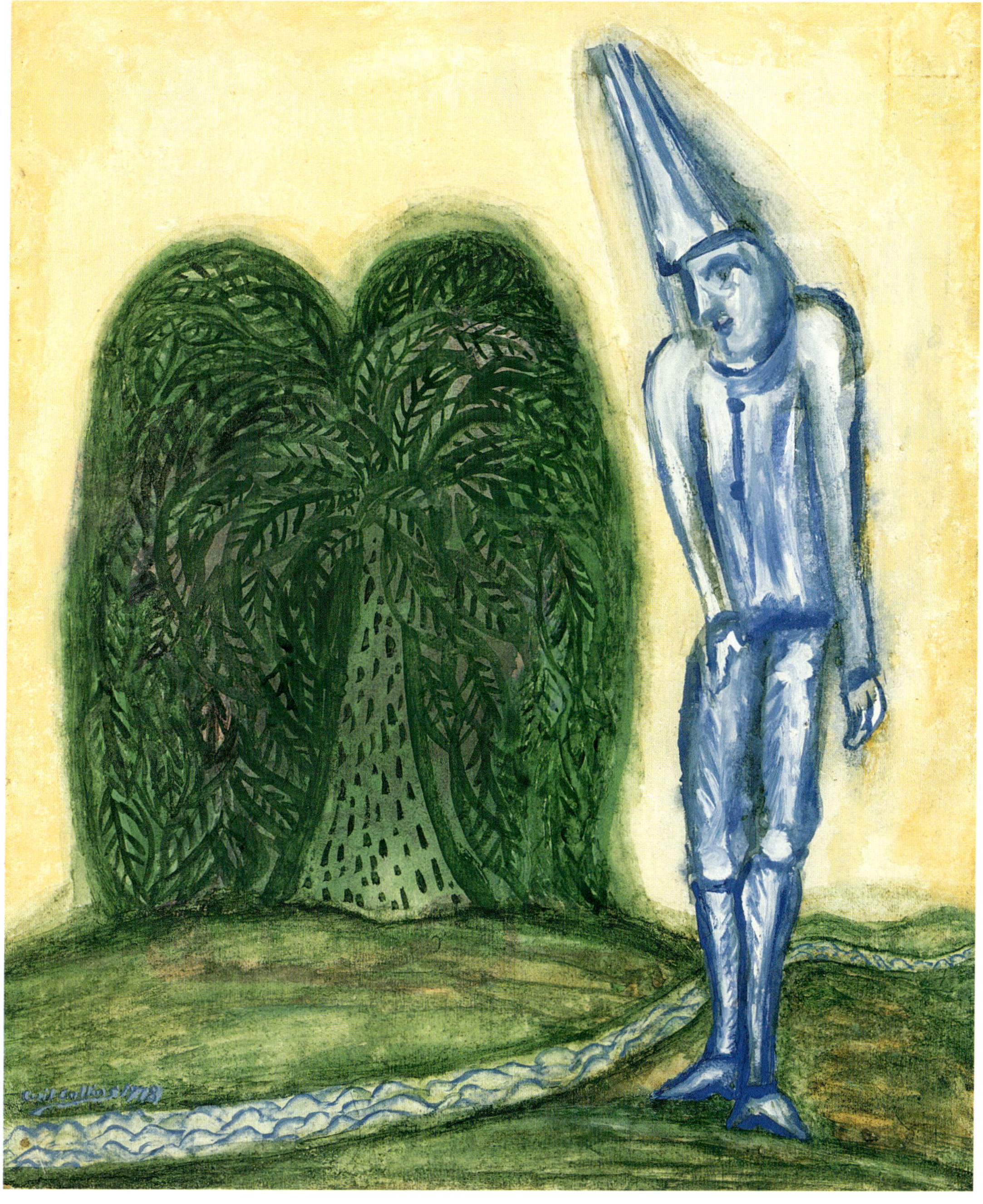

21 **Fool and Landscape** 1978

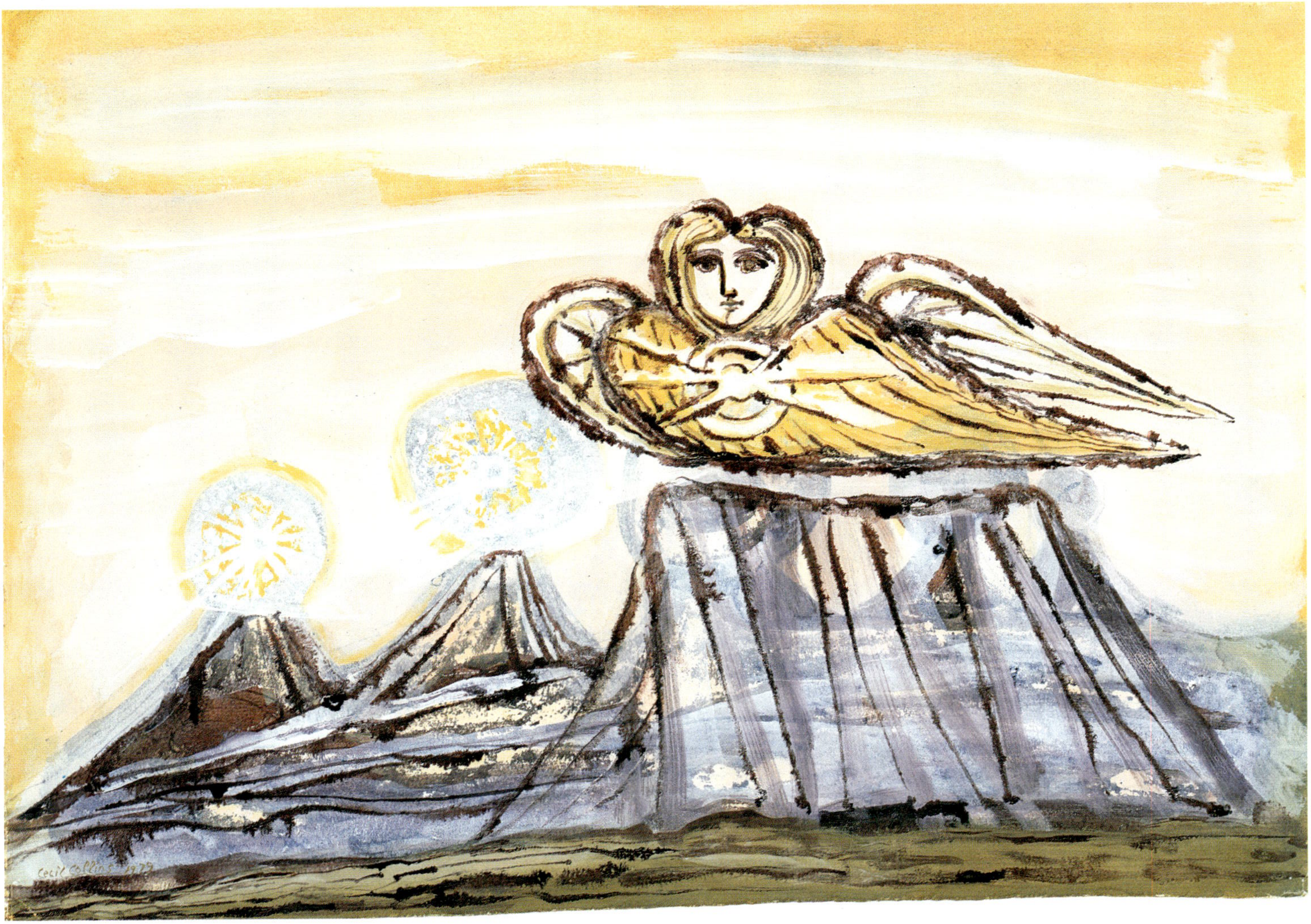

22 The Divine Land 1979

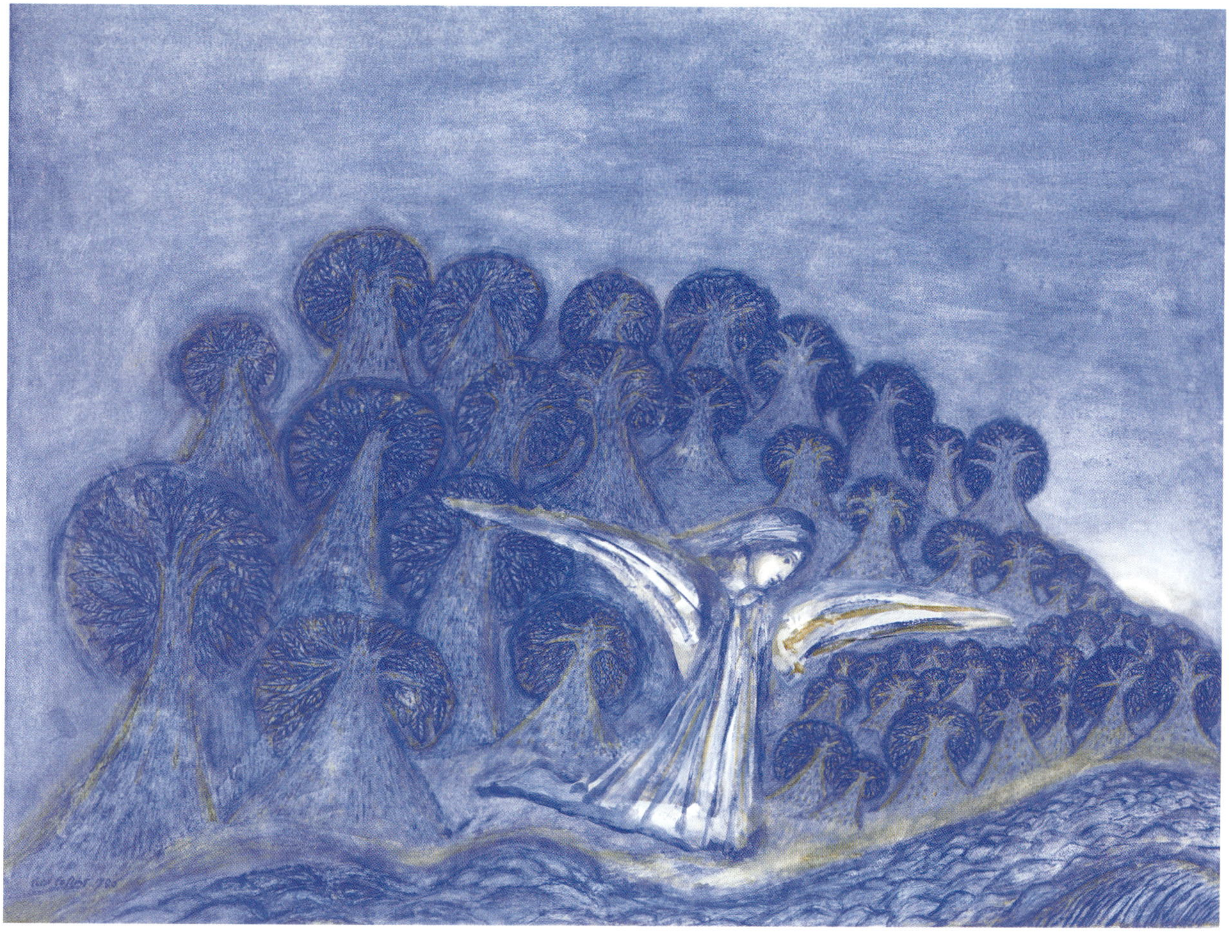

23 **By the Waters** 1980

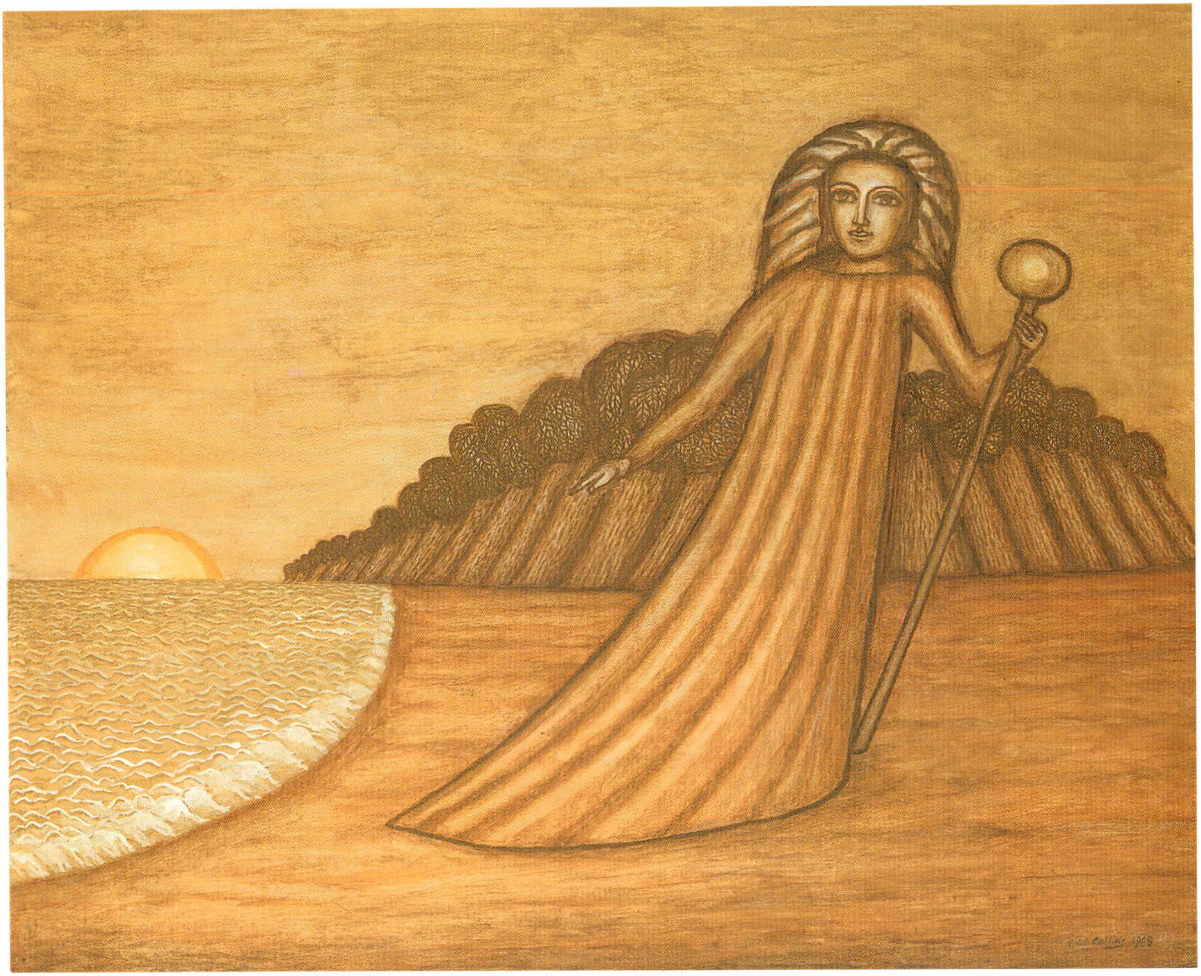

24 **The Music of Dawn** 1988

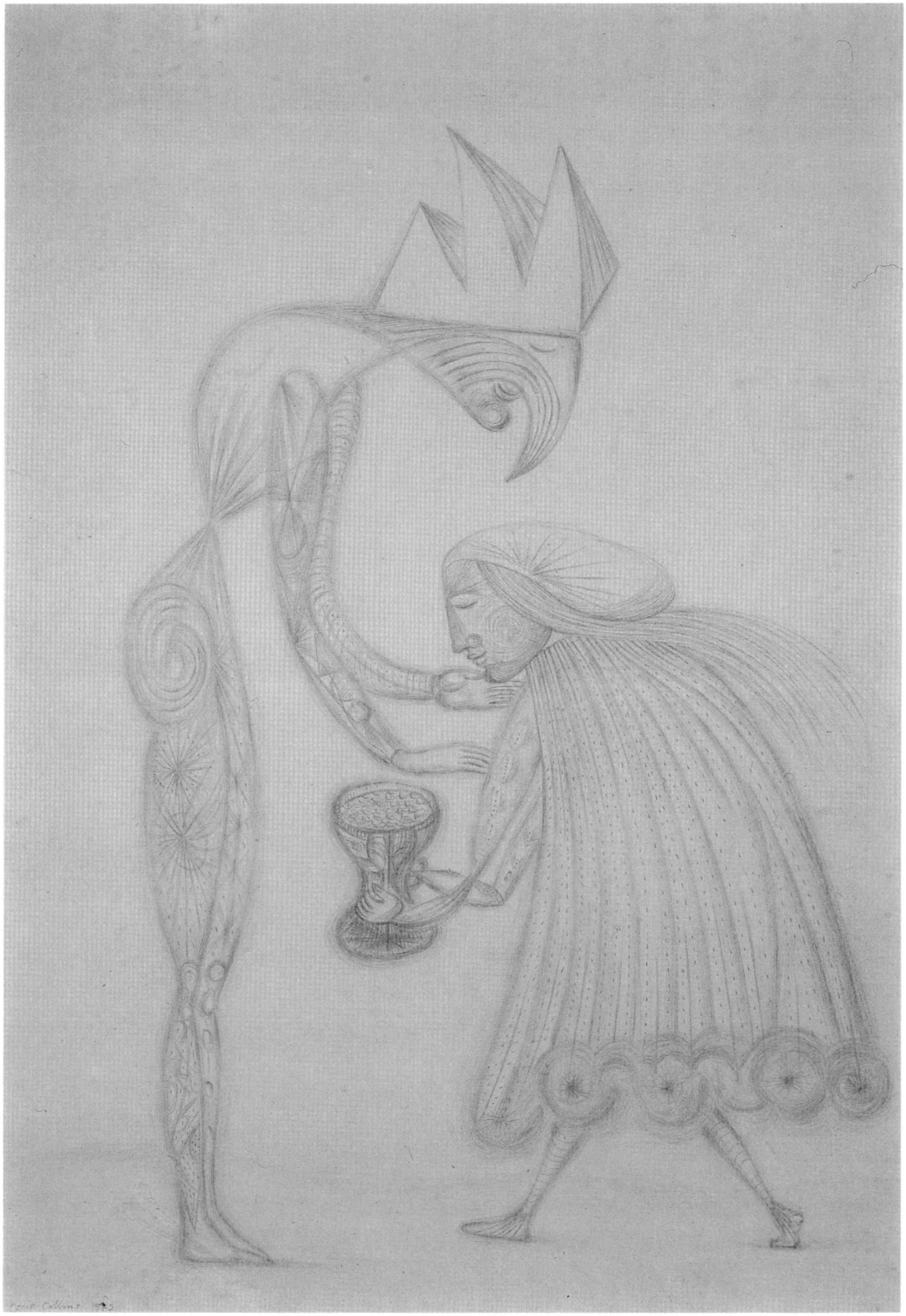

25 The Peace of the Fool 1942

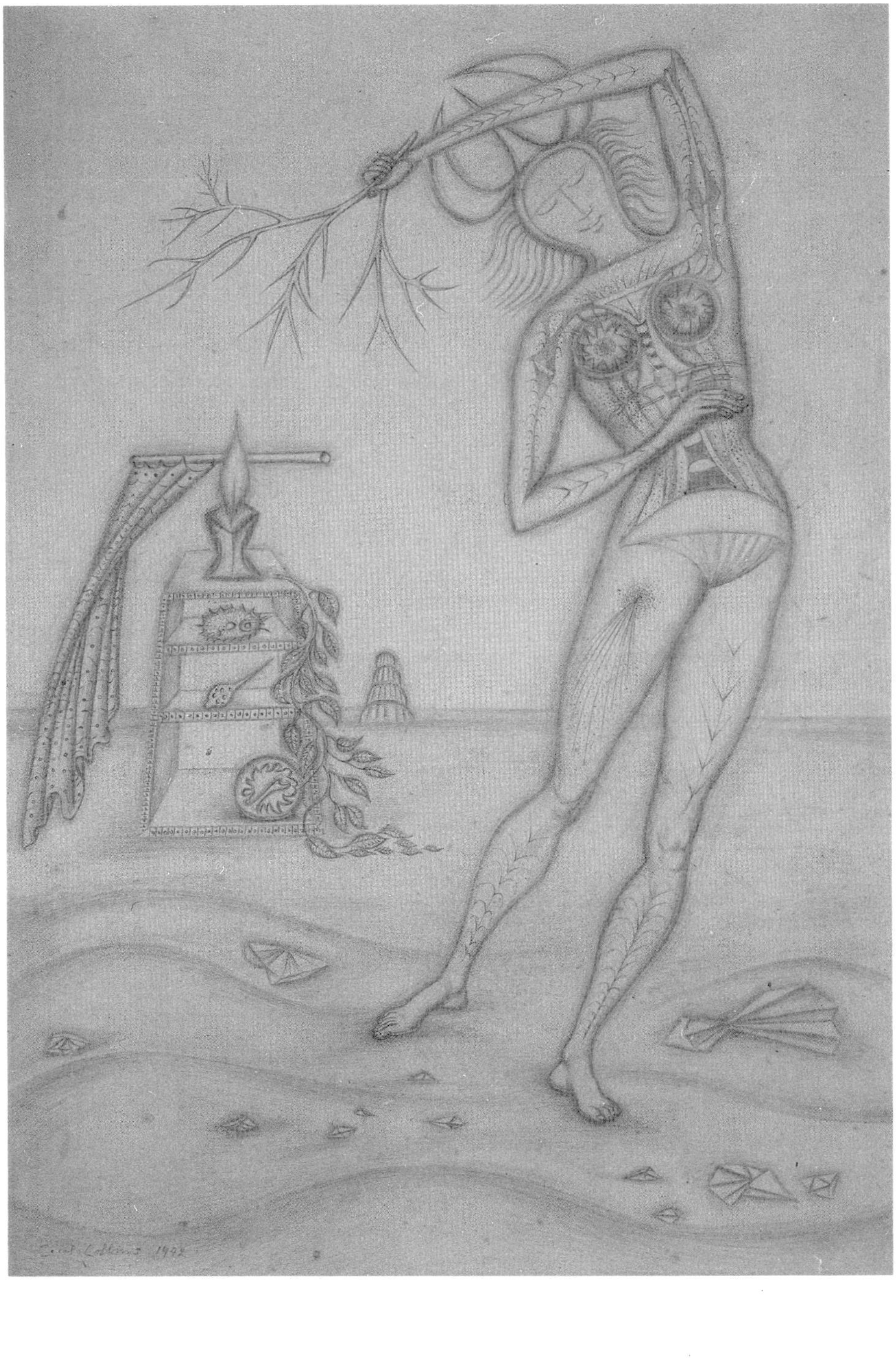

26
The Sybil
1942

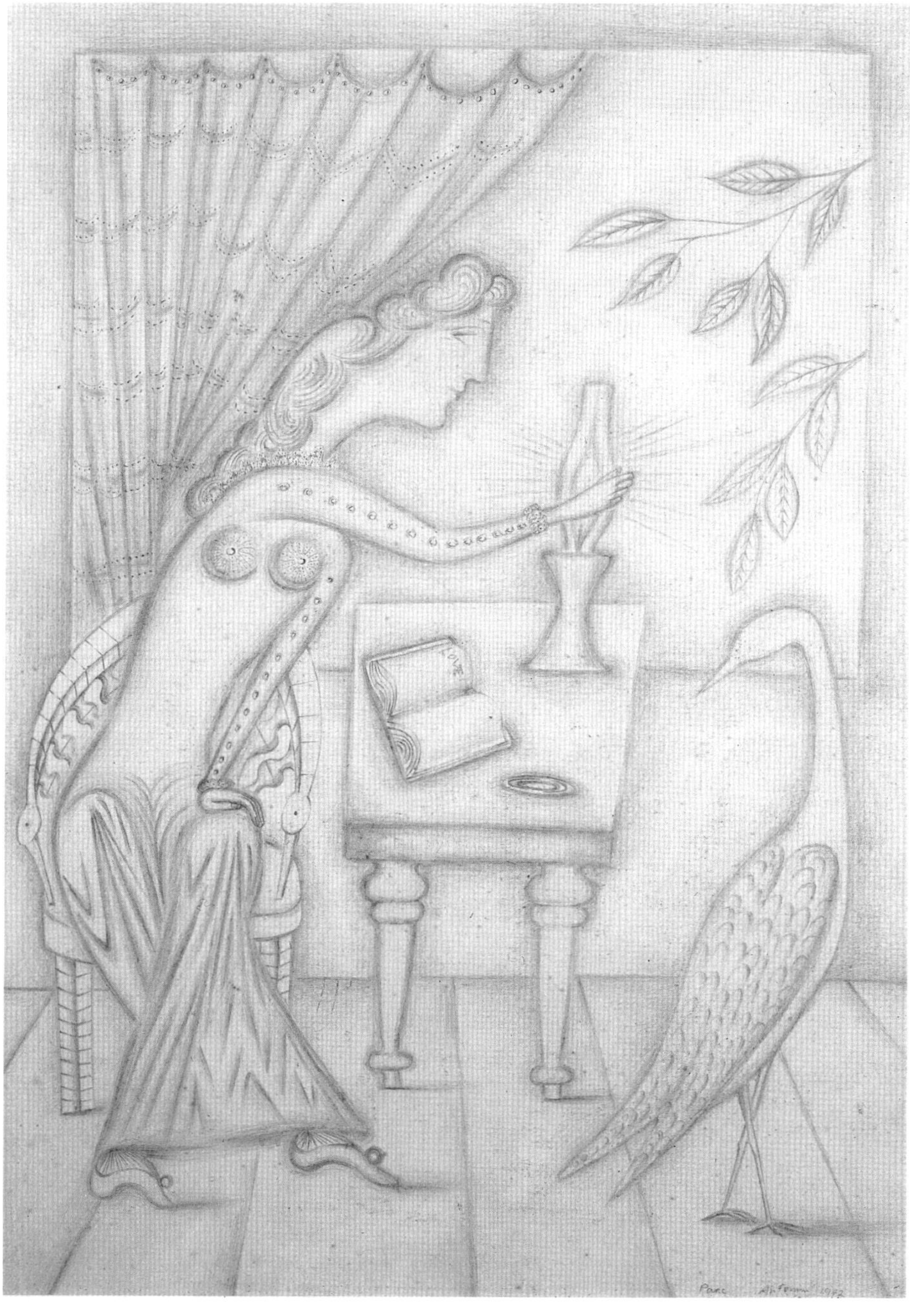

27
The Artist's Wife Lighting a Lamp
1942

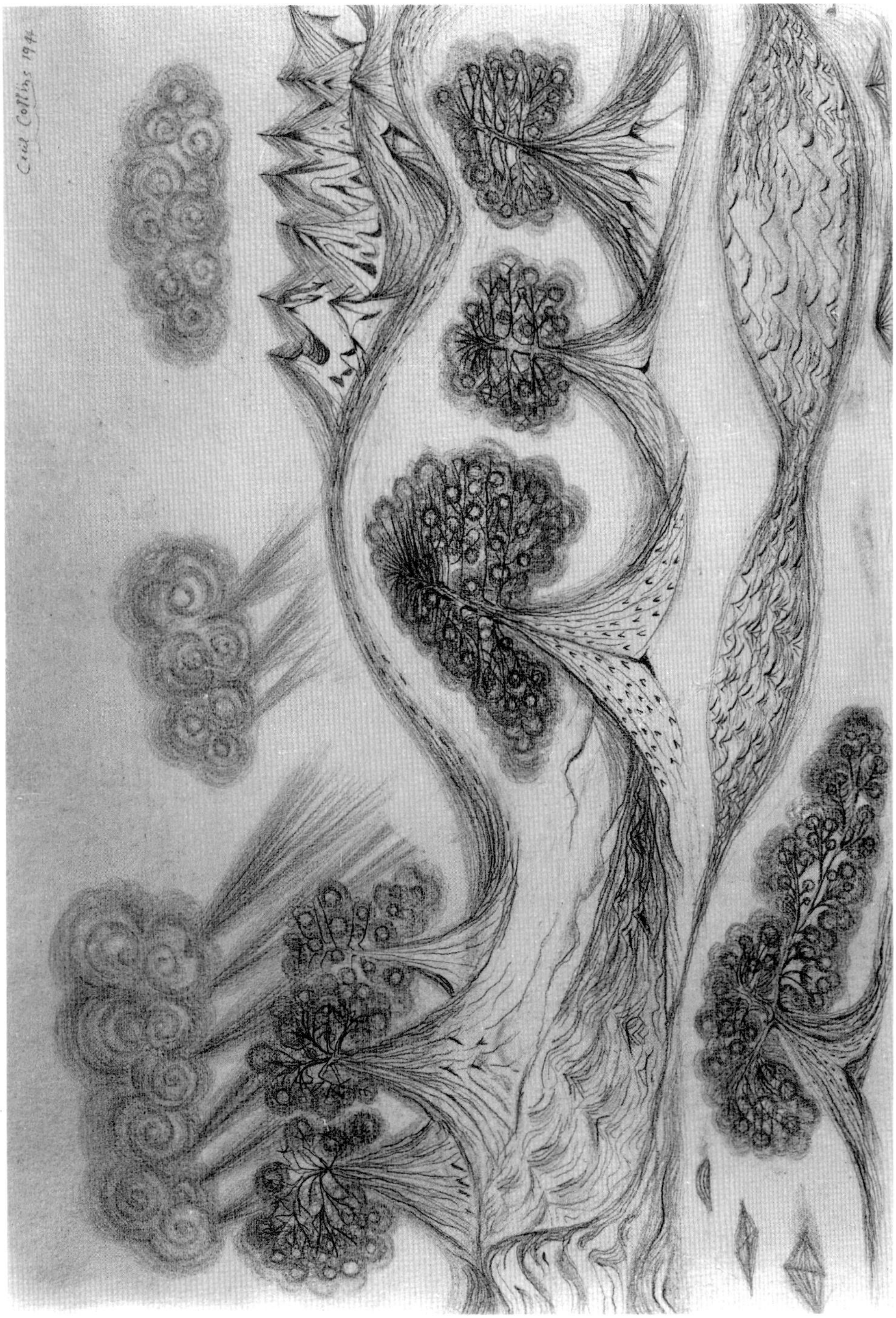

28 **Landscape** 1944

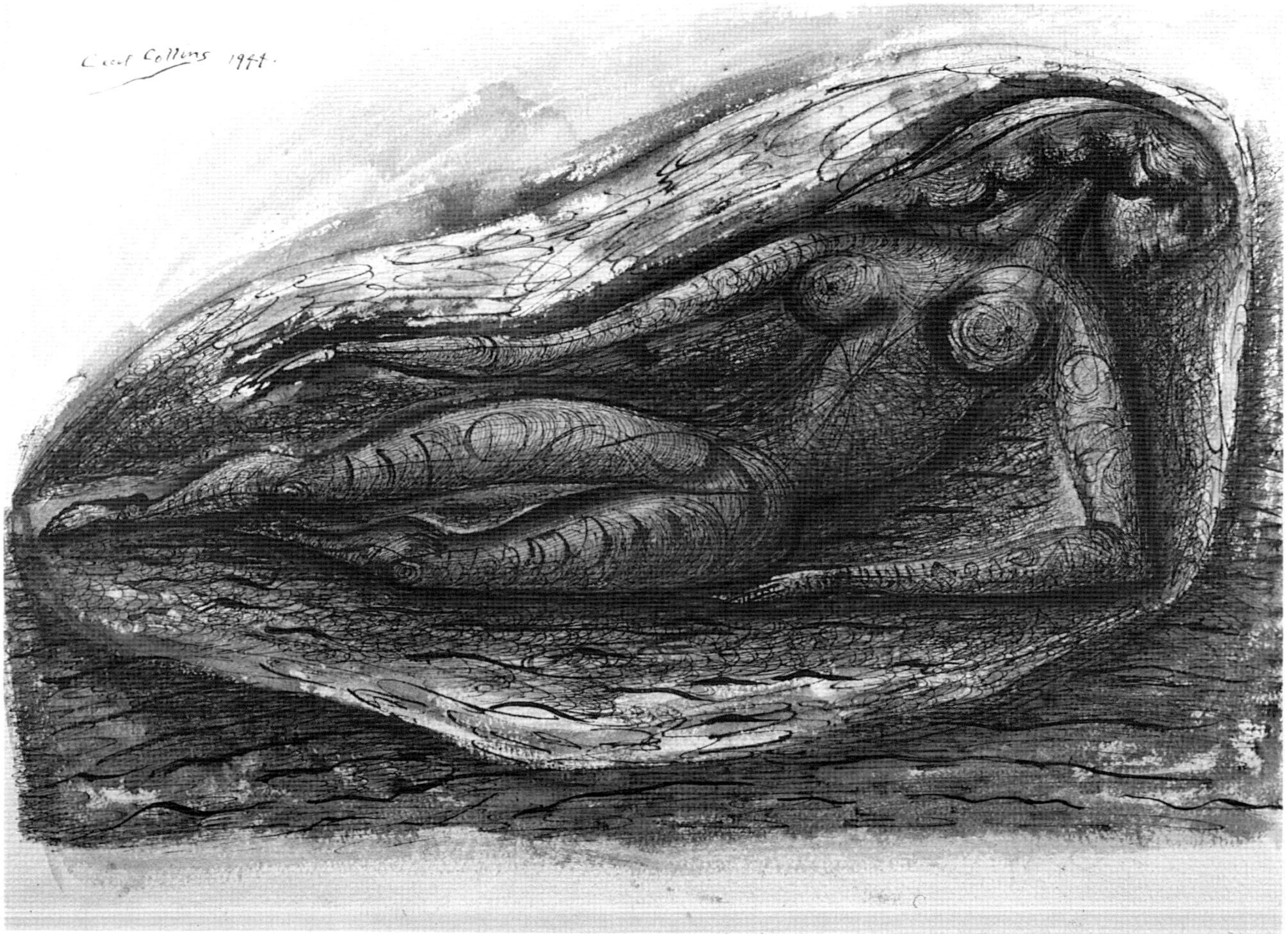

29 Woman in Shell 1944

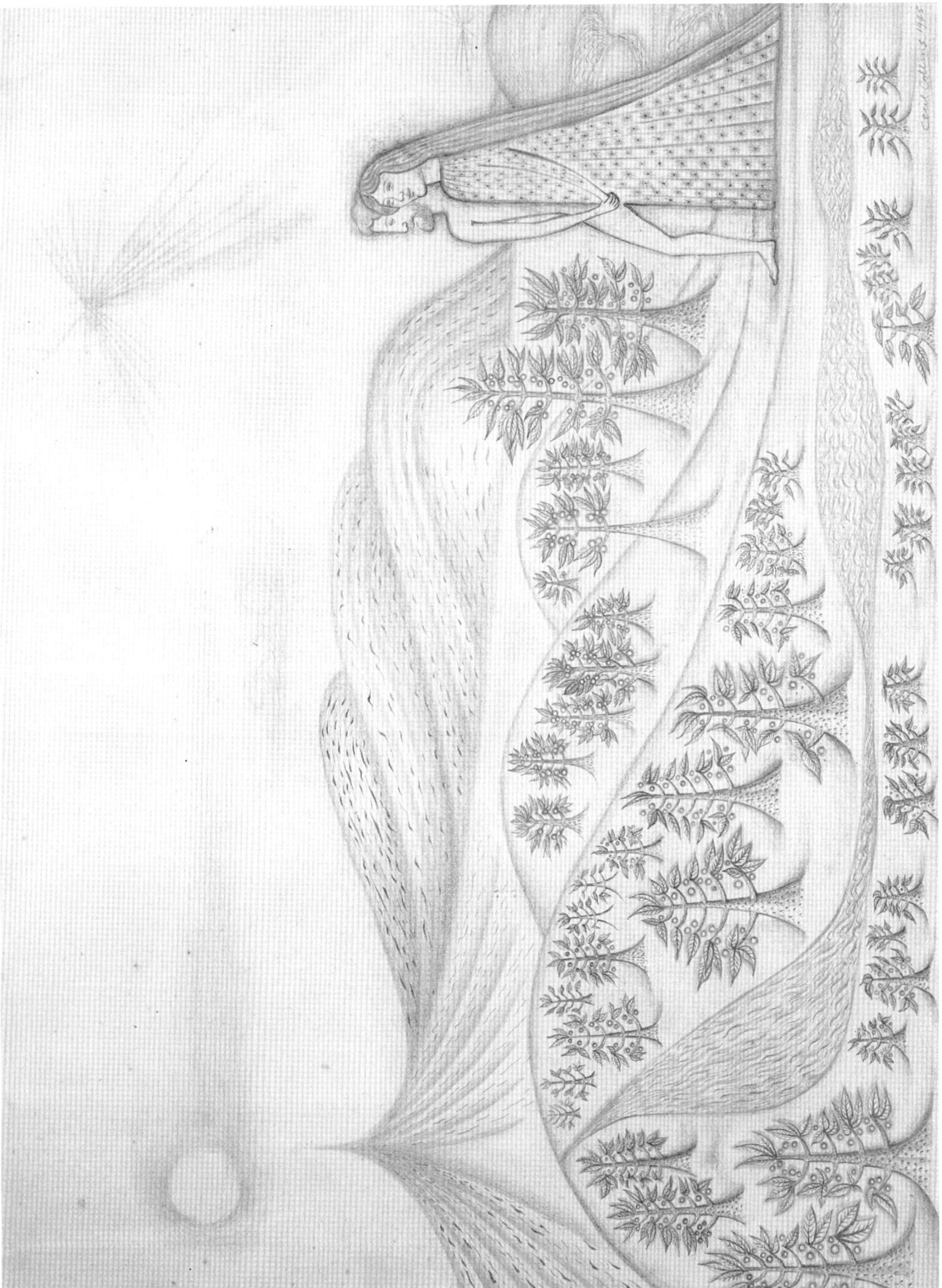

30 The Artist and his Wife Walking in a Landscape 1945

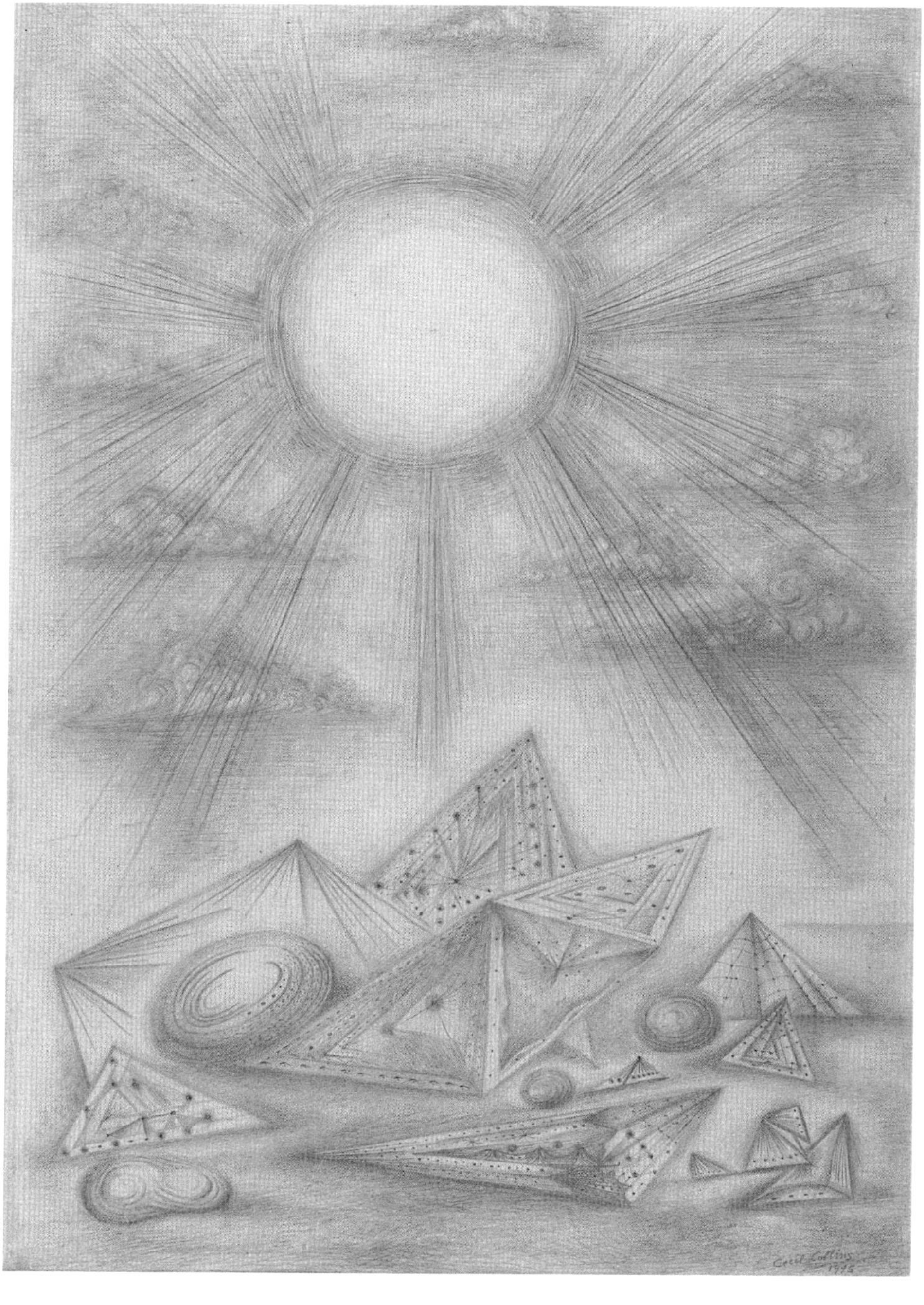

31
The Sun Blessing Stones
1945

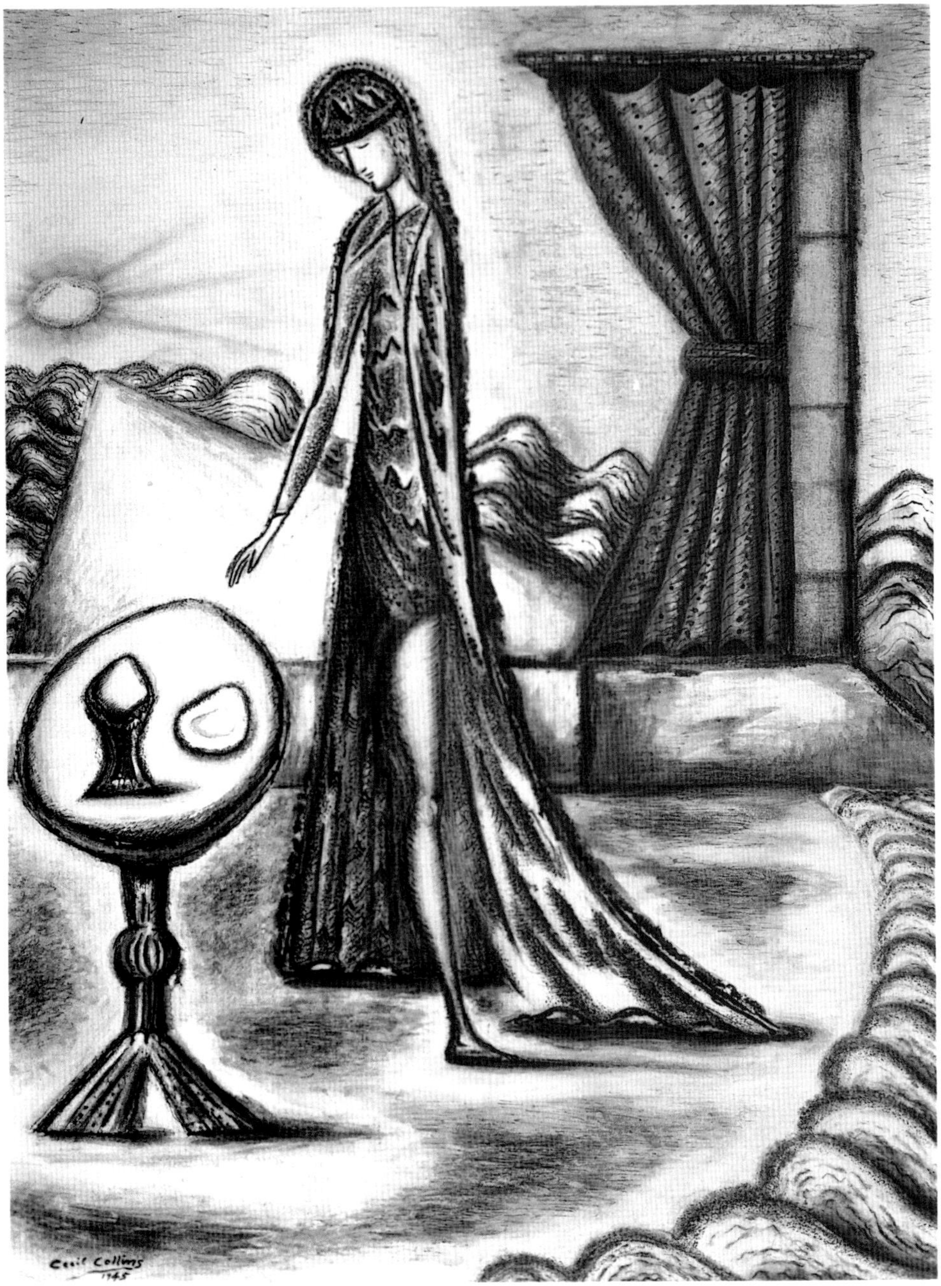

32
The Gift
1945

RIGHT: 33
Evening
1947

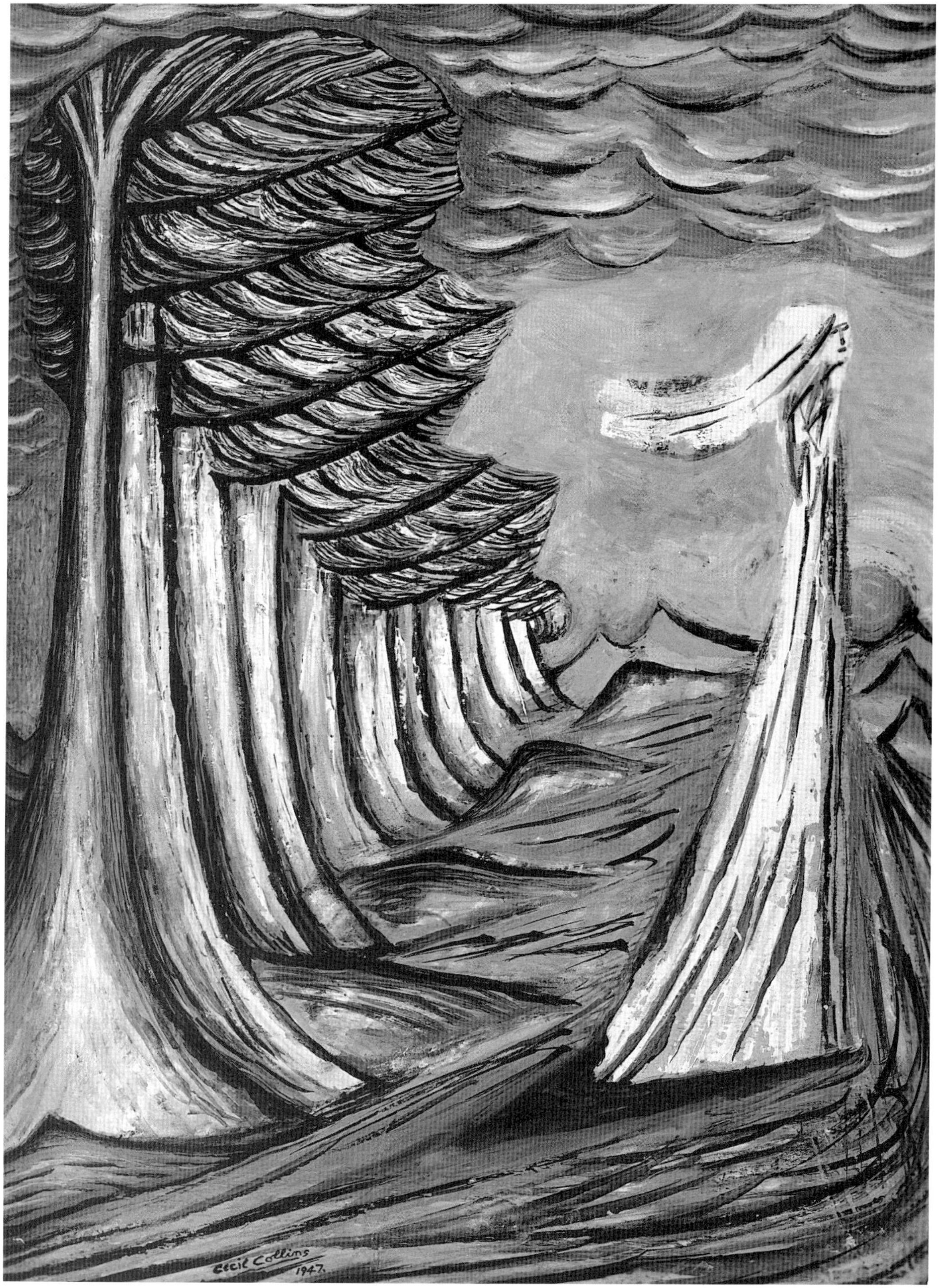
Cecil Collins
1947.

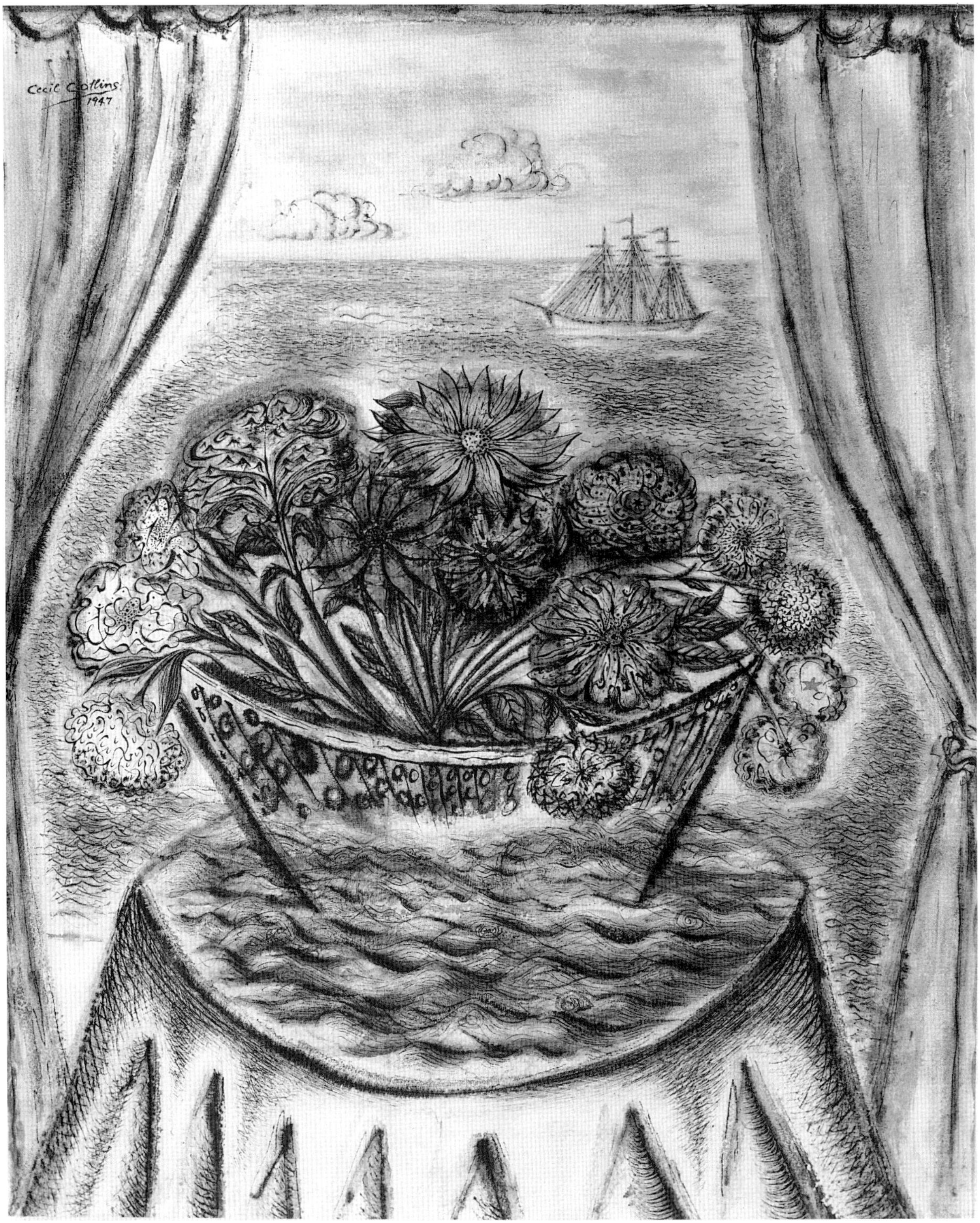
Cecil Collins
1947

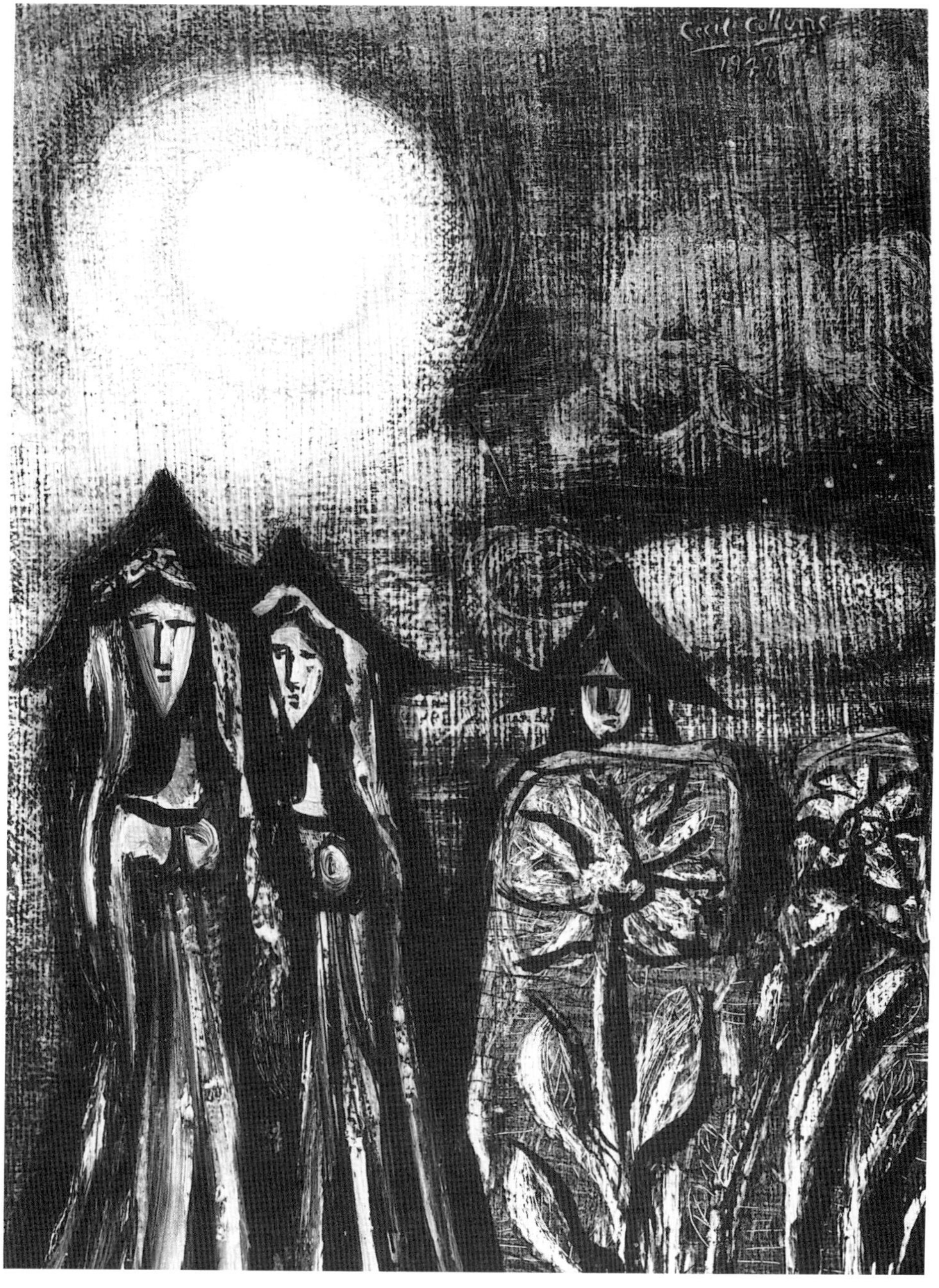

35 **Nocturne** 1948

FAR LEFT: 34
Still Life
1947

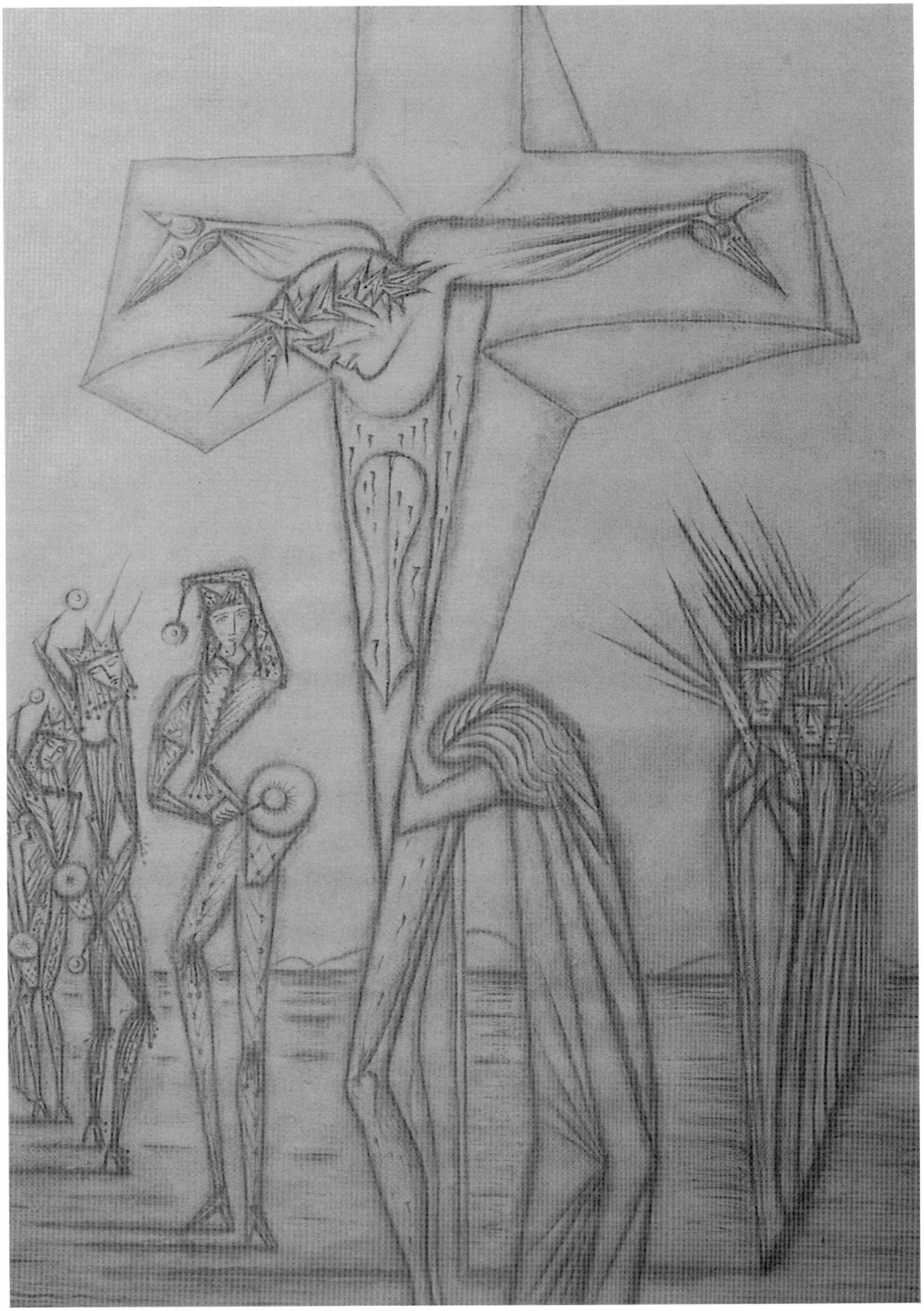

36 **The Crucifixion** 1952

RIGHT: 37
The Resurrection
1952

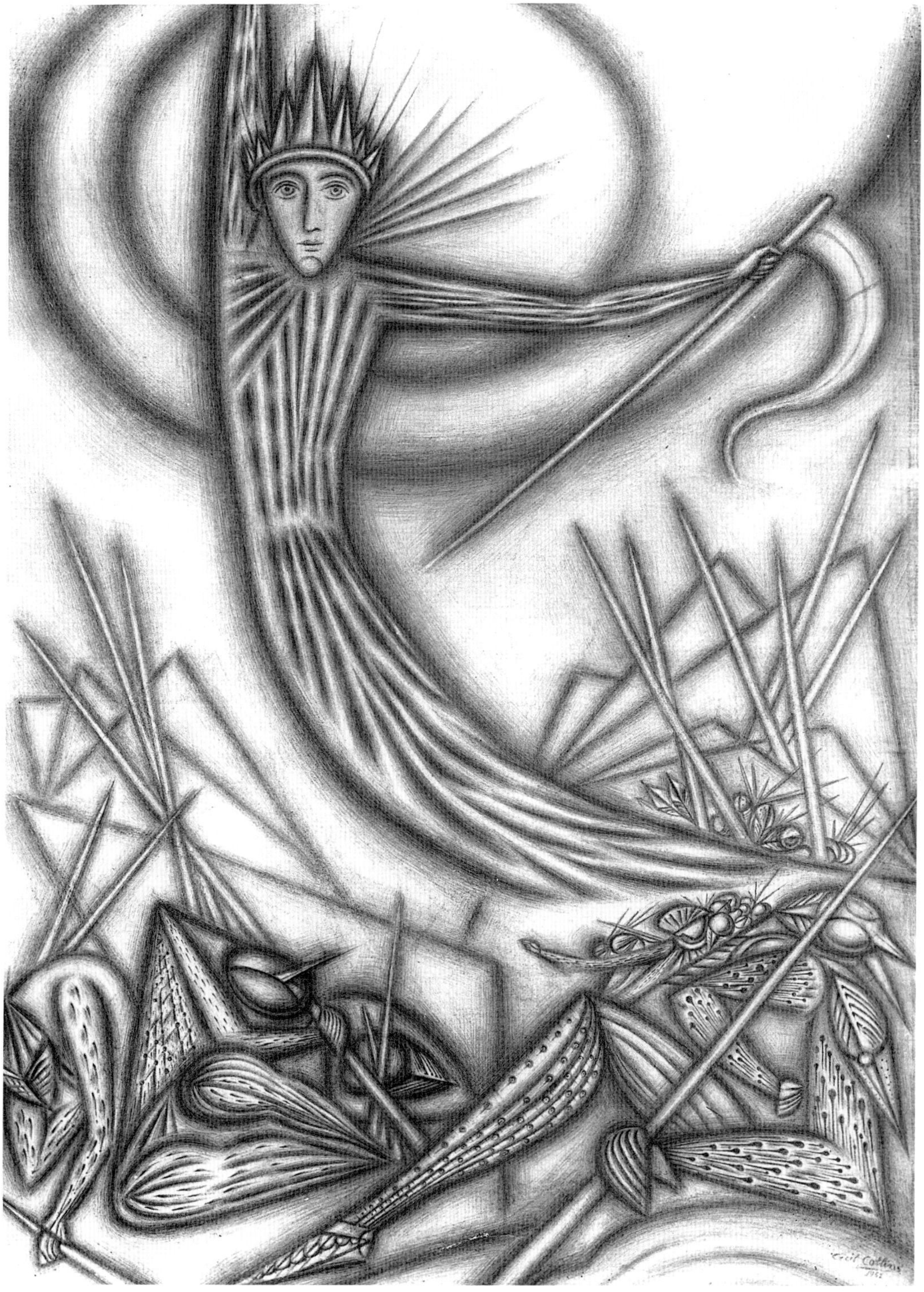

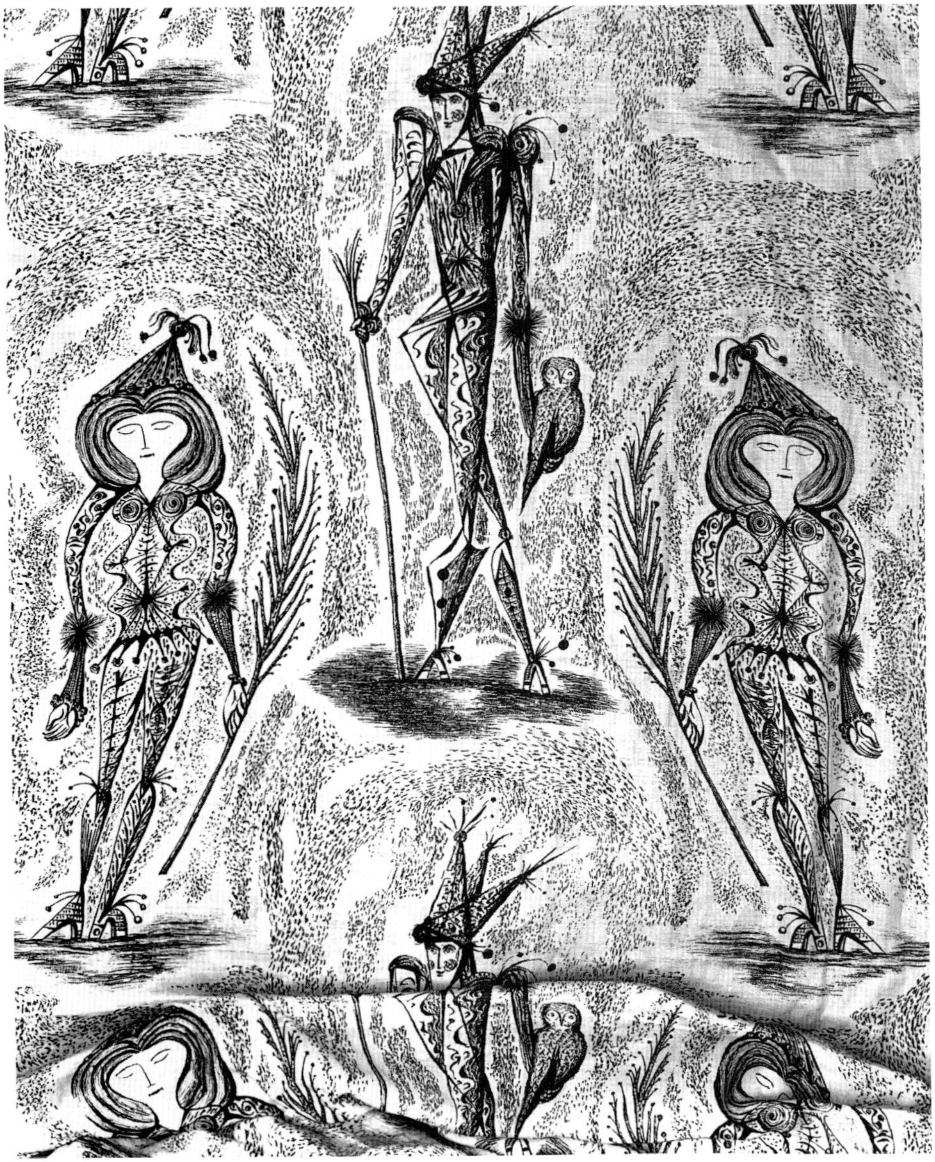

38 **The Fools** 1956

Right: 39
A Song
1960

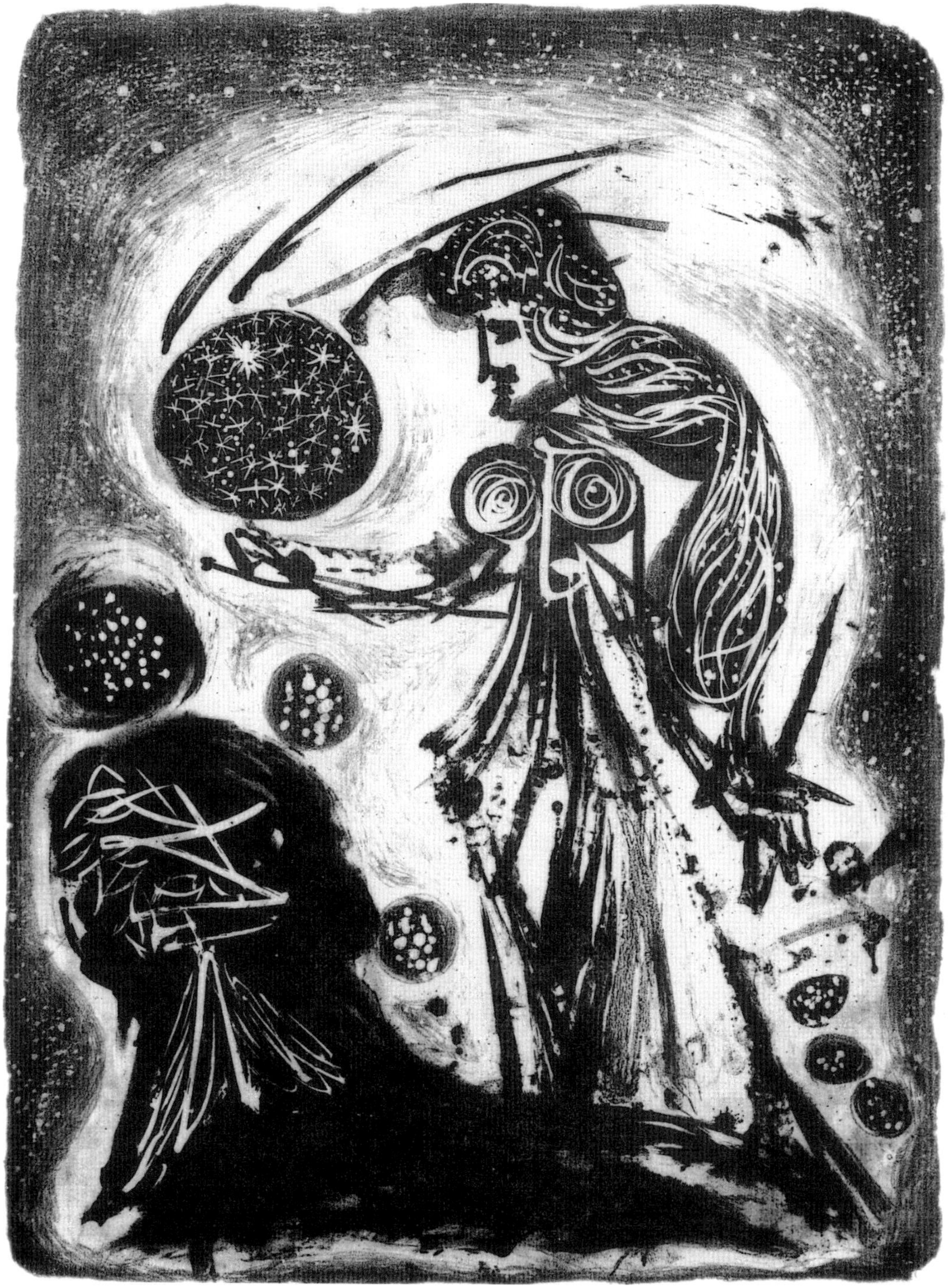

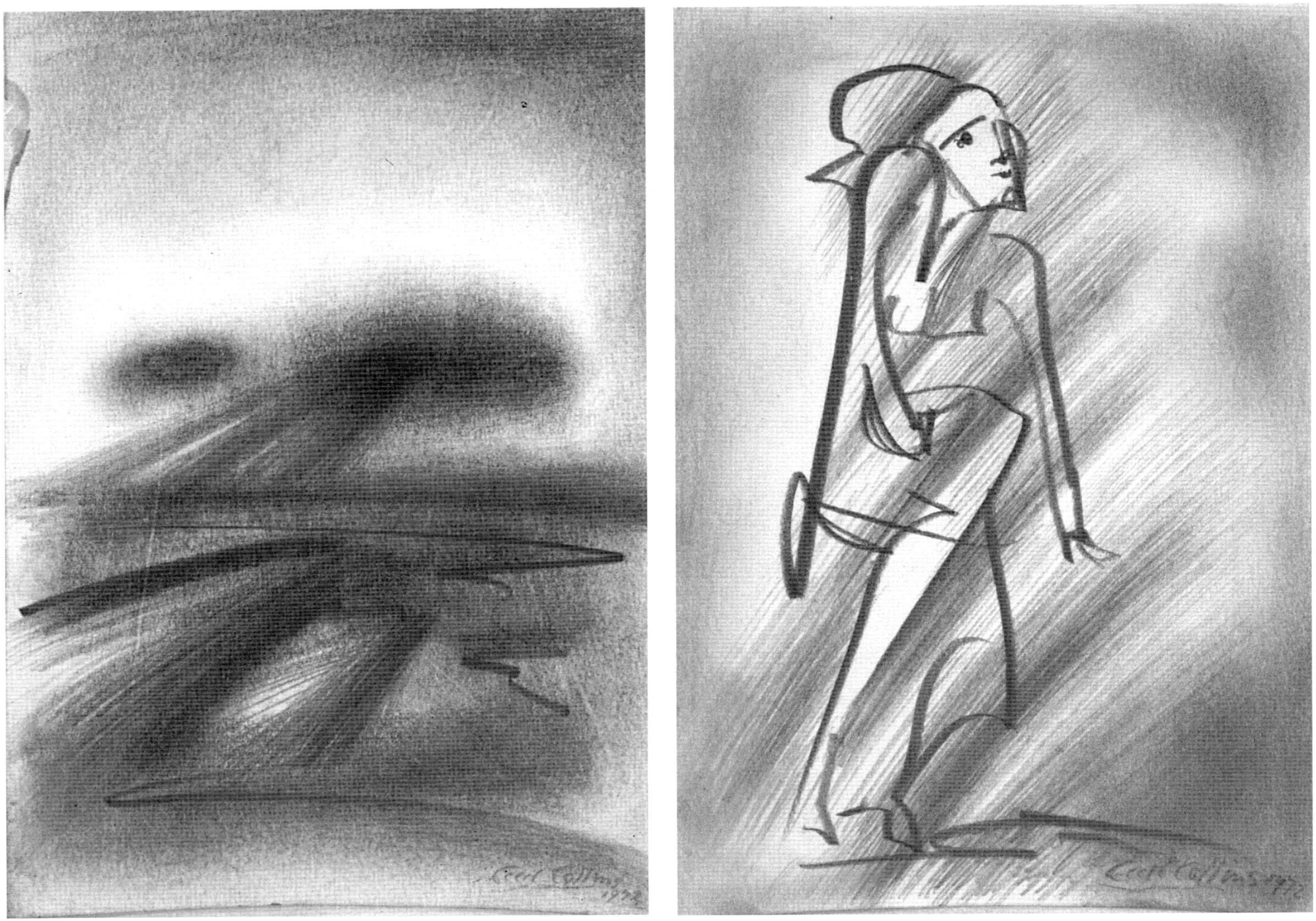

40 Two pages from a sketchbook 1972

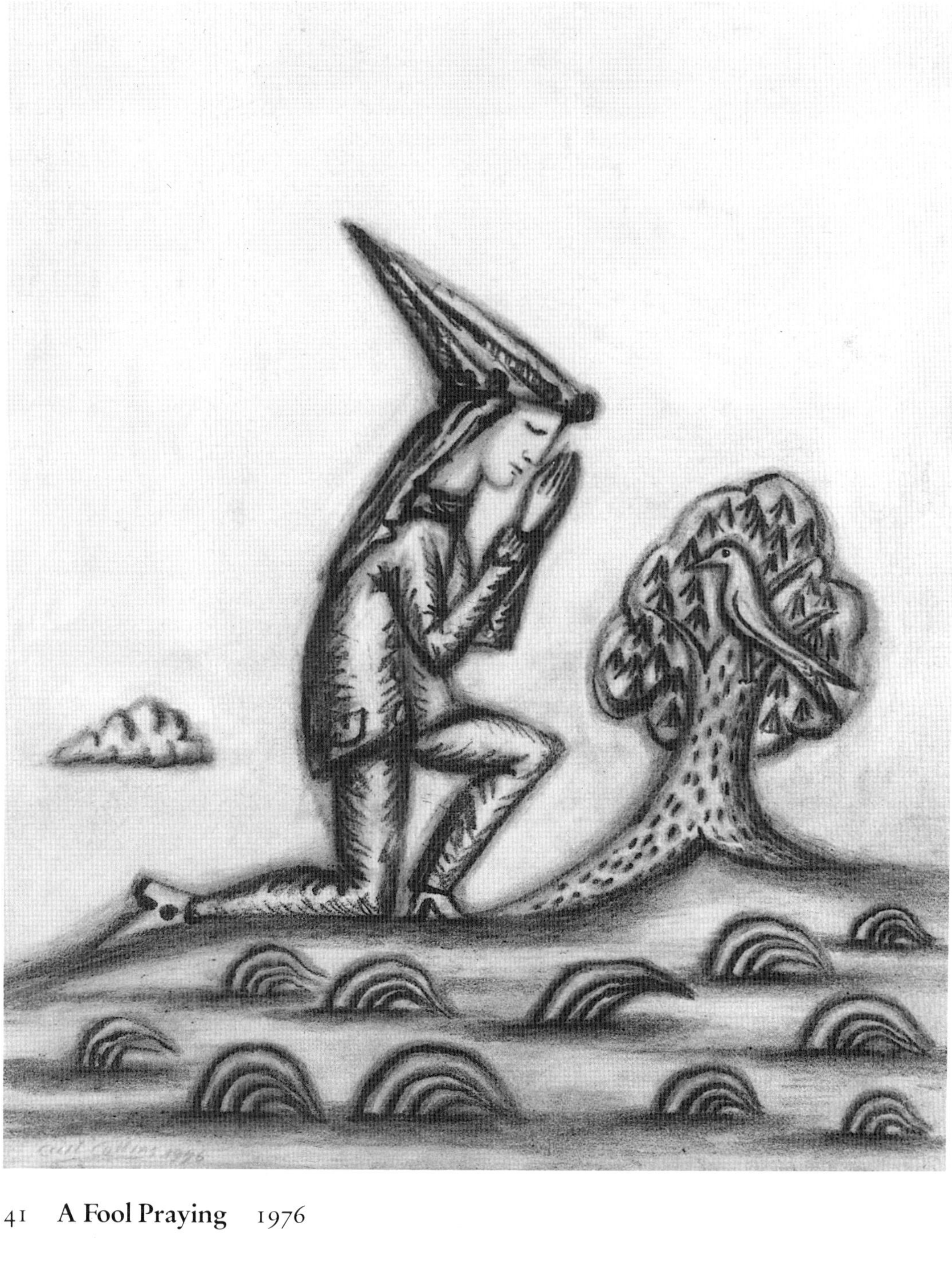

41 **A Fool Praying** 1976

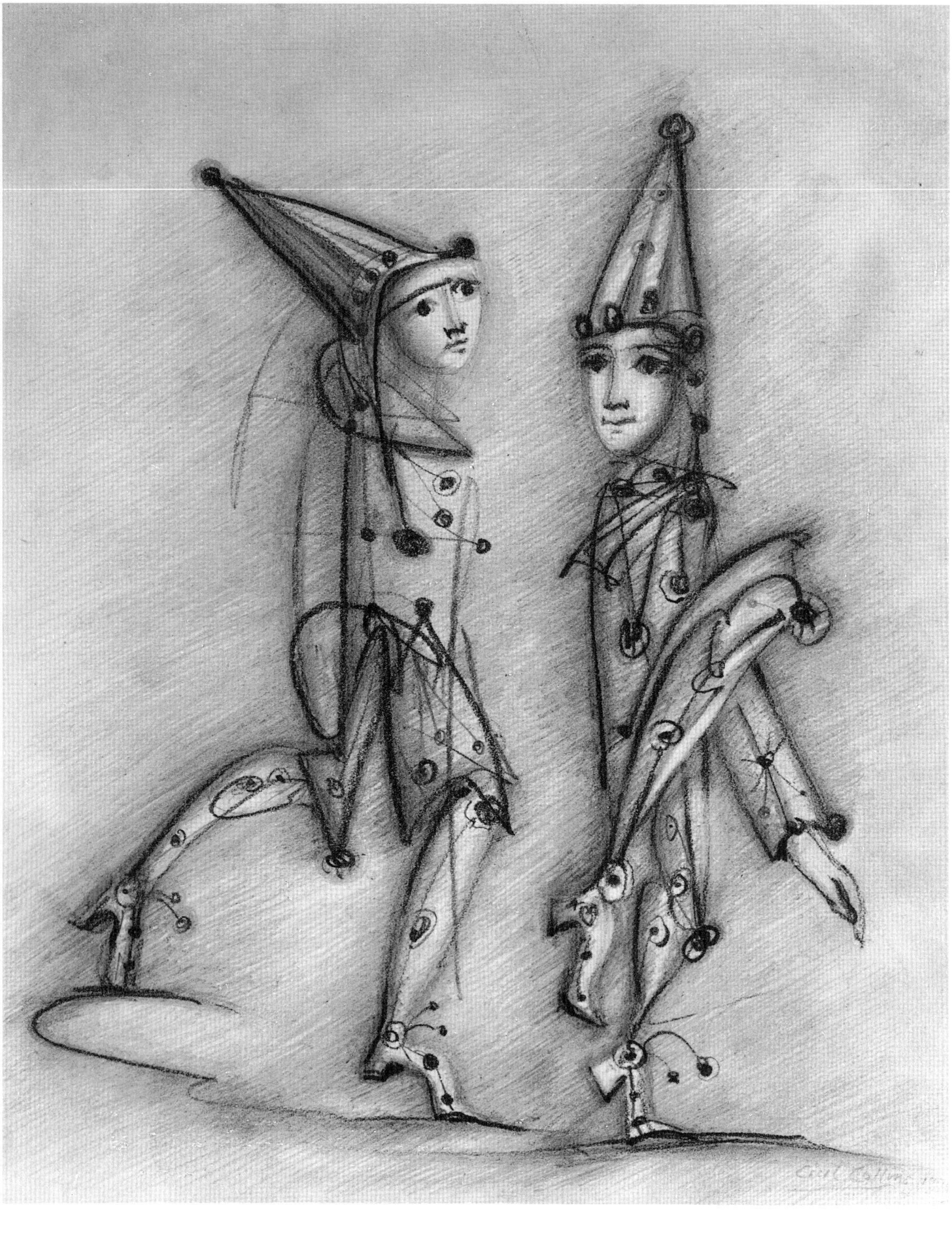

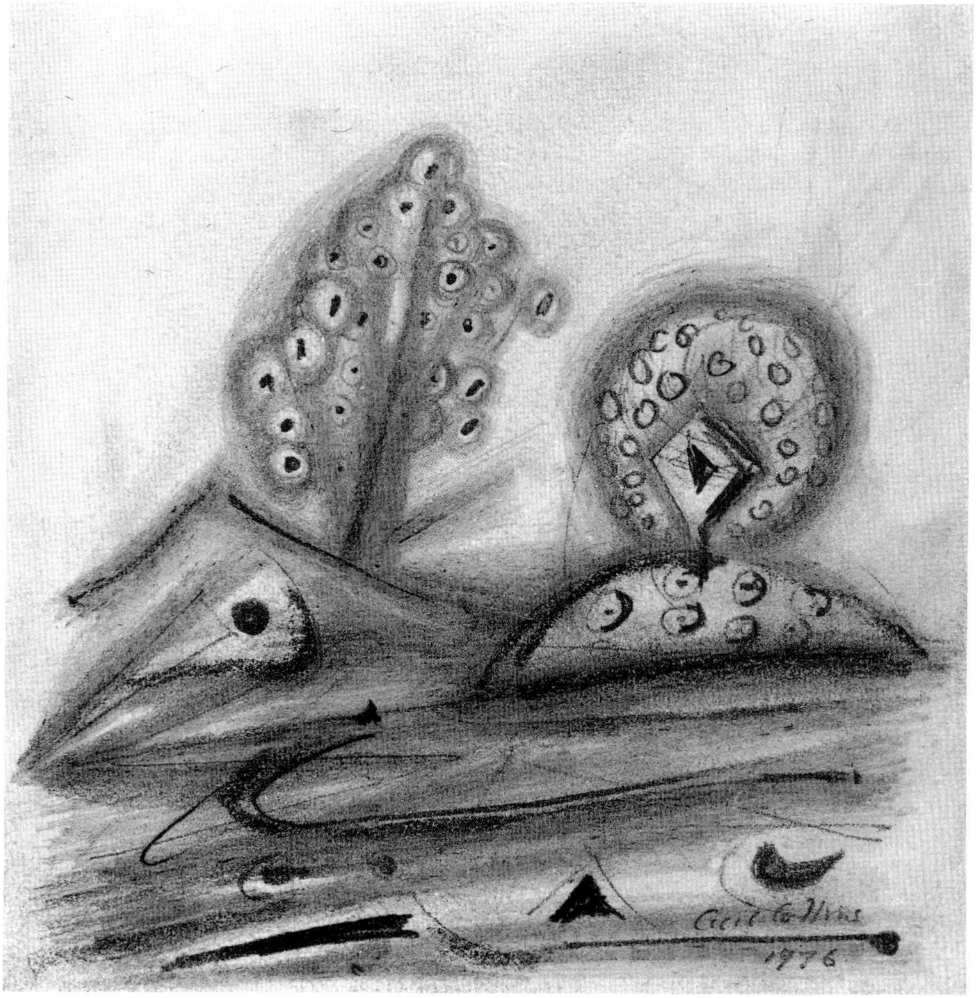

43 **Landscape** 1976

LEFT: 42
Two Fools Dancing
1976

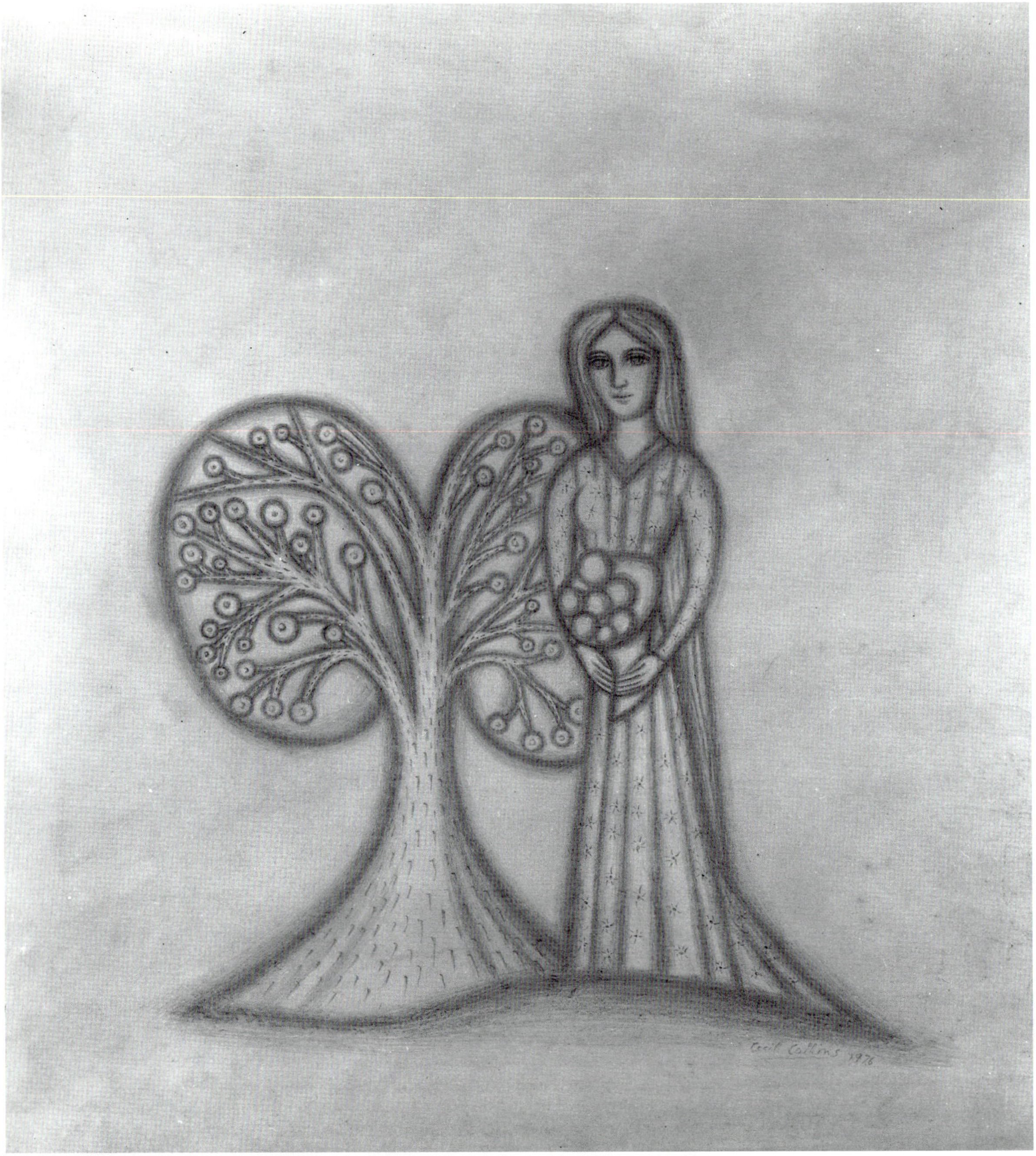

44 **Paradise** 1976

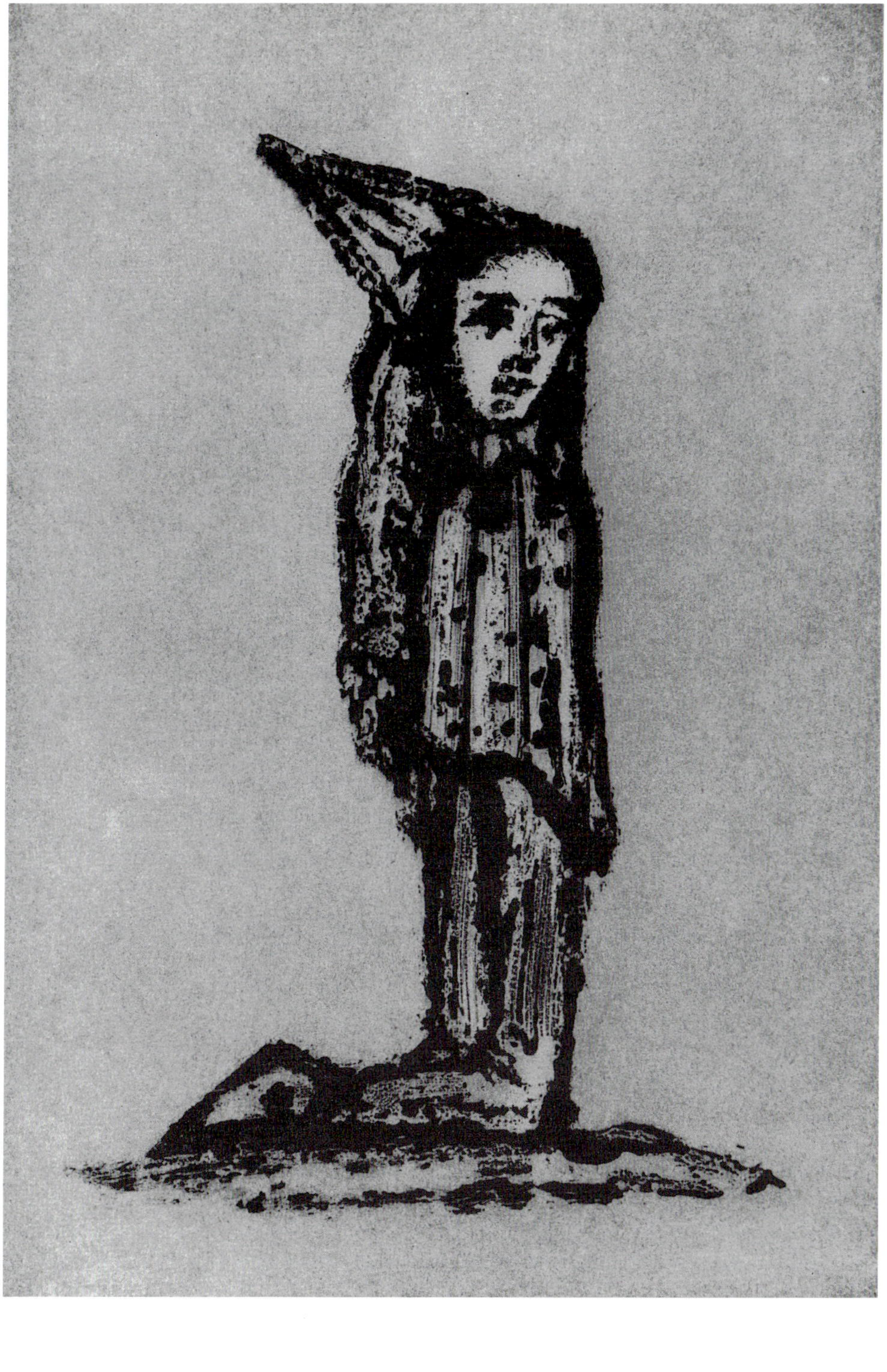

45
Kneeling Fool
1977

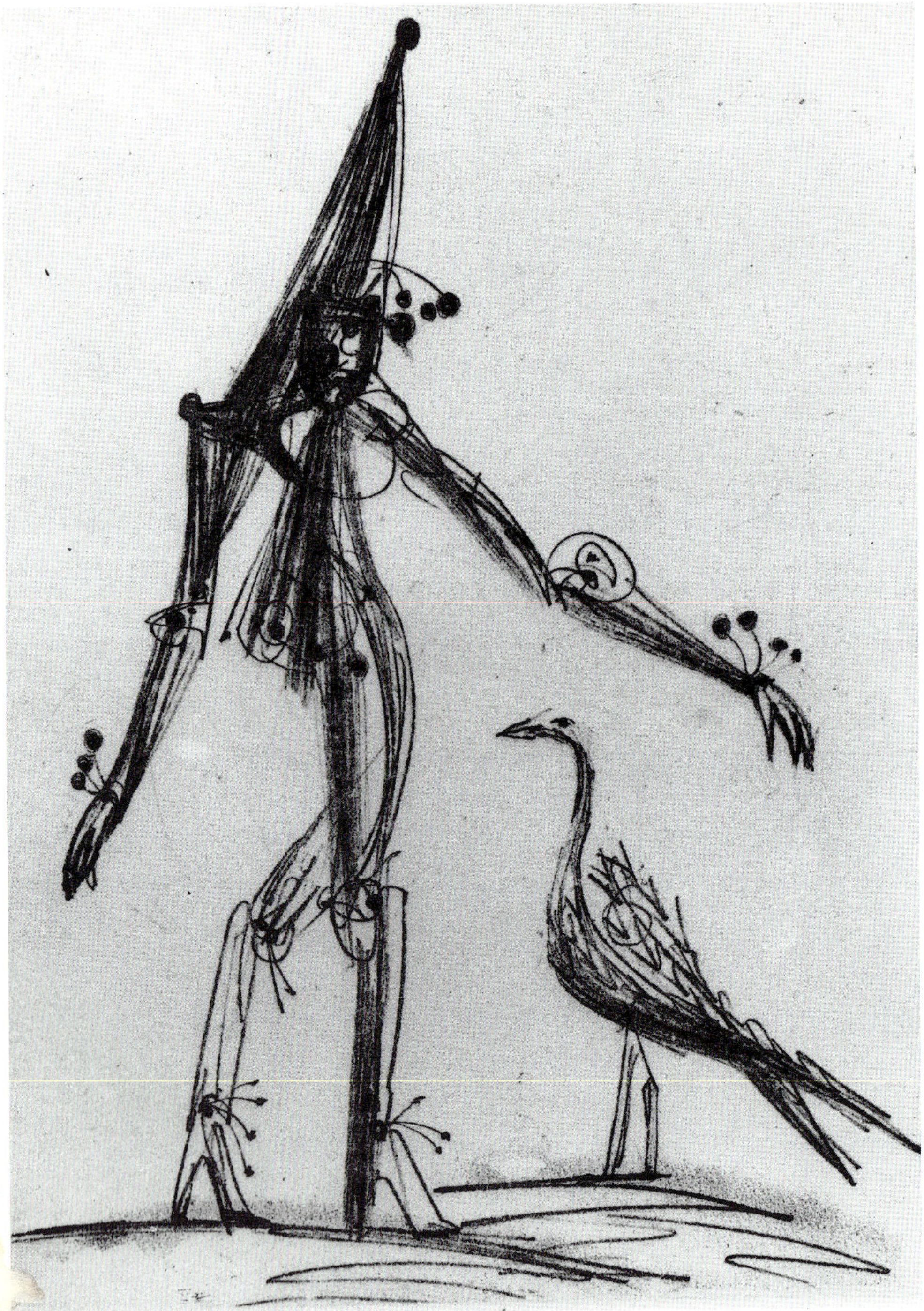

46 **Fool and Bird** 1978

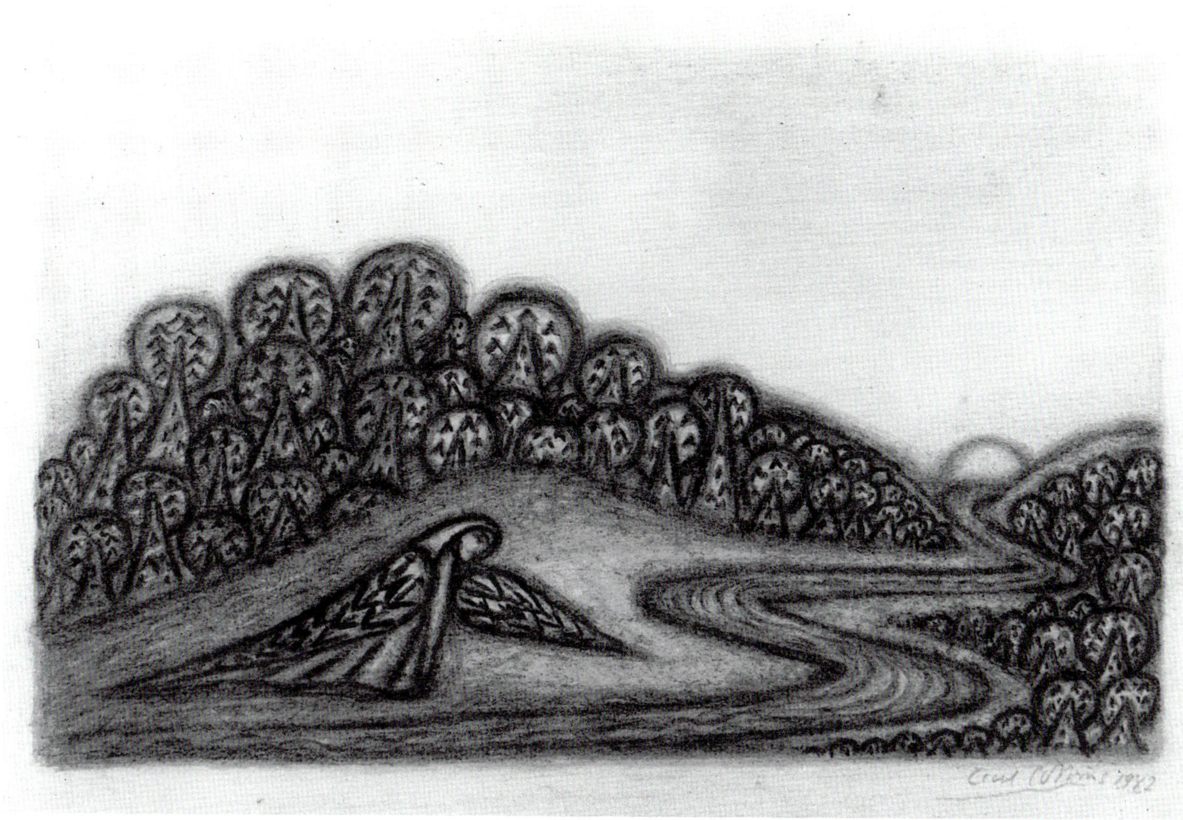

47 **By the Waters** 1982

Acknowledgements

A book such as this could not be compiled without the help of many people. I am chiefly indebted to Elisabeth Collins for her enthusiastic encouragement at all stages of the book's preparation. No less encouraging and supportive has been Robin Baring's efforts towards seeing the work successfully completed. Without their contribution the work simply could not have been done. Peter Nahum and John and Maryanna Tavener very generously sponsored the addition of a number of colour plates and supervised the photography of several of the works. This added greatly to the quality of the final choice of illustrations. A grant from The Henry Moore Foundation made it possible in the first instance to consider the inclusion of colour plates. Clive Hicks kindly gave me access to his photographic archive of the artist's work. To him goes the photographic credit for plates 6, 8, 9, 10, 11, 12, 13, 19, 29 and 36. Also, the Anthony d'Offay Gallery allowed me access to their photographic archive. Their help has been invaluable.

Kathleen Raine and Philip Sherrard read an early draft of the Introduction and, as often in the past, challenged me to do better. Susan Breakell of the Tate Gallery archive department unfailingly responded to my urgent requests for information. It is a pleasure to record once again my indebtedness to Rita Langford who so patiently and accurately transcribed the original tapes of the interview with the artist. Genevieve Overy faultlessly typed several sections of the manuscript. I must thank my friend and typesetter Alan Goodfellow for his heroic indulgence in accepting to work against the clock with a manuscript of deplorable untidiness. As on previous occasions and under similar conditions, his staff worked miracles of accuracy and typographic refinement. Not for the first time my wife Janet spent many hours helping me with the chore of proof-reading, the burden this time lightened by personal memories of the artist. I am grateful to John Lane and Satish Kumar for permission to quote from the interview with the artist first published in *Resurgence*. For their contribution I would like to thank Lord Marks, Judith Collins, Raphael Nadal, Bryan Robertson, Bryce McKenzie-Smith, Robin Vousden and Robert Violette of the Anthony d'Offay Gallery, the Derby City Art Gallery and the Trustees of the Britten-Pears Foundation, Aldeburgh. To all of these I am deeply grateful.